D1636779

THE
LAST
THINGS

THE LAST THINGS

by

Very Rev. James Alberione, S.S.P., S.T.D.

*"In whatever you do,
remember your last days,
and you will never sin."*

SIRACH 7:36

ST. PAUL EDITIONS

NIHIL OBSTAT:
   SHAWN G. SHEEHAN
      Diocesan Censor

IMPRIMATUR:
   ✠ RICHARD CARDINAL CUSHING

ISBN 0-8198-0072-4 cloth
      0-8198-4420-9 paper

Library of Congress Catalog Card Number: 64-17751

Printed in the U.S.A. by the Daughters of St. Paul
50 St. Paul's Ave., Boston, MA 02130

The Daughters of St. Paul are an international congregation of
religious women serving the Church with the communications
media.

*"In all your actions,
remember your last end,
and you will never sin."*

The "Last Things" are ever new truths, powerful incentives, considerations that sanctify.

The thought of them casts a brilliant light on life and points out its true meaning. They are sparks which set on fire a tremendous love—a love that consists in striving to reach God, our final Goal and the Supreme Good. The thought of the Last Things is a prayer with the power to move the most indifferent hearts and inspire souls to generous resolutions. For meditation is mental prayer.

May every reader find in reflection on the Last Things the Way, the Truth and the Life!

The lay man or woman, the priest or the religious who builds his spiritual life on the Last Things builds on the most solid foundation: "And the rain fell, and the floods came, and the winds blew and beat against that house, but it did not fall, because it was founded on rock" (Matt. 7:25).

Homo aeternitatis sum!—"I am a man destined for eternity!"

THE AUTHOR

CONTENTS

DEATH

PARTICULAR JUDGMENT

PURGATORY

HEAVEN

HELL

THE GENERAL JUDGMENT

DEATH

I

WHAT DEATH IS

Let us offer these reflections for the grace to be delivered from an untimely death. This is the grace our Rosaries aim to obtain through the intercession of our Blessed Mother. We say, in fact, "pray for us NOW AND AT THE HOUR OF OUR DEATH." *Many times our Divine Master advised us to be prepared, because death comes "like a thief in the night." Out of deference to His warning, let us ask Him to help us keep ourselves ready to die—always, everywhere, and with the best dispositions.*

The man who should fear that he will meet a bad end is the man who is not prepared every moment to die. The person who may confidently look forward to a good death is he who resolves each morning to spend the day as though it were his last, and after examining his conscience each evening, can say, "If death were to come tonight, I could confidently present myself before the judgment seat of God."

Death–punishment for sin

The Lord God planted a garden in Eden, to the east, and he put there the man he had formed. The Lord God made to grow out of the ground all kinds of trees pleasant to the sight and good for food, the tree of life also in the midst of the garden, and the tree of the knowledge of good and evil. A river rose in Eden watering the garden; and from there, it separated into four branches.

The Lord God took the man and placed him in the garden of Eden to till it and keep it. And the Lord God commanded the man thus, "From every tree of the garden you may eat; but from the tree of the knowledge of good and evil you must not eat; for the day you eat of it, you must die."

Both the man and his wife were naked, but they felt no shame.

Now the serpent was more cunning than any beast of the field which the Lord God had made. He said to the woman, "Did God say, 'You shall not eat of any tree of the garden'?" The woman answered the serpent, "Of the fruit of all the trees in the garden we may eat; but 'Of the fruit of the tree in the middle of the garden,' God said, 'you shall not eat, neither shall you touch it, lest you die.'"

But the serpent said to the woman, "No, you shall not die; for God knows that when you eat of it, your eyes will be opened and you will be like God, knowing good and evil." Now the woman saw that the tree was good for food, pleasing to the eyes, and desirable for the knowledge it would give. She took of its fruit and ate it, and also gave some to her husband and he ate. Then the eyes of both were opened, and they realized that they were naked; so they sewed fig-leaves together and made themselves coverings. When they heard the sound of the Lord God walking in the garden in the cool of the day, the man and his wife hid themselves from the Lord God among the trees of the garden. But the Lord God called the man and said to him, "Where are you?" And he said, "I heard you in the garden, and I was afraid because I was naked; and I hid." Then he said, "Who told you that you were naked? You have eaten then of the tree of which I commanded you not to eat." The man said, "The woman you placed at my side gave me fruit from the tree and I ate." Then the Lord God said to the woman, "Why have you done this?" The woman said, "The serpent deceived me and I ate."

Then the Lord God said to the serpent: "Because you have done this, cursed are you among all animals, and among all beasts of the field; on your belly shall you crawl, dust shall you eat, all the days of your life. I will put enmity between you and the woman, between your seed and her seed; he shall crush your head, and you shall lie in wait for his heel." To the woman he said: "I will make great your distress in child-bearing; in pain shall you bring forth children; for your husband shall be your longing, though he have dominion over you." And to Adam he said, "Because you have listened to your wife, and have eaten of the tree of which I commanded you not to eat: cursed be the ground because of you; in toil shall you eat of it all the days of your life; thorns and thistles shall it bring forth to you, and you shall eat the plants of the field. In the sweat of your brow you shall eat bread, till you return to the ground, since out of it you were taken; for dust you are and unto dust you shall return. (Gen. 2:8-10; 15-17, 25; 3:1-19.)

Death, then, is a punishment for sin. Paying no heed to the warning given them by God, Adam and Eve ate the forbidden fruit, and thus the sentence fell: "You shall die."

Death is certain, but the time of its coming is not. It could come anytime, anywhere, when we least expect it. This uncertainty is due to our nature itself, to God's mercy, and to the demands of justice.

Our very nature, first of all, makes the time of death uncertain because our body is composed of corruptible matter. It takes but the event of a moment to end our lives—an accident, a fall, a slash of a vein, a stubborn fever, pneumonia, a heart-attack—and we are gone. Every day the newspapers carry reports of sudden deaths. Some are from internal causes and some from external, such as accidents on land or sea or in the air. The human vessel is a very fragile one. It can break at any moment. At times, one germ is all it takes! In a twinkling, we can pass into eternity.

The mercy of God is another reason for the uncertainty surrounding death. Precisely because He is merciful, God often calls souls into eternity suddenly. He sees that if a young man were to grow into adulthood, he would fall into sin and seriously endanger his salvation. Hence He calls the boy to Himself while he is still innocent: "He was taken away lest wickedness should alter his understanding" (Wis. 4:11). They die young who are dear to Heaven! At other times, the Lord grants a long life out of mercy, i. e., when a soul is doing good. For His own glory and the greater merit of zealous apostles who have given themselves entirely to Him and are spreading His Kingdom, God grants them long lives, full of graces. It was said of St. Titus that he died "full of years and merits."

Death comes unexpectedly for a third reason: the justice of God. It is sin which brings it on: "Through sin death" (Rom. 5:12); "The sting of death is sin" (1 Cor. 15:56). What brings on death is sin, that is, acts of ingratitude toward the Divine Mercy. How many times we are at a loss to explain early, sudden death, but God has His reasons and we shall see them one day at the General Judgment. He forgives some souls ten times, some twenty, and there are those who are snatched away at their first sin, or their second or their third. It is not the same for all. When the number determined by God is up, the punishment comes. God's mercy is infinite, but the acts of this mercy are numbered for each soul. Let us then be vigilant since we "know neither the day nor the hour" (Matt. 25:13). Let us always live in a kind of holy fear, on our guard, watchful, realizing that our body is subject to corruption. May our lives by ruled by trust in the mercy of God and a salutary fear of His justice.

A good practice is the frequent recitation of the **Our Father** to ask deliverance from an untimely death. Now we shall conclude by reciting Psalm 111, for there is much to be learned from its praise of the "man who fears the Lord" and wisely orders his days and his every action toward the eternal goal.

PSALM 111

The Blessings of the Just Man

Happy· the man who fears the Lord,
who greatly delights in his commands.
His posterity shall be mighty upon the earth;
the upright generation shall be blessed.
Wealth and riches shall be in his house;
his generosity shall endure forever.
He dawns through the darkness, a light for the upright;
he is gracious and merciful and just.
Well for the man who is gracious and lends,
who conducts his affairs with justice;
He shall never be moved;
the just man shall be in everlasting remembrance.
An evil report he shall not fear;
his heart is firm, trusting in the Lord.
His heart is steadfast; he shall not fear
    till he looks down upon his foes.
Lavishly he gives to the poor;
his generosity shall endure forever;
his horn shall be exalted in glory.
The wicked man shall see it and be vexed;
he shall gnash his teeth and pine away;
the desire of the wicked shall perish.

Our Father ...

From a bad death, deliver us, O Lord (three times).

The uncertainty of death

A man named Ananias, with Sapphira his wife,
sold a piece of land and by fraud kept back part
of the price of the land, with the connivance of his

wife, and bringing a part only, laid it at the feet of the apostles. But Peter said, "Ananias, why has Satan tempted thy heart, that thou shouldst lie to the Holy Spirit and by fraud keep back part of the price of the land? While it yet remained, did it not remain thine; and after it was sold, was not the money at thy disposal? Why hast thou conceived this thing in thy heart? Thou hast not lied to men, but to God." And Ananias, hearing these words, fell down and expired. And great fear came upon all who heard of it. And the young men got up and removed him and, carrying him out, buried him.

About three hours later his wife, not knowing what had happened, came in. And Peter said to her, "Tell me, did you sell the land for so much?" And she said, "Yes, for so much." And Peter said to her, "Why have you agreed to tempt the Spirit of the Lord? Behold the feet of those who have buried thy husband are at the door, and they will carry thee out." And she fell down immediately at his feet and expired. And the young men, coming in, found her dead, and carrying her out they buried her beside her husband. And great fear came upon the whole church and upon all who heard of this.   (Acts 5:1-11.)

We do not know where, when or how we will die.

Death can overtake us in any place—on the street, in bed, at table, in church, at work, anywhere.

I remember a man who died just as he arose from his knees after going to confession, a woman who dropped dead at the Communion rail right after receiving Our Lord, another man who came out of church on Assumption Day after assisting at a solemn high Mass and collapsed at my feet, dead. Death can surprise us in any place.

It can overtake us at any time. When death is mentioned, young people are easily tempted to look at their elders and think: going in order, you are first. Yes, if we passed into eternity in order by age, we could know exactly when our turn was coming! But the fact is that we do not always go in order of age. Older people do not live beyond a certain maximum number of years, it is true; however, many young people die, too. People die at every age. Every day approximately one hundred forty thousand pass into eternity. It cannot be said that death spares those who are strong and in the best of health. No one can be sure from morning to night. When we rise in the morning, we do not know whether we will return safe and sound to our bed at night. At night we do not know whether we shall still be alive in the morning. How many have been snatched by death during sleep! Each New Year's Day, we can all say: I do not know whether I shall see December 31st. We may say the same thing at the beginning of every month, on the first day of the week, at the dawn of each new day: I am not sure of finishing out this month, I am not sure of reaching the end of the week, or of the day. A young seminarian went home on vacation, fell sick and died in a matter of days. We are not sure at any age.

The worst aspect of the uncertainty of death is that we are not sure **how** we will die. Will ours be a good death or a bad one? Our fear of death itself should be moderate. What we must fear is a bad death. Every day we can be tempted to sin, we can fall, and death can surprise us in that state. Consequently, who can help but fear? Who does not have reason to fear?

Even if death is preceded by sickness, we cannot be sure that those who take care of us will tell us on time of death's approach. We do not know whether a good priest will be on hand to attend to our spiritual needs and whether we shall be calm enough to make a good examination of conscience and confess ourselves as we should. We do not know whether we shall have sorrow for our sins so as to obtain forgiveness. Who can feel sure in this matter? Ordinarily Our Lord does not reveal this aspect of the future even to the best souls.

Hence the grace of a good death is one of the most beautiful graces for which to ask. Let us pray for it every day and many times a day. Final perseverance is a special gift of God. In the **Hail Mary,** we always make the same plea to Our Lady: to pray for us now and **at the hour of our death.**

Often recite the "De Profundis", and seven
Hail Marys in honor of Mary's seven sorows, for the
grace to be delivered from a bad death, a bad end.
May death not surprise us in sin!

PSALM 129

Prayer for Pardon and Mercy

Out of the depths I cry to you, O Lord;
Lord, hear my voice!
Let your ears be attentive
to my voice in supplication:
If you, O Lord, mark iniquities,
Lord, who can stand?
But with you is forgiveness,
that you may be revered.
I trust in the Lord;
my soul trusts in his word.
My soul waits for the Lord
more than sentinels wait for the dawn.
More than sentinels wait for the dawn,
let Israel wait for the Lord,
For with the Lord is kindness
and with him is plenteous redemption;
And he will redeem Israel from all their iniquities.

Hail Mary.... (seven times).
From a bad death, deliver us, O Lord (three times).

Preparation for a good death

But the souls of the just are in the hand of
God, and no torment shall touch them. They
seemed, in the view of the foolish, to be dead;

and their passing away was judged an affliction
and their going forth from us, utter destruction.
But they are in peace. For if before men, indeed,
they be punished, yet is their hope full of immortality; chastised a little, they shall be greatly
blessed, because God tried them and found them
worthy of himself. As gold in the furnace, he
proved them, and as sacrificial offerings he took
them to himself. In the time of their visitation they
shall shine, and shall dart about as sparks through
stubble; they shall judge nations and rule over peoples, and the Lord shall be their King forever. Those
who trust in him shall understand truth, and the
faithful shall abide with him in love: because grace
and mercy are with his chosen ones.

But the wicked shall receive a punishment to
match their thoughts, since they neglected justice
and forsook the Lord. For he who despises wisdom
and instruction is doomed. Vain is their hope,
fruitless are their labors, and worthless are their
works. Their wives are foolish and their children
wicked; accursed is their brood.

(Wisdom 3:1-12.)

The lot awaiting the just is quite different from
what awaits the wicked.

Preparation for a good death entails at least the
following:

1. **Absence of mortal sin.** Sin is the only true
evil. It may be a word, a thought, a desire, an action,
or an omission forbidden by the law of God. With
the crown of thorns, Jesus made reparation for sins
of thought. Sins of the heart caused the cruel sword-

wound in His side. Sins of sight cost Him many tears. Sins of gluttony made Him drink gall and myrrh. With the blows and spittle, Jesus made up for our sins of vanity, of speech, of inordinate love for comfort and pleasure.

What damage sin does to the soul in depriving it of God's grace! Woe to the person who lives in mortal sin! What would happen to him if God were to call him suddenly? The fact is that sin is like a magnet continually attracting death. It is like a call to creatures to take revenge for the offense given the Creator. Just as a barren fruit tree invites the axe, so sin calls for divine revenge.

2. **Avoidance of venial sin.** Venial sins lead to lukewarmness. Moreover, they must be paid for in Purgatory. We should detest venial sin and strive never deliberately to commit it. Some imperfections are natural weaknesses, but what we must avoid is venial sin to which we consent, which we commit with eyes wide open, so to speak.

3. **Total satisfaction for sin beforehand.** Confession does not always take away all the temporal punishment due to sin. Perhaps after the sin has been forgiven, some reparation remains to be made either in this life or in the next. Let us do penance, therefore, and make use of the treasures of indulgences. St. Augustine tells us that no one, even if his life was not bad, should approach death without

spending some time in penance and mortification. God sees the affairs of our soul much better than we do. How many times a little bit of vanity is indulged in! How frequently there is less zeal, less energy in the service of God than there should be. . . .

4. **Gaining of merit while there is time.** Death is the time of the harvest; we shall find neither more nor less than what we have sown. The hands of the just will be full: "They shall come back rejoicing, carrying their sheaves" (Ps. 125:6). The hands of the lazy, instead, will be empty. These negligent souls will be forced to moan, "The time has gone, but our lamps are without oil."

5. **Effort to become saints!** Sanctity is the aim of every devout soul. This is the grace for which many ask morning and night with the ejaculation, "Virgin Mary, Mother of Jesus, make us saints!" This is the pupose–the whole purpose and the only one–for which we live. It matters little whether a person be gifted or not, in good health or bad, famous or unknown, rich or poor. What does matter is that he become a saint: "This is man's all" (Eccl. 12:13). And St. Paul adds: "This is the will of God, your sanctification" (1 Thess. 4:3).

Let us conclude these reflections by saying the Litany of Our Lady, whom we await at the hour of our death, and also, a prayer for a good death.

LITANY OF THE BLESSED VIRGIN

Lord, have mercy on us.
Christ, have mercy on us.
Lord, have mercy on us.
Christ, hear us.
Christ, graciously hear us.
God, the Father of heaven, have mercy on us.
God, the Son, Redeemer of the world, have mercy on us.
God, the Holy Spirit, have mercy on us.
Holy Trinity, One God, have mercy on us.
Holy Mary,
Holy Mother of God,
Holy Virgin of virgins,
Mother of Christ,
Mother of divine grace,
Mother most pure,
Mother most chaste,
Mother inviolate,
Mother undefiled,
Mother most amiable,
Mother most admirable,
Mother of good counsel,
Mother of our Creator,
Mother of our Redeemer,
Virgin most prudent,
Virgin most venerable,
Virgin most renowned,
Virgin most powerful,
Virgin most faithful,
Mirror of justice,
Seat of wisdom,
Cause of our joy,
Spiritual vessel,
Vessel of honor,
Vessel of singular devotion,

pray for us.

Mystical rose,
Tower of David,
Tower of ivory,
House of gold,
Ark of the covenant,
Gate of heaven,
Morning star,
Health of the sick,
Refuge of sinners,
Comforter of the afflicted,
Help of Christians,
Queen of Angels,
Queen of Patriarchs,
Queen of Prophets,
Queen of Apostles,
Queen of Martyrs,
Queen of Confessors,
Queen of Virgins,
Queen of all Saints,
Queen conceived without original sin,
Queen of the most holy Rosary,
Queen of peace,

pray for us.

Lamb of God, who takest away the sins of the world,
spare us, O Lord,

Lamb of God, who takest away the sins of the world,
graciously hear us, O Lord.

Lamb of God, who takest away the sins of the world,
have mercy on us, O Lord.

v. Pray for us, O holy Mother of God.

r. That we may be made worthy of the promises of
Christ.

Let us Pray

O God, whose only-begotten Son by his life, death and
resurrection, has purchased for us the rewards of eternal
salvation, grant, we pray, that meditating upon these mys-

teries in the most holy Rosary of the Blessed Virgin Mary, we may imitate what they contain and obtain what they promise. Amen.

PRAYER FOR A GOOD DEATH

Lord, my Creator and Redeemer, I accept in the spirit of adoration, the sentence of death which You have pronounced over me.

I intend to die as a devout child of the Church and pass into eternity with the best dispositions of faith, of hope, of charity and of sorrow for my sins, renewing at the time, at least mentally, my Baptismal vows (and my religious profession).

I intend that every circumstance, even the most painful, which will attend my passing into eternity, as also every detachment I must make and the humiliation of the grave, should be reparation for my many sins and thanksgiving for the vocation with which You have honored me.

With all my heart, I invoke the three great models of a good death, from whom I expect the most merciful assistance: my crucified Jesus, with Whom I intend to pronounce the words, "Father, into Your hands I commend my spirit"; the Virgin Mother of God and my Mother, so that she will pray for me now and at the hour of my death; and St. Joseph, that he may obtain for me a holy life so as to merit a holy death, similar to his.

O Christ, in agony on the cross, O Mary most holy, who died of pure love of God, O St. Joseph, the protector of the dying, I ask you for these graces:

1. Not to be surprised by a sudden death, but rather to be able to receive in time, and with full awareness, the Sacraments of Confession, Viaticum, Extreme Unction, and also the plenary indulgence.

2. To go to Confession frequently and to make a retreat when I am able, so as to find myself each day prepared to die.

3. To correspond fully in my life to all the plans which You, O Lord, had for me in creating me, giving me the grace of Baptism, and calling me to my state in life.

4. To use for the Lord all my talents, natural and supernatural, and my special graces, so that my life may render the maximum fruit of glory to God, merit for me, and peace to souls.

5. O Lord, reward with Your mercy all those who were good to me in life; accept the offering of my life for those to whom I was of bad example, or to whom I should have done more good, or who offended me. Apply to me the merits of my crucified Redeemer.

O Lord, accept my prayers, actions and sufferings, which I offer You in union with the heart of Mary and according to the intentions for which Jesus continuously immolates Himself on the altars.

To obtain these graces, O Lord, I promise to assist diligently every dying person to whom I am obliged for reasons of charity or duty, and to suggest that each recite as many times as possible:

Jesus, I believe in You!

Jesus, I hope in Heaven!

Jesus, I love You with all my heart!

Jesus, forgive me all my sins!

Jesus, Mary and Joseph, I give you my heart and my soul.

Jesus, Mary and Joseph, assist me in my last agony.

Jesus, Mary and Joseph, may I breathe forth my soul in peace with you.

II

JESUS, MODEL FOR THE DYING

The Divine Master instituted the Holy Eucharist not only to be the Sacrifice of the New Law, but also to be food for our souls and a memorial of His passion and death.

Jesus in the Tabernacle is our lifetime Companion, and, on our deathbed, He will be our Viaticum for the voyage to eternity.

It is well to acquire the habit of asking for the grace of a good death.

Let us ask for it as the grace crowning all others.

Let us ask for it from our dying Master, from our Crucified Savior.

Let us ask for it in virtue of the merits of His passion and agony.

Let us ask for it for ourselves and for all our dear ones.

Above all, let us ask for the grace of a holy preparation for death, for he who lives a holy life will certainly have a holy end.

Jesus is condemned to death

Now at festival time it was necessary for him (Pilate) to release to them one prisoner. But the whole mob cried out together, saying, "Away with this man, (Jesus) and release to us Barabbas!" —one who had been thrown into prison for a certain riot that had occured in the city, and for murder. But Pilate spoke to them again, wishing to release Jesus. But they kept shouting, saying, "Crucify him! Crucify him!" And he said to them a third time, "Why, what evil has this man done? I find no crime deserving of death in him. I will therefore chastise him and release him."

But they persisted with loud cries, demanding that he should be crucified; and their cries prevailed. And Pilate pronounced sentence that what they asked for should be done. So he released to them him who for murder and riot had been put in prison, for whom they were asking; but Jesus he delivered to their will.

And as they led him away, they laid hold of a certain Simon of Cyrene, coming from the country, and upon him they laid the cross to bear it after Jesus. Now there was following him a great crowd of the people, and of women, who were bewailing and lamenting him. But Jesus turning to them said, "Daughters of Jerusalem, do not weep for me, but weep for yourselves and for your children. For behold, days are coming in which men will say, 'Blessed are the barren, and the wombs that never bore, and breasts that never nursed.' Then they will begin to say to the mountains, 'Fall upon us,' and to the hills, 'Cover us!' For if in the case of green wood they do these things, what is to happen in the case of the dry?"

(Luke 23:17-31.)

Let us contemplate our Master before Pilate. He listens to the death sentence and bows His head. It was the will of His Father that His death should be our life, salvation for all men, and should give Him greater glory. Jesus accepted death. He did not protest to Pilate, who was turning Him over to His enemies. He did not reject the cross given Him, the instrument of His torture and martyrdom. He embraced it, kissed it and laid it on His shoulders. Without complaint of any kind, without a moan, He let Himself be led like a lamb to the slaughter (Isa. 53:7). In dying, Jesus gave the greatest glory to the Father.

God is the Master of life and death. The act of total submission, and therefore the act which gives God the greatest glory, is the acceptance of death. When we resign ourselves to the sentence condemning us to death, to the separation of soul and body, to the destruction, so to speak, of our being as men, to the descent into the grave, we acknowledge God to be the absolute Lord of life and death. We truly submit to Him and give Him our lives: "No one loves more than he who lays down his life."

Martyrs give their lives by accepting a violent death; others make the offering for various reasons and in diverse circumstances. All of us can accept death with both the certainty and uncertainty connected with it, with all the suffering preceding it, and with all the detachment and humiliation it will entail for our body. Our corpse, in fact, will be abandoned by men, enclosed in a grave, left to decompose. A deep humiliation this! Yet our sins merit it. Sin, a rebellion against God, leads us to exalt ourselves unreasonably. Death, submission to God, forces us to humble ourselves as is proper.

Let us offer up this act of acceptance of death:

"My Lord, wholeheartedly and with full consent I accept from Your hands whatever form of death it shall please You to send me, together with all the sufferings, sorrows and anxieties which accompany my last journey."

A plenary indulgence is attached to this act. Hence whoever goes to confession and communion, then recites this or a similar act, and never revokes it, will receive a plenary indulgence at the point of death. Note that the indulgence comes at the exact moment of death, not before.

Let us pray from our hearts: "May Your will, not mine, be done, O Lord—in death, in judgment, and in eternity"; then let us pray the first station of the cross.

I STATION

Jesus Is Condemned to Death

We adore You, O Christ, and we bless You. Because by Your holy cross You have redeemed the world.

The most innocent Jesus accepts, for our love, and in payment for our sins, the unjust sentence of death pronounced against Him by Pilate.

Most loving Jesus, for Your love, and in penance for my sins, I accept my death with all the pains, sorrows and afflictions which will accompany it.

May Your will and not mine be done, O Lord. Grant that I may taste the consolation of those who fulfill Your holy will.   *Our Father, Hail Mary, Glory be.*

Have mercy on us, O Lord.
Have mercy on us.

Holy Mother, pierce me through,
In my heart each wound renew
Of my Savior crucified.

Through her heart, His sorrow sharing,
All His bitter anguish bearing,
Now at length the sword had passed.

Jesus, model for the dying

And they brought him to the place called
Golgotha, which translated, is the Place of the
Skull. And they gave him wine to drink mixed with
myrrh; but he did not take it. Now it was the third
hour and they crucified him. And the inscription
bearing the charge against him was, "The King of
the Jews."

And they crucified two robbers with him, one
on his right hand and one on his left. And the
Scripture was fulfilled, which says, "And he was
reckoned among the wicked."

(Mark 15:22-23; 25-28.)

And Pilate also wrote an inscription and had
it put on the cross. And there was written, JESUS
OF NAZARETH, THE KING OF THE JEWS.
Many of the Jews therefore read this inscription,
because the place where Jesus was crucified was
near the city; and it was written in Hebrew, in
Greek and in Latin. The chief priest of the Jews
said therefore to Pilate, "Do not write, 'The king
of the Jews,' but, 'He said, I am the King of the

Jews.'" Pilate answered, "What I have written, I have written."

The soldiers therefore, when they had crucified him, took his garments and made of them four parts, to each soldier a part, and also the tunic. Now the tunic was without seam, woven in one piece from the top. They therefore said to one another, "Let us not tear it, but let us cast lots for it, to see whose it shall be." That the Scripture might be fulfilled which says, "They divided my garments among them; and for my vesture they cast lots." These things therefore the soldiers did.

(John 19:19-24.)

Now the passers-by were jeering at him, shaking their heads, and saying, "Thou who destroyest the temple, and in three days buildest it up again, save thyself! If thou art the Son of God, come down from the cross!" In like manner, the chief priests with the Scribes and the elders, mocking, said, "He saved others, himself he cannot save! If he is the King of Israel, let him come down now from the cross, and we will believe him. He trusted in God; let him deliver him now, if he wants him; for he said, 'I am the Son of God.'" And the robbers also, who were crucified with him, reproached him in the same way.

(Matt. 27:39-44.)

Let us turn our thoughts to our Divine Master, model for the dying. Jesus is about to die. His eyes behold a heart-breaking sight: men drawing lots for His clothes, ungrateful men in that crowd whom He has fed with miraculous bread and nourished with His divine words. He sees those whom He has helped now laughing over His shameful death and joining sides with His enemies. He hears the blasphemies and mocking challenges to His power, as we know from the Gospel. His mouth is bitter with gall and myrrh. His hands and feet are pierced by nails. All of Christ's senses may be said to have been crucified—the internal as well as the external, for His heart and spirit were plunged into a sea of sorrow. With His mind's eye He saw soul upon soul tumbling into hell, despite His bloody passion and death.

May Christ's death be our preparation for death.

Our sight will fade out little by little. Our hearing will fail, and at a certain point we shall no longer understand what is said to us. We shall not be able to make out even one word. Our tongue will be stilled. Questions will be put to us and we will make an effort to reply, but no words will come. Our hands and feet will grow cold first, because the extremities are the first members to die. Life gathers around the heart.

Our imagination will place before our eyes our past life, and many things perhaps will cause regrets at the thought of the approaching judgment, the outcome of which we will wish we knew. Our spirit will be sunk in mortal sadness, our heart tempted to despair or presumption, depending on what God permits.

This, then, is what will precede death. Hence, through the merits of Jesus Crucified, the thirst He suffered, the wounds of His hands and feet, all the sufferings He bore in His heart and in His spirit, let us ask the grace of good dispositions at the moment of death. Let us offer now, for that moment, the loss of all our senses in the inexorable onward march of death. Let us ask for that moment the grace to suffer patiently, as Jesus suffered.

The crucifix always shows us a calm, serene Divine Master, fully conscious and fully resigned to the divine will: "Into your hands, Father, I commend my spirit" (Luke 23:46).

Let us ask for the grace of a good death. Let us pray that in that final hour we may overcome every temptation, the last great temptations the devil will hurl at us: "The devil has gone down to you in great wrath, knowing that he has but a short time" (Apoc. 12:12)! We must pray **now** for **then.** May Jesus come in that moment to console us in our agony!

"I await Him, that agonizing Crucified Savior, hope and comfort of the dying. I await Him and I invoke Him now."

An appropriate way to conclude this meditation is with the recitation of the Fourth Sorrowful Mystery of the Rosary.

FOURTH SORROWFUL MYSTERY

Condemned to death, Jesus carries the heavy cross to Calvary. Let us admire our Savior's patience and ask for patience in our sufferings.

Jesus dies

Now one of those robbers who were hanged was abusing him, saying, "If thou art the Christ, save thyself and us!" But the other in answer rebuked him and said, "Dost not even thou fear God, seeing that thou art under the same sentence? And we indeed justly, for we are receiving what our deeds deserved; but this man has done nothing wrong." And he said to Jesus, "Lord, remember me when thou comest into thy kingdom." And Jesus said to him, "Amen I say to thee, this day thou shalt be with me in paradise."

(Luke 23:39-43.)

Now there were standing by the cross of Jesus his mother and his mother's sister, Mary of Cleophas, and Mary Magdalene. When Jesus, therefore, saw his mother and the disciple standing by, whom he loved, he said to his mother, "Woman, behold thy son." Then he said to the disciple, "Behold thy mother." And from that hour the disciple took her into his home.

(John 19:25-27.)

And when the sixth hour came, there was darkness over the whole land until the ninth hour. And at the ninth hour Jesus cried out with a loud voice, saying, "Eloi, Eloi, lama sabacthani?" which, translated, is, "My God, my God, why hast thou forsaken me?" And some of the bystanders on hearing this said, "Behold, he is calling Elias."

(Mark 15:33-35.)

After this Jesus, knowing that all things were now accomplished, that the Scripture might be fulfilled, said, "I thirst." Now there was standing there a vessel of common wine.

(John 19:28-29.)

And immediately one of them ran and, taking a sponge, soaked it in common wine, put it on a reed and offered it to him to drink. But the rest said, "Wait, let us see whether Elias is coming to save him."

(Matt. 27:48-49.)

And Jesus cried out with a loud voice and said, "Father, into thy hands I commend my spirit." And having said this, he expired.

(Luke 23:46.)

The tremendous scene appears before our eyes: a hill, two crucified thieves, and between them the Divine Master, dying. There is an eclipse of the sun, and the whole earth darkens. At the foot of the Crucifix stands a woman rigid with grief–Mary. Jesus Crucified leaves us His Mother as His last bequest. He prays for His very crucifiers and forgives them. He attests to having fulfilled His mission, which means having preached the truth, instituted the Church and the Sacraments, and taught men the way to Heaven. He expresses thirst, but His thirst is a thirst for souls. We contemplate Him now recommending His spirit to His Father and then letting His head fall forward in death.

In virtue of the death of Our Savior Jesus Christ, let us ask the grace of a holy life, so as to merit a holy death. In that last moment, we will have no reason to trust in ourselves. Looking back over our lives, we shall find many, many failings. Our only consolation will be acts which now perhaps we think lightly of, such as certain hidden sacrifices, temptations overcome, and inner struggles. On the other hand, we will not even want to recall many things which give us so much joy at present.

Our only hope will be the Crucifix: "My hope is in Your wounds." "Lord, I have no merits; my merits are Your wounds." St. Therese of the Child Jesus beautifully expressed the theology of St. Paul on this point: "Seeing myself without merits, I take the merits of Jesus, of Jesus Crucified." This is sublime theology of the Redemption put in the simplest terms by a soul who understood the things of God more than many of the world's geniuses.

The Crucifix, then, is our hope. May the Crucified Savior cover us—His crown of thorns on our head, His hands on our hands, His heart on our heart, His feet on our feet. When the Eternal Father looks upon us, may He see only His Son: "Look upon the face of Thy Christ." This, then, is why we want to diminish and present ourselves at the judgment seat of God with the merits of Jesus only. From this we see the value of the Mass, the reason why it is such an immense treasure, why it is said every morning. We see why we must take refuge behind the Sacred Host, so that only the Host will be seen, and our sins will be covered by the wounds, the blood, the shadow of the figure of Christ, the Son of God, Who is always pleasing to the Father.

Let us prepare ourselves for death with great distrust of ourselves and great trust in the Crucifix. At the point of death, we want to disappear from sight—we and our whole lives—so that the Father will see only Jesus in us: "in whom I am well pleased" (Luke 3:22).

Let us close with the prayer, "Soul of Christ," and the Fifth Sorrowful Mystery of the Rosary.

SOUL OF CHRIST

Soul of Christ, sanctify me,
Body of Christ, save me.
Blood of Christ, inebriate me.
Water from the side of Christ, wash me.
Passion of Christ, strengthen me.
O good Jesus, hear me.
Within Your wounds hide me.
Permit me not to be separated from You.

From the malignant enemy defend me.
In the hour of my death call me.
And bid me come to you.
Forever and ever. Amen.

FIFTH SORROWFUL MYSTERY

Jesus is crucified, suffers for three hours and dies on the Cross in order to save us from hell. Let us love the Holy Mass, which is the renewal of the Sacrifice on Calvary.

III

Preparation for Death

Let us ask the Divine Master for the grace to be able to prepare ourselves properly for that last step we must take in the final moments of our life. In particular, let us ask the grace to make every confession well, as though it were our last, and thus our last confession will be a good one. Let us ask also to receive Extreme Unction with holy dispositions.

May Jesus Master, in His mercy, grant every dying person the grace of receiving the Last Sacraments, or at least the grace to depart from this life perfectly reconciled to God, rich in merits only, without any debt to pay the Divine Justice.

Our concluding proposal will be to confess ourselves well always, as we hope to do at the point of death; to receive every Holy Communion as though we were to die immediately afterwards; and to develop a great devotion to St. Joseph, Patron of the dying.

The grace of good confessions

When it was late that same day, the first of the week, though the doors where the disciples gathered had been closed for fear of the Jews, Jesus came and stood in the midst and said to them, "Peace be to you!" And when he had said this, he showed them his hands and his side. The disciples therefore rejoiced at the sight of the Lord. He therefore said to them again, "Peace be to you! As the Father has sent me, I also send you." When he had said this, he breathed upon them,

and said to them, "Receive the Holy Spirit; whose
sins you shall forgive, they are forgiven them; and
whose sins you shall retain, they are retained."
(John 20:19-23.)

The Divine Master conferred upon the Apostles and through them, upon their successors and
all priests, the divine power of forgiving sins. When
we lie on our deathbed weary, sick, and fearful,
our thoughts will fly to our past life, to the debts
we have contracted with Divine Justice. Stunned,
we shall face the thought of the approaching judgment. We shall picture ourselves before Christ our
Judge and imagine a devil on hand to reel off the
sad story of certain past days. Truly, our horror
would lead to desperation if we did not think to
turn towards the crucifix on the wall, the comfort
of those who hope in their Savior.

Before conferring the power to forgive sins,
Jesus showed His Apostles the wounds of His hands
and His open side. Behold our hope—the blood and
the passion of Jesus Christ, the wounds in the hands
and feet of our Divine Savior! His side is still open,
because the sword that pierced it did not close it.
Sin wounded that Heart, but the mercy of God has
kept this wound open so that we may take shelter
in it any day or moment of our life. Our hearts may
rejoice in a new hope, in that divine power which
the crucified and risen Savior gave His Apostles:

"Whose sins you shall forgive, they are forgiven them" (John 20:23).

May our Lord grant us the grace to receive the Last Sacraments at the point of death. "Those who show respect to priests," says St. Alphonse, "deserve to be assisted at death by a good priest." St. Teresa used to say that she would willingly kiss the ground on which a priest had walked. She declared that for her the hand of a priest, destined to release her from her debts with God, was as sacred as the hand of Jesus Christ. Let us respect priests, then, for a priest will open to us the gates of heaven in the hour of our death.

At that time, there will certainly be many factors making Confession difficult: the sickness and fever that usually accompany death, the limited time, the fear of confessing certain falls, the devil of desperation showing us sins perhaps too numerous and too grave. Then we shall need confidence—confidence in the wounds of Jesus, in His open side. This confidence will certainly be given to those who habitually confess themselves well. A monthly day of recollection is an excellent sign of fervor, writes a holy author, if made regularly and well, because thus in every month accounts are settled with God.

With Psalm 116, "Praise the Lord, all you nations!", let us give glory to Jesus Master for having instituted the Sacrament of Penance, the anchor of salvation for those who have lost their innocence. Let us also say the Litany of the Dying.

PSALM 116

Doxology of All the Nations

Praise the Lord, all you nations;
glorify him, all you peoples!
For steadfast is his kindness toward us,
and the fidelity of the Lord endures forever.

LITANY FOR THE DYING

Lord, have mercy on us.
Christ, have mercy on us.
Lord, have mercy on us.
Holy Mary, pray for him.
 All ye holy Angels and Archangels,
Holy Abel,
All ye choirs of the Just,
Holy Abraham,
St. John the Baptist,
St. Joseph,
All ye holy Patriarchs and Prophets,
St. Peter,
St. Paul,
St. Andrew,
St. John,
All ye holy Apostles and Evangelists,
All ye holy Disciples of our Lord,
All ye holy Innocents,
St. Stephen,
St. Lawrence,

pray for him.

All ye holy Martyrs,
St. Sylvester,
St. Gregory,
St. Augustine,
All ye holy Bishops and Confessors,
St. Benedict,
St. Francis,
St. Camillus,
St. John of God,
All ye holy Monks and Hermits,
St. Mary Magdalene,
St. Lucy,
All ye holy Virgins and Widows,

pray for him.

All ye holy Saints of God, make intercession for him.
Be merciful, spare him, O Lord!
Be merciful,
From thy anger,
From the danger of death,
From an ill death,
From the pains of hell,
From all evil,
From the power of the devil,
Through Thy Nativity,
Through Thy Cross and Passion,
Through Thy Death and Burial,
Through Thy glorious Resurrection,
Through Thy admirable Ascension,
Through the grace of the Holy Spirit, the Comforter,
In the day of judgment,

deliver him, O Lord!

We sinners, beseech Thee, hear us.
That thou spare him, we beseech Thee, hear us.
Lord, have mercy.
Christ, have mercy.
Lord, have mercy.

O St. Joseph, foster father of Jesus Christ, and true spouse of the Virgin Mary, pray for us and for the dying of this day.

The grace of
a holy reception of Viaticum

The Jews said to Jesus, "Our fathers ate the manna in the desert, even as it is written, 'Bread from heaven he gave them to eat.'"

Jesus then said to them, "Amen, amen, I say to you, Moses did not give you the bread from heaven, but my Father gives you the true bread from heaven. For the bread of God is that which comes down from heaven and gives life to the world."

They said therefore to him, "Lord, give us always this bread."

But Jesus said to them, "I am the bread of life. He who comes to me shall not hunger, and he who believes in me shall never thirst."

(John 6:31-35.)

With these words, Christ promised the Holy Eucharist. At the point of death, when this earthly life is slipping away from us, we shall delight more than ever before in the beauty of this divine promise: "He who eats my flesh. . . shall live forever." Realizing that our hours are already counted and that there are but few left, with this promise of life everlasting uppermost in our mind, how much comfort and consolation the thought of Holy Communion will give us! The Sacred Host is a divine germ of life. The tree of natural life will be cut down. But a new shoot will come forth from the ashes of that tree: "Thou hast been cut off from the wild olive tree... and hast been grafted into the cultivated olive tree" (Rom. 11:24). And this shoot will be vivified by the life of Jesus Christ. We are His members. We shall feel that by uniting ourselves to Jesus in the Eucharist, we shall live of His eternal life. Let us always ask the Lord the grace to receive Holy Communion at the point of death and to receive well. But let us merit it by making good Communions now.

If for years and years a soul has faithfully and lovingly received Holy Communion daily, even at the cost of sacrifice, he deserves much from the Lord. Now behold this good servant of God lying sick and worn-out on his deathbed. His lips can hardly form the words of a prayer; pain has nailed him to the bed and he can barely move. But his heart is on fire with love for Jesus. And now Jesus leaves the neighboring church carried by the consecrated hands of a good priest. That dying soul sought no one else but Jesus; he gave Him his heart every day. Jesus has loved him in return, and now they meet like two close friends on that deathbed. What a joyous encounter! The soul exclaims, "I am consumed by love!" Jesus answers: "And I am the Supreme Good. I shall be with you." "I am your reward exceedingly great" (Gen. 15:1).

A second means of meriting the grace to receive Holy Viaticum well is to make the nine First Fridays. For Jesus Himself gave us this great promise: "In the excess of my mercy, I promise that whoever receives Communion for nine consecutive months on the first Friday will not die unprepared, without the Sacraments, or in My disgrace."

This is a tremendous promise connected to a very simple practice: receive Communion on the first Friday of nine consecutive months. For the religious or devout soul, Holy Communion is so much a part of daily life that at times he may receive hardly remembering that it is a First Friday. But once the intention is placed, it is sufficient to receive even if one forgets that it is a First Friday. Above all, let the reception be fervent!

The prayer the priest says in assisting the dying is sublimely beautiful. Let us say a part of the "Recommendation of a Departing Soul" now.

PRAYER

Depart, O Christian soul, from this world, in the name of God, the Father Almighty, Who created you; in the name of Jesus Christ, Son of the living God, Who suffered and died for you; in the name of the Holy Spirit, Who sanctified you; in the name of the glorious and Blessed Virgin Mary, Mother of God; in the name of Blessed Joseph, chaste Spouse of the same Virgin; in the name of the Angels and in the name of the Archangels; the Thrones and Dominations; in the name of the Principalities and Powers; in the name of the Virtues, Cherubim and Seraphim; in the name of the Patriarchs and Prophets; in the name of the holy Apostles and Evangelists; in the name of the Holy Martyrs and Confessors; in the name of the Holy Monks and Hermits; in the name of the holy Virgins and of all the Saints of God: may your place be this day in peace, and your abode in holy Sion. Through the same Christ our Lord.   Amen.

O merciful God, O benign God, O God, Who according to the abundance of Thy mercy, dost blot out the sin of those who repent, and dost graciously remit the guilt of past offences; look favorably upon this Thy servant N.; and in Thy mercy hear him as he craves, with heartfelt confession, full remission of all his sins. Renew within him, O most loving Father, whatsoever hath been corrupted through human weakness, or violated through the deceit of the devil; and associate him as a redeemed member to the unity of the body of Thy church. Have pity, O Lord, on his groanings; have pity on his tears; and admit him who hath no hope except in Thy mercy, to the sacrament of Thy reconciliation. Through Christ our Lord. Amen.

The grace of receiving
the Anointing of the Sick well

Is any one among you sick? Let him bring in the presbyters of the Church, and let them pray over him, anointing him with oil in the name of the Lord. And the prayer of faith will save the sick man, and the Lord will raise him up, and if he be in sins, they shall be forgiven him. Confess, therefore, your sins to one another, and pray for one another, that you may be saved. For the unceasing prayer of a just man is of great avail.   (James 5:14-16.)

The principal effect of the Anointing of the Sick is to free the soul from its final debts to God, that is, from venial sins and from certain sins that perhaps were forgotten or could no longer be confessed; to cancel at least in part, the punishment for sin still left to be suffered in the next life; and to restore bodily health should this be the will of God, for the benefit of our soul. In particular, the Anointing of the Sick brings comfort, patience, serenity, love of God, and readiness to support suffering and accept death willingly, if such be God's will.

Often, through negligence, this Sacrament is given to the sick when they are already in a coma, as though the most sacred things should be restricted to the time when the ill are unconscious, that is, when the Sacrament cannot help, or rarely, and then but little. What an insult to God! And it is done under the pretext of charity toward the sick! This is truly an inconceivable kind of charity on the part of believing Christians—a cruel charity.

But we want to merit the grace of receiving the Anointing of the Sick on time and with the proper dispositions. Here are some ways to merit this blessing:

a) Be of real assistance to the sick and dying entrusted to our care. When someone is ill, the first thing to be thought of is his soul. For some people, sickness becomes as spiritually helpful as a long retreat. They reflect seriously and take a good look at themselves to see what they really are. If, with the help of God, they recover, they leave their sickbed greatly changed for the better. Others, on the contrary, and the young especially, get well physically but become ill in spirit. Suffering and periods of illness must be sanctified.

b) Exhort the sick to be patient, to be united to God, and to hope in the Crucified. It is well to help them to say frequent prayers, no matter how brief. They should be urged to kiss the Gospel and to read short passages from it, making a kind of novena of this practice. In particular, they might read passages referring to Our Lord's passion. What beautiful triduums and novenas can be made in this manner!

c) If the person's condition becomes worse, take care to provide the Sacraments on time, and, with great charity, help him to receive them. St. Camillus de Lellis who was so devoted to Jesus in agony, lovingly assisted the sick. At times the right words to say to them were suggested to him by angels audibly whispering in his ear. And the name of this great lover of the suffering has been added to the litany of the saints.

d) See to it that the sick receive the Sacraments on time. Let us never be afraid to act too quickly. It is never too soon to become saints, especially when it seems that the end of life is drawing near. While there is still time, no time must be lost! Delays are risky! There is no room for false security when eternity hangs in the balance, warns St. Augustine.

e) Another means of meriting a good death is devotion to St. Joseph, patron of the dying. He had the grace of dying in the arms of Jesus and Mary. Let us, then, develop this special devotion to St. Joseph, protector of souls in their last agony. Let us frequently offer fervent ejaculations, the litany in his honor, and special prayers to him. Especially, let us strive to sanctify the first Wednesday of every month, and the month of March, dedicated to his name.

We shall conclude by reciting another part of the "Recommendation of a Departing Soul."

PRAYER

Receive, O Lord, Thy servant into the place of salvation, which he hopes for from Thy mercy. Amen.

Deliver, O Lord, the soul of Thy servant from all the dangers of hell, and from the bonds of punishments, and from all tribulations. Amen.

Deliver, O Lord, the soul of Thy servant as thou didst deliver Enoch and Elias from the common death of the world. Amen.

Deliver, O Lord, the soul of Thy servant, as thou didst deliver Noe from the flood. Amen.

Deliver, O Lord, the soul of Thy servant, as Thou didst deliver Abraham from Ur of the Chaldeans. Amen.

Deliver, O Lord, the soul of Thy servant, as Thou didst deliver Job from his sufferings. Amen.

Deliver, O Lord, the soul of Thy servant, as Thou didst deliver Isaac from being sacrificed by the hand of his father Abraham. Amen.

Deliver, O Lord, the soul of Thy servant, as Thou didst deliver Lot from Sodom, and from the flames of fire. Amen.

Deliver, O Lord, the soul of Thy servant, as Thou didst deliver Moses from the hands of Pharaoh, king of the Egyptians. Amen.

Deliver, O Lord, the soul of Thy servant, as Thou didst deliver Daniel from the lions' den. Amen.

Deliver, O Lord, the soul of Thy servant, as Thou didst deliver the three Children from the flaming furnace and from the hands of a wicked king. Amen.

Deliver, O Lord, the soul of Thy servant, as Thou didst deliver Susanna from a false accusation. Amen.

Deliver, O Lord, the soul of Thy servant, as Thou didst deliver David from the hands of Goliath. Amen.

Deliver, O Lord, the soul of Thy servant, as Thou didst deliver Peter and Paul from prison. Amen.

And as Thou didst deliver Thecla, Thy most blessed Virgin and Martyr, from the most cruel torments, so vouchsafe to deliver the soul of this Thy servant, and make it rejoice with Thee in the bliss of Heaven. Amen.

IV

USE OF THE MEANS
OF SANCTIFICATION

Let us ask God to grant us the grace of making good use of all the means of sanctification—the body the Lord gave us, the time that remains to us, and especially the spiritual means at our disposal, i.e., religious instruction, prayer, and good works.

Someday we shall look back over the truly great outpouring of blessings the Lord made available to us that we might become saints. It will be of little avail then to bemoan our negligence. The prudent man provides for his needs on time. St. Robert Bellarmine wrote a book entitled, "The Art of Dying Well." In the first section, he lists sixteen means of preparing for a holy death.

Good use of the body

I will give myself up to complaint; I will speak from the bitterness of my soul. I will say to God: Do not put me in the wrong! Let me know why you oppose me. Is it a pleasure for you to oppress, to spurn the work of your hands, and smile on the plan of the wicked?

Have you eyes of flesh? Do you see as man sees? Are your days as the days of a mortal, and are your years as a man's lifetime, that you seek for guilt in me and search after my sins, even though you know that I am not wicked and that none can deliver me out of your hand?

Your hands have formed me and fashioned me; will you then turn and destroy me? Oh, remember that you fashioned me from clay! Will you then bring me down to dust again? Did you not pour me out as milk, and thicken me like cheese? With skin and flesh you clothed me, with bones and sinews knit me together.

(Job 10:1-11.)

The body is the soul's companion on life's journey. A rational soul and an organic body form man. Man is destined to live forever, but death temporarily separates body from soul. Death is precisely that–a temporary separation of body and soul. If the soul is to be contained in the body, certain conditions of the body must be verified. Now, if through illness, accident, or some other cause, the body is no longer in the state required to contain the soul, the latter leaves. When a bottle holding a costly liquor is broken, the liquor flows out. The body will die and descend into the grave to be purified. The Lord did not make us pure spirits, like the angels. He gave us a body to serve the soul, which in turn serves God. Thus, both soul and body attain to the eternal reward.

The body is endowed with senses–hearing, sight, smell, taste, touch, speech, sentiment, imagination, etc. Because it is spiritual, the soul is superior; because it is rational, it must lead.

The **eyes** can be a source of merit because we can use them to instruct ourselves and to observe what should be learned, and we can mortify them when it is a matter of what should not be looked at.

The soul makes good use of its **hearing** by listening to the word of God, by heeding the cry of the needy, by paying attention to instructions being given, by mortifying curiosity, and refraining from listening to talk that is displeasing to God.

The **tongue** must be used well. It is destined to utter many holy things, to teach, to express thought, to maintain social relations, to praise the Lord, to pray, to preach, and so forth. However, the soul can also abuse the gift of speech. How often the tongue is the cause of great harm!—so much so that St. James calls it a flame that sets everything on fire.

The soul must use its **physical powers** properly. There are some who know so well how to regulate the sentiments of their heart that they love only the Lord. They keep their imagination well controlled; they fill it only with good, holy images. There are souls who keep a good check on their body and mortify all inordinate appetites. Blessed is the soul that is a true leader of the body, a rational guide, capable of urging it on to hard work in a wise, orderly manner at the right time, and capable, too, of mortifying it in a prudent way, even with regard to lawful matters.

The moment will come when our weary body will find itself on its deathbed. Our breathing will become more and more labored until finally we breathe our last. Let us now imagine that a soul departing from the body turns for a last word to the corpse on the bed. The soul that has controlled the body well will say, "Go to repose in the grave. Meanwhile I will go to heaven and prepare the place you, too, have merited. I will come back for you!"

But what a despairing farewell would come from the soul that gave in to all the disorderly appetites of the body. It would say, "To please you, I have damned myself and you. I am going to await you in the torments of hell!"

Let us offer the first sorrowful mystery of the Holy Rosary to ask our suffering Jesus to free us from such a miserable end. Through His bloody sweat in the garden, may He grant us the grace to bid farewell at death to our body as our companion in merit. May our last word to it be a happy "See you soon! I'll be back for you. I'll come to take you with me to Heaven in glory."

FIRST SORROWFUL MYSTERY

In the Garden of Gethsemane, Jesus sweats blood and prays with humility, confidence and perseverance. The angel comforts Him. Let us ask for the spirit of prayer.

With death, time ends

Grace and favor you granted me, and providence has preserved my spirit.

Yet these things you have hidden in your heart; I know that they are your purpose: If I should sin, you would keep a watch against me, and from my guilt you would not absolve me. If I should be wicked, alas for me, filled with ignominy and sodden with affliction! If righteous, I dare not hold up my head; should I raise it, you hunt me like a lion. Repeatedly you show your wondrous power against me, bringing new witness to confront me; while you continue your displeasure with me, in waves your troops come against me.

Why then did you bring me forth from the womb? I should have died and no eye have seen me. I should be as though I had never lived; I should have been taken from the womb to the grave. Are not the days of my life few? Let me alone, that I may recover a little before I go whence I shall not return, to the land of darkness and of gloom, the black, disordered land where darkness is the only light.

(Job 10:12-22.)

Man is destined to live forever. His life begins on this earth, but it lasts only a few days so to speak. Then he enters his eternal home, where life will never end. Time, so brief in comparison to eternity, is, nevertheless, the key to eternity. It is a key which can open the door to Heaven or the door to hell. Whoever uses his time in accordance with the will of God will find Heaven open to him. Likewise, whoever wastes his time opens for himself the gates of hell.

Suppose two young men of the same age and profession spent most of their time together as children, boys and then adults, and finally died on the same day. They would both have received exactly the same amount of time, but depending on how they used it, it could be for one the key to heaven and for the other the key to hell. The fact that they were near in life, worked in the same place, were the same height and build, lived the same number of days–all this matters not at all. "One will be taken, and the other will be left" (Luke 17:34). In a group of people all about the same age, some may have acquired abundant merit, some very little, and some may even be in mortal sin.

Time is a treasure. Used well, it buys another treasure–heaven. Used wrongly or wasted, it renders us blameworthy in God's eyes and becomes our condemnation: "You could have used it well, and you did not." Meanwhile, death comes. Time ends, and what was done remains forever.

To make a comparison, should a young man inherit a fortune from his father, he could either put it to work and multiply it, or go through it in no time and end up in bankruptcy and disgrace.

Evening is a good symbol of death. Every evening a conscientious person examines his actions of the day. He asks himself: Did I give them my all, did I work fervently, with upright intention and care for exactness? Did I do what I could? If the answer is yes, he acquired much merit that day. On the other hand, when the negligent soul casts a backward glance over his day, he realizes that there were many imperfections, many evidences of weakness. How much time in Purgatory he accumulated! And if it is a question of an evil soul, at nightfall, he would be forced to admit: "Today was a black one! Poor me if death should overtake me now! This was a day lost! I wasted it!"

There have been young people who died very early in life and yet, because they made good use of the short time allowed them, they are saints. St. Aloysius Gonzaga, St. Dominic Savio, St. Stanislaus Kostka, St. John Berchmans and St. Agnes are just a few examples of the many young people who achieved sanctity. In contrast, many souls who are given a long life do not sanctify themselves. As the **Imitation of Christ** puts it, "A long life is not always the best."

Let us make good use of our time. It can be wasted in four ways: by committing sin; by losing time in empty, useless pursuits; by doing good poorly; and by doing good without the right intention, that is, to win praise or for some other natural purpose.

Good use of time, on the other hand, demands that we spend it in performing good works, and performing them in a holy manner—that is, in the grace of God, with the right intention, and with as much perfection as possible; and finally, that we do everything with great love of God, making up for lost time by doing the penance required.

Now let us say the second sorrowful mystery of the Rosary to ask Our Lord for the grace to make good use of the priceless treasure of time.

SECOND SORROWFUL MYSTERY

Jesus is tied to the pillar and cruelly scourged in reparation for so many sins of impurity. Let us ask for the virtue of chastity.

The means of salvation end with death

Man, born of woman, is short-lived and full of trouble. Like a flower that springs up and fades, swift as a shadow that does not abide, even so he wastes away like a rotten thing; like a garment that the moth has consumed. Upon such a one will you cast your eyes so as to bring me into judgment before you? Can a man be found who is clean of defilement? There is none, however short his days. You know the number of his months; you have fixed the limit which he cannot pass. Look away from him and let him be, while, like a hireling, he completes his day.

For a tree there is hope, if it be cut down, that it will sprout again and that its tender shoots will not cease. Even though its root grow old in the earth, and its stump die in the dust, yet at the first whiff of water it may flourish again and put forth branches like a young plant. But when a man dies, all vigor leaves him; when man expires, where then is he? As when the waters of a lake fail, or a stream grows dry and parches, so men lie down and rise not again. Till the heavens are no more, they shall not awake, nor be roused out of their sleep.

Oh, that you would hide me in the nether world and keep me sheltered till your wrath is past; would fix a time for me, and then remember me! When a man has died, were he to live again, all the days of my drudgery I would wait, until my relief should come. You would call, and I would answer you; you would esteem the work of your hands. Surely then you would count my steps, and not keep watch for sin in me.

(Job 14:1-16.)

God gave us truth, which is light for our minds. At our disposition, we have the teachings of the Church, the Holy Bible, and the writings of the Fathers of the Church; we can profit from sermons, instructions, and exhortations; we have the benefit of interior lights from God, good books, and the teachings of various persons on the divine truths.

Moreover, we are in a position to practice Christian virtues—faith, hope, charity, mortification, humility, chastity, and so forth. On this earth, we can carry out a mission, we can correspond to our vocation. Every single individual on earth has a job to do. He must courageously and faithfully follow his own path, fulfilling the mission assigned him by God. At the end, everyone must be able to say: "I have finished the course" (2 Tim. 4:1). Woe to the man who has to confess that he missed the right road or travelled it unworthily, or did not make good use of the talents he received from the Lord, or hid them and left them idle!

How many means of grace we have at our disposal–the Sacraments of Confession and Communion, prayer, meditation, examination of conscience, Holy Mass, devotion to our Divine Master in the Blessed Sacrament, to our Blessed Mother, to the Saints, to our Guardian Angel, and so forth. Our Lord has, then, provided us with many means, and the Church offers them to us. Blessed is the soul who enriches himself with them. Truly to be pitied is he who makes ill use of them. Happy the man who can present himself to God with the words: "Lord, you gave me five talents, and I have earned another five."

We make our own eternity, good or bad. The decision is ours, and we have no one else to blame. Even in the worst situations imaginable, we can always produce the best results–resignation, patience, and love of God. Moreover, those who have to suffer earn much more merit than they who work only.

To ask for the grace of using the means of sanctification well, let us say the third sorrowful mystery of the Rosary, followed by the Litany of St. Joseph.

THIRD SORROWFUL MYSTERY

Jesus is crowned with thorns and mocked in reparation for so many evil thoughts and sentiments. Let us ask for purity of mind and heart.

LITANY OF ST. JOSEPH

Lord, have mercy on us.
Christ, have mercy on us.
Lord, have mercy on us.
Christ, hear us.
Christ, graciously hear us.
God the Father of heaven,
God the Son, Redeemer of the world,
God the Holy Spirit,
Holy Trinity, One God,

have mercy on us.

Holy Mary,
St. Joseph,
Renowned offspring of David,
Light of Patriarchs,
Spouse of the Mother of God,
Chaste guardian of the Virgin,
Foster-father of the Son of God,
Diligent protector of Christ,
Head of the Holy Family,

pray for us.

Joseph, most just,
Joseph most chaste,
Joseph most prudent,
Joseph most strong,
Joseph most obedient,
Joseph most faithful,
Mirror of patience,
Lover of poverty,
Model of artisans,
Glory of home life,
Guardian of Virgins,
Pillar of families,
Solace of the wretched,
Hope of the sick,
Patron of the dying,
Terror of demons,
Protector of Holy Church,

pray for us.

Lamb of God, who takest away the sins of the world,
spare us, O Lord!
Lamb of God, who takest away the sins of the world!
graciously hear us, O Lord!
Lamb of God, who takest away the sins of the world!
have mercy on us.

V. He made him the lord of His household.
R. And prince over all His possessions.

LET US PRAY

O God, in Your ineffable providence, You were pleased to choose Blessed Joseph to be the spouse of Your most holy Mother; grant, we beseech You, that we may be worthy to have him for our intecessor in heaven whom on earth we venerate as our protector. Who lives and reigns, world without end. Amen.

V

THE DETACHMENT DEATH DEMANDS

Let us beg Our Lord to give us the grace to detach our hearts from pleasures, wealth, and the esteem of men. Death will detach us from it all, anyway, but that will be a forced separation, whereas if done now, it is free, deliberate and wholly inspired by love. Fortunate are they who are wise enough to make the sacrifice while they are young, or at least, while they are still far from life's end! The sacrifice made at the point of death, if offered resignedly, may be meritorious, too, but it is far more meritorious when made in good health, or better, in the springtime of life. St. Paul tells us to use the things of this world without enjoying them, which means to make use of them as aids to serve God better. We have to attain salvation, to reach heaven, and to become saints. Everything—be it joy or sorrow, wealth or poverty, honor or dishonor—is simply a means to this end. "For those who love God, all things work together unto good" (ROM. 8:28).

Our hearts must be detached from the desire for esteem and from too natural affection

But the just man, though he die early, shall be at rest. For the age that is honorable comes not with the passing of time, nor can it be measured in terms of years. Rather, understanding is the hoary crown for men, and an unsullied life, the attainment of old age. He who pleased God was loved; he who lived among sinners was trans-

ported—snatched away, lest wickedness pervert
his mind or deceit beguile his soul; for the witchery
of paltry things obscures what is right and the
whirl of desire transforms the innocent mind. Having become perfect in a short while, he reached the
fullness of a long career; for his soul was pleasing
to the Lord, therefore he sped him out of the midst
of wickedness. But the people saw and did not
understand; nor did they take this into account:
That God's grace and mercy are with his holy ones
and his care with his elect.   (Wisdom 4:7-15.)

Life is always long enough, even though the
actual number of days be few, when in the time al-
lotted us, we become saints. Contrariwise, life is
ever too long when we make use of it to commit sin
and merit hell. The desire for honor is a powerful
charm which at times ensnares even those who apparently scorn the judgments of their fellowmen.
Unfortunately, many sacrifice their duties to gain
the esteem and affection of others. Out of human
respect, they neglect to do good; for the same reason, many commit sin. If it were not for the company they keep, there are many who would be much
holier. They hear the invitation of God's grace, and
they would like to heed it, but they refrain because
of the sarcastic smile of some poor sinner who has
more reason to cry over his own sins than to laugh
at others.

How many things are done for perverse ends!
Some people have only one thought—to win acclaim.

How much good is ruined by being done for praise!
Our daily performance of duty and, at times, even
our prayer is thus spoiled. Yet why seek the praise
and admiration of those who are as changeable as
ourselves? Everything vanishes–possessions, acclaim,
and men themselves.

Let us consider for a moment what happens
when someone finds himself on the point of death.
The onlookers gradually leave the bedroom, whispering to one another. Others, curious, ask how
many hours or days he can last. The doctor shrugs
his shoulders, replying that there is nothing more
medical science can do. The only ones who remain
in the end are the few holier souls, of whom the
dying man had heretofore taken little notice. "When
a man is prosperous," goes the saying, "he has many
friends. But if his luck runs out, so do his friends."

Those who praised us with their own advantage
in mind, hoping, perhaps, to win our favors and
our confidence, will leave us when we lie dying.
What will be said of us in the room where we expire? Will we be praised or censured? And which
one of our acquaintances will come to plead our
cause at God's tribunal? If we attempted to offer
excuses to the supreme Judge for our life, what
could we say? Perhaps that the others were not
holy? Jesus would answer: Each of them will render

his own personal account; you have to answer for **your** soul!

The body will be accompanied to church by a few and then to the cemetery. As the coffin is lowered into the grave, some tears will be shed by those closest to us, but once the earth has covered it up, everyone will go away, leaving us alone with the gravediggers, alone with the silent dead. Night will fall. The din of the world, the thin smoke of vanity, the echo of shouts of praise will all have vanished in that silent darkness where lie those who sleep the sleep of death.

Yes, let us love, but in Christ. No more for us the foolish desire to win men's admiration, for does it not all cease with death? Let us begin to desire God alone, to want Christ to be pleased with us, so that at our judgment, we may hear: "Well done, good and faithful servant; . . . enter into the joy of thy master" (Matt. 25:21). That is true praise, with eternal consequences, for it comes from God.

At this point, let us offer the following Act of Resignation:

PRAYER

O my God, supreme Lord of life and death, with an immutable decree, for the punishment of sin, You established that all men shall die once. Behold me humbly prostrate before Your tremendous majesty, resignedly submissive to this law of Your justice. With my whole heart I detest my past sins, because of which I have deserved death a thousand times. Therefore I accept it as expiation for my sins, or to obey Your will. Yes, my God, send death to me when, where, and as it pleases You. I on my part will make the most of the days or years You deign to grant me to detach myself from this world and sever all ties holding me to this land of exile. I shall prepare my soul to appear before Your judgment seat with full confidence. So I abandon myself to Your fatherly care. May Your divine Will be done now and always. Amen.

Death separates us from wealth

Yes, the just man dead condemns the sinful who live, and youth swiftly completed condemns the many years of the wicked man grown old. For they see the death of the wise man and do not understand what the Lord intended for him, or why he made him secure. They see, and hold him in contempt; but the Lord laughs them to scorn. And they shall afterward become dishonored corpses and an unceasing mockery among the dead. For he shall strike them down speechless and prostrate and rock them to their foundations; they shall be utterly laid waste and shall be in grief and their memory shall perish.

Fearful shall they come, at the counting up of their misdeeds, and their trangressions shall convict them to their face.   (Wisdom 4:16-20.)

Blessed are they who voluntarily became poor for Jesus' sake. What they gave the Lord will be changed into eternal wealth. Blessed are the poor, for theirs is the kingdom of heaven.

Many, unfortunately, allow themselves to be dragged into sin by love for the wealth and good things of this earth. They violate the seventh Commandment, which becomes their undoing. Or, out of love for a comfortable life, they leave the road to heaven. They keep accumulating wealth, delighting in the luxuries it affords, and never feel they have enough. At times, so great is greed that they seem incapable even of enjoying what they have.

What consolation will come to the man who from his deathbed can view only a simply furnished room, witness to his detachment from this world's goods! He will experience comfort at having no wealth of which to dispose, since he possessed little and desired nothing. He will have no earthly care at that moment, not even concerning his burial and his grave.

In contrast, what a bed of thorns do many lie on who reach the end of their life with their hearts still attached to goods actually possessed or desired. They are attended by those who have a selfish interest in them, who have at heart not them but what they may leave behind. It sometimes happens that even while the poor patient is in his last agony, or perhaps has just expired, those surrounding him are already carrying off the possessions he accumulated at the price of great effort.

Did it pay to take such exquisite care of that body which is destined to become a skeleton? If we were to ask those who repose now in the cemeteries what they think of their poor graves and the abandonment in which the living have left them, they would answer: "That does not interest us at all. The only thing that matters is that the soul be rich in merit."

What does it profit a man, therefore, if he gain the whole world and suffer the loss of his soul? A bare room, a poor bed, plain fare, and simple but dignified apparel are of greater consolation to the dying than luxurious clothes and furnishings, tasty delicacies, and a wealthy mansion. We can never forget that our Lord Jesus Christ was extremely poor. He died on a cross, and not even that was His own! The Apostles, too, were very poor. How absurd it would be to desire a life of comfort and ease and yet hope to find ourselves as holy as those who sacrificed everything for the Lord! No one can serve two masters. Either a man serves pleasure and greed or he serves Our Lord Jesus Christ. The choice must be made. The Gospel is very explicit on this point, and not one word of it will ever fail.

Let us ask Christ to strip our hearts of all earthly desires. We want to choose Christ's own poverty and love it. "He who follows Me does not walk in darkness, but will have the light of life" (John 8:12).

Let us now recite the prayer for a good death.

PRAYER FOR A GOOD DEATH

Jesus Lord, God of goodness, Father of mercy, I present myself before You with a confused and contrite heart. I recommend to You my last hour and that which awaits me after it.

When my immobile feet warn me that my career in this world is about to end, *merciful Jesus, have pity on me.*

When my hands, trembling and benumbed, cannot any longer clasp the Crucifix, and in spite of myself I let it fall upon my bed of pain, *merciful Jesus, etc.*

When my gaze, dim and distorted by the horror of approaching death, fixes upon You, *merciful Jesus, etc.*

When my lips, cold and trembling, pronounce Your adorable name for the last time, *merciful Jesus, etc.*

When my cheeks, pale and livid, inspire the bystanders with compassion and terror, and my brow, wet by the sweat of death, announces that my end is near, *merciful Jesus, etc.*

When my ears, soon to be closed forever to the words of men, open to hear Your voice pronouncing the irrevocable sentence, which will settle my fate for all eternity: *merciful Jesus, etc.*

When my spirit, upset by the sight of my iniquities and by the fear of Your justice, fights against the angel of darkness striving to deprive me of the consoling thought of Your mercies and cast me into a pit of despair, *merciful Jesus, etc.*

When my weak heart, oppressed by sickness, is overcome by the horrors of death and exhausted by the efforts it has made against the enemies of my salvation, *merciful Jesus, etc.*

When I shed my last tears, receive them as an expiatory sacrifice, so that I may expire a victim of penance, and in that terrible moment, *merciful Jesus, etc.*

When my relatives and friends, standing around me, are moved by my sufferings to invoke You on my behalf, *merciful Jesus, etc.*

When I have lost the use of my senses and the entire world has disappeared from me, and I groan in the anguish of my last agony and in the fear of death, *merciful Jesus, etc.*

When my heart's last throbs force my soul to depart from my body, accept these as signs of a holy impatience to come to You, and *merciful Jesus, etc.*

When my soul goes forth forever from this world and leaves my body pale, cold and lifeless, accept the destruction of my being as a homage which I come to render to Your Divine Majesty, and then, *merciful Jesus, etc.*

Finally, when my soul appears before You and sees the immortal splendor of Your Majesty for the first time, do not reject it from Your presence, but deign to receive me into the loving bosom of Your mercy, so that I may eternally sing Your praises. *Merciful Jesus, etc.*

Let us pray.

O God, in condemning us to die, you have hidden from us the hour and the moment. Grant that by spending all the days of my life in justice and holiness, I may merit to depart out of this world in Your holy love. Through the merits of Our Lord Jesus Christ, who lives and reigns with You, in the unity of the Holy Spirit. Amen.

Death will detach us from earthly pleasures

Then shall the just one with great assurance stand before his oppressors who set at nought his labors. Seeing this, they shall be shaken with dreadful fear, and amazed at the unlooked-for salvation. They shall say among themselves, rueful and groaning through anguish of spirit: "This is he whom we once held as a laughingstock and as a type for mockery, fools that we were! His life we deemed madness, and his death dishonored. See how he is accounted among the sons of God; how his lot is with the saints! We, then, have strayed from the way of truth, and the light of justice did not shine for us, and the sun did not rise for us. We had our fill of the ways of mischief and of ruin; we journeyed through impassable deserts, but the way of the Lord we knew not. What did our pride avail us? What have wealth and its boastfulness afforded us? All of them passed like a shadow and like a fleeting rumor." (Wis. 5:1-9.)

Many souls are lost because of an unrestrained thirst for pleasure. Man was created for happiness, but often he fixes his heart on the wrong goal, and instead of loving God, loves what is earthly. Among adults, the majority lose their souls because of impurity, or at least, not without it. Desiring to enjoy what the world offers, they will be tormented by these pleasures and left bitterly disillusioned. Their bodies will descend into the grave and decompose little by little until all that is left of them is a handful of dust which will be scattered with time.

Witness the destruction that continues in the grave, says St. Alphonse. There death goes on with its work and completes it. The body begins to decompose and is slowly consumed, until at last it is impossible even to tell where it lay. Everything disappears—bones, skull, the coffin itself and finally every trace of it. Likewise, nowhere on earth are to be found the prints of that man's footsteps during life. This is the way things end for man's body.

Is it not about time to start serving the God who will be our eternal joy? When St. Francis Borgia saw the corpse of Queen Isabella, who had been called the most stunningly beautiful woman of her day, he paused to contemplate the horrible sight the opened coffin presented. He and the other nobles were on hand to testify that it was really the body of the Queen which they were about to bury. When the casket was opened, so terrible was the spectacle of the rotting body and the accompanying stench that all but Francis fled in horror. The Saint remained and meditated long on that once beautiful face now decaying, on the eye sockets crawling with worms. Then and there he said to himself: I resolve to begin loving God alone and serving Him. Creatures come and go, but God remains forever!

Delights of this world finish soon enough, leaving in their wake both remorse and anguish. After tasting every kind of earthly pleasure, Solomon exclaimed, "Everything is vanity!" **The Imitation of Christ** says: "Vanity of vanities! All is vanity, except to love God and serve Him alone."

Let us dearly love the Lord. Our love in this life will be the beginning of an eternal love in heaven. "Charity never fails" (1 Cor. 13:8).

We shall conclude by saying the Chaplet to the Divine Master.

CHAPLET TO THE DIVINE MASTER

1. Jesus, Divine Master, we adore You as the Word Incarnate sent by the Father to instruct men in the truths which give life. You are uncreated Wisdom; You are the Light, the only Master. You alone have words of eternal life. We thank You for having given us the light of reason and the light of faith, and for having called us to the light of glory. We believe, submitting our whole mind to You and to the Church, and we condemn all that the Church condemns. Master, show us the treasures of Your wisdom. Let us know the Father, make us true disciples of Yours. Increase our faith so that we may arrive at the eternal vision in heaven.

Jesus Master, Way, Truth, and Life, have mercy on us.

2. Jesus, Divine Master, we adore You as the delight of the Father, object of His satisfaction, the sole way to go to Him. We thank You for making Yourself our model. You have left us examples of the highest perfection, You have invited men to follow You on earth and in heaven. We contemplate You in the various periods of Your earthly life. We docilely place ourselves in Your school and condemn every moral teaching which is different from Yours. Draw us to You so that by following in Your footsteps and renouncing ourselves, we may seek only Your will. Increase in us active hope, and the desire to be found similar to You at the judgment, and to possess You forever in heaven.

Jesus Master, etc.

3. Jesus, Divine Master, we adore You as the only Son of God, come on the earth to give life, the most abundant life, to man. We thank You for dying on the cross to merit life for us, which You give to us in Baptism and nourish in

Holy Communion and the other Sacraments. Live in us, O Jesus, with the effusion of the Holy Spirit, that we may love You with all our mind, strength, and heart, and our neighbor as ourselves for Your love. Increase charity in us, so that when we are called from the sepulchre to the glorious life, we may be united with You in eternal happiness in heaven.   *Jesus Master, etc.*

4. Jesus, Divine Master, we adore You living in the Church, Your mystical body, and our sole ark of salvation. We thank You for having given us this infallible and unfailing Mother, in whom You continue to be for men the way, the truth and the life. We pray that all unbelievers may come to Her inestinguishable light, that those in error may return to her, and all humanity be united in faith, hope, and charity, as God is one, as the redemption is one, as heaven is one. Exalt the Church! May she find men docile to her work. Assist the Pope, sanctify the priests and the souls consecrated to You. Lord Jesus, our sigh is Yours: that there may be one fold under one Shepherd, so that we may all be reunited in the Church Triumphant in heaven.

Jesus Master, etc.

5. Jesus, Divine Master, we adore You with the angels who sang the reasons for Your incarnation: "Glory to God and peace to men." We thank You for having called us to participate in Your own apostolate. Enkindle in us Your same flame of zeal for God and for souls. Fill all our powers with Yourself; live in us so that we may diffuse You through the apostolates of prayer and of suffering, of example and of deeds. Send good laborers into Your vineyard. Enlighten preachers, teachers, and writers. Infuse in them the Holy Spirit with His seven gifts. Prepare minds and hearts to receive the light, the guidance and the grace of Your priests. Come, Master and Lord! teach and reign, through Mary our Mother, Teacher and Queen.

Jesus Master, etc.

VI

THE WAY TO PREPARE FOR DEATH

There are three ways of preparing to die well: 1) THINK *of death,* 2) ACT *with a view to death, and* 3) PRAY *for a good death.*

In our own hands lies the key to a good or evil end. On His part, God has created us, redeemed us, and sanctified us. Now it is up to us to correspond.

Man is free. He is master of his eternal destiny.

Thinking of death

"The land of a certain rich man brought forth abundant crops. And he began to take thought within himself, saying, 'What shall I do, for I have no room to store my crops?' And he said, 'I will do this: I will pull down my barns and build larger ones, and there I will store up all my grain and my goods. And I will say to my soul, Soul, thou hast many good things laid up for many years; take thy ease, eat, drink, be merry.' But God said to him, 'Thou fool, this night do they demand thy soul of thee; and the things that thou hast provided, whose will they be?' So is he who lays up treasure for himself, and is not rich as regards God."

(Luke 12:16-21.)

This parable presents a man who thinks of nothing but this earth. And he is labelled a fool!

We must think of death and eternity. A thousand thoughts and cares, a thousand worries and problems occupy man's mind here below. We think about our reputation, about our meals, and about our clothes. Much precaution is taken when it is a matter of the health of the body. But what about the soul? Do we give it thought? And what about death? When the Church places blessed ashes on our foreheads, she tells us: "Remember you are dust!" The Holy Spirit admonishes us: "Think of your last end!"

The brother of the famous monk, à Kempis, had built a beautiful home furnished in the most luxurious manner desirable. One day he invited à Kempis to visit it. After showing him all through it, he asked, "What do you think of my house now? Isn't it beautiful and comfortable? Haven't I provided everything?"

His brother, growing serious, replied, "This house would be truly beautiful, for you have thought of just about everything. But . . . I see one defect in it, a big defect."

Surprised, the other said, "Tell me what it is. I can still remedy it."

"You cannot remedy it," replied à Kempis.

"What is this defect?"

"Your trouble is that you have made a door!"

"The door! Since when is a door in a house a defect?! Why, it's essential! . . ."

"It's a defect," the monk repeated, "because you will one day go out that door for the last time, carried by pallbearers, and the house will be left to someone else. Blessed will you be if you think of that and make sure you build another house– the home of your eternal happiness." "Man goes to his lasting home" (Eccles. 12:5).

One evening I spoke to a group briefly on the need to prepare for death. The next morning I received the following message: "Kindly do not come again in the evening to speak on death. It's frightening. I, for one, was unable to sleep."

Death is frightening for those who do not want to think of it. But faced squarely, realistically, it brings great serenity, as is the case with saints.

Presenting him with a ring, Pope Pius IX told a man, "Wear it every day. At night, before you retire, read the two words engraved on it: **Memento mori**–Remember, you will die." The man carried out the advice for several nights, but indifferently, almost without thought. One night, however, as he prepared for bed, those words made a deep impression on him. "I am going to die," he thought, "and am I ready? If tonight were my last night on earth, in what state would I find myself as I faced the judgment of God?" The result was that he changed his way of life.

Let us make use of a holy little trick: when we wake up each morning and when we retire in the evening, let us look at the palms of our hands and, seeing the two "M's" traced thereon, think of the Latin phrase **Memento mori**–"Remember you must die." In the morning our thought will be: Today I want to live as if this were the last day of my life. I want to make a perfect act of contrition. In the evening: If death should come tonight, I want to be ready.

If more thought were given to death, how fewer sins there would be! How much less excess and agitation! How much more virtue, prayer, and merit!

Let us now recite the Fourth Psalm and then pray the Thirteenth Station of the Way of the Cross, asking our Blessed Mother to receive us at death as she received her Son.

PSALM 4

Joyful Confidence in God

When I call, answer me, O my just God,
you who relieve me when I am in distress;
Have pity on me, and hear my prayer!
Men of rank, how long will you be dull of heart?
Why do you love what is vain and seek after falsehood?
Know that the Lord does wonders for his faithful one;
the Lord will hear me when I call upon him.

Tremble, and sin not;
reflect, upon your beds, in silence.
Offer just sacrifices,
and trust in the Lord.
Many say, "Oh, that we might see better times!"
O Lord, let the light of your countenance shine upon us!
You put gladness into my heart,
more than when grain and wine abound.
As soon as I lie down, I fall peacefully asleep,
for you alone, O Lord,
bring security to my dwelling.

Glory be, etc.

XIII STATION

We adore You, O Christ and we bless You.

Because by Your holy cross, You have redeemed the world.

The Sorrowful Mother receives into her arms her Son, Who was taken down from the cross.

Mary contemplates in His wounds the horrible work of our sins and Jesus' infinite love for us.

Devotion to Mary is a sign of salvation. O Mother and our Co-redemptrix, give me Your love. Grant me the grace to pray to You every day. Assist me now and especially in the hour of my death.

Our Father, Hail Mary, Glory be.

Holy Mother, pierce me through
In my heart, each wound renew
Of my Savior crucified.
By the cross with you to stay
There with you to weep and pray,
Is all I ask of you to give.

Acting with death in mind

Acting with a view to death means doing now what we will then want to have done, and rejecting or avoiding now what we will then want to have avoided.

"There was a certain rich man who used to clothe himself in purple and fine linen, and who feasted every day in splendid fashion. And there was a certain poor man, named Lazarus, who lay at his gate, covered with sores, and longing to be filled with the crumbs that fell from the rich man's table; even the dogs would come and lick his sores. And it came to pass that the poor man died and was borne away by the angels into Abraham's bosom; but the rich man also died and was buried in hell. And lifting up his eyes, being in torments, he saw Abraham afar off and Lazarus in his bosom. And he cried out and said, 'Father Abraham, have pity on me, and send Lazarus to dip the tip of his finger in water and cool my tongue, for I am tormented in this flame.'

"But Abraham said to him, 'Son, remember that thou in thy lifetime hast received good things, and Lazarus in like manner evil things; but now here he is comforted whereas thou art tormented. And besides all that, between us and you a great gulf is fixed, so that they who wish to pass over from this side to you cannot, and they cannot cross from your side to us.'

"And he said, 'Then, father, I beseech thee to send him to my father's house, for I have five brothers, that he may testify to them, lest they too come into this place of torments.' And Abraham said to him, 'They have Moses and the Prophets: let them hearken to them.' But he answered, 'No, father Abraham, but if someone from the dead goes to them, they will repent.' But he said to him, 'If they do not hearken to Moses and the Prophets, they will not believe even if someone rises from the dead.'"

(Luke 16:19-31.)

"Night is coming, when no one can work" (John 9:4). Let us pretend that our last hour is fast approaching and ask our conscience: what will I wish to have done in my life? The answer will certainly be easy. It will spring from the depths of the heart with devastating conviction: Ah, if only I had become a saint! To the dying comes the thought: I lived forty (or twenty or sixty) years. In that same length of time, others have become saints. Oh, how blessed would I be if I were holy now! But such desires then are useless. A farmer who has sown no seed cannot look for a crop to harvest! We reap what we sow. Let us sanctify ourselves now. We still have hours and minutes at our disposal. Even a little while is enough!

"If I want, from this day forward, I will become a saint, by directing all my thoughts, all my aspirations, all my sentiments to God. I embrace His will wholeheartedly, I cling with my whole being to His heart, I unite myself to Him in life and death."

Whoever wants to become a saint will become one. Blessed will we be if at our death we see ourselves surrounded by good deeds—deeds which seem to say to us: "We were performed by you and we shall go with you to the judgment-seat of God."

Let us do now what we shall be unable to do then. Such was the great motto of the saints. St. Alphonse has a whole meditation on this one point. Let us reject now what we will wish then to have avoided—sin. What a sad harvest it would be to leave this world with a heart still loaded down with sin!

May we detest every sin and cleanse our souls with good confessions! May we resolve to sin no more, to prefer death instead, no matter what. No special friendship, no pleasure, no empty pride, no love of comfort must succeed in swerving us from our firm decision to do good.

Let us pray the beautiful Psalm 90 which begins, "You who dwell in the shelter of the Most High...", and then say the first two parts of the Chaplet to St. Joseph.

PSALM 90

Security under God's Protection

You who dwell in the shelter of the Most High,
who abide in the shadow of the Almighty,
Say to the Lord, "My refuge and my fortress,
my God, in whom I trust."
For he will rescue you from the snare of the fowler,

from the destroying pestilence.
With his pinions he will cover you,
and under his wings you shall take refuge;
his faithfulness is a buckler and a shield.
You shall not fear the terror of the night
nor the arrow that flies by day;
Not the pestilence that roams in darkness
nor the devastating plague at noon.
Though a thousand fall at your side,
ten thousand at your right side,
near you it shall not come.
Rather with your eyes shall you behold
and see the requital of the wicked,
Because you have the Lord for your refuge;
you have made the Most High your stronghold.
No evil shall befall you,
nor shall affliction come near your tent,
For to his angels he has given command about you,
that they guard you in all your ways.
Upon their hands they shall bear you up,
lest you dash your foot against a stone.
You shall tread upon the asp and the viper;
you shall trample down the lion and the dragon.
Because he clings to me, I will deliver him;
I will set him on high because he acknowledges my name.
He shall call upon me, and I will answer him;
I will be with him in distress;
I will deliver him and glorify him;
with length of days I will gratify him
and will show him my salvation.

CHAPLET TO ST. JOSEPH

1. O St. Joseph, faithful cooperator in our redemption,
have pity on poor mankind still enfolded in many errors,
vices and superstitions. You were a docile instrument in the

hands of the Heavenly Father, in all arrangements for the birth and infancy of Jesus, for the preparation of the Victim, the Priest, and the Divine Master of men. May you be blessed, you who often, even without understanding, let yourself be guided entirely by heavenly inspirations and the words of the angel! Obtain for us the apostolic spirit, so that with prayer, words and works, we may humbly cooperate in the Christianization of the world. May iniquity be wiped out, and may everyone receive Jesus Christ, the Way, Truth and Life.   St. Joseph, pray for us.

2. O St. Joseph, model of every virtue, obtain for us the grace to possess your spirit. In loving, fruitful silence, in the practice of all religious and civil precepts, in docility to every manifestation of God's will, you arrived at a high degree of sanctity and of heavenly glory. Obtain for us an increase of faith, hope and charity, an ample infusion of prudence, justice, fortitude, and temperance, an abundance of the gifts of wisdom, understanding, knowledge, counsel, piety, fortitude and fear of God. From heaven assist us so that we may always better know the end for which we were created, the wisdom of those who do good, and direct every action of our life towards heaven.

St. Joseph, pray for us.

Praying for a good death

"Let not your heart be troubled. You believe in God, believe also in me. In my Father's house there are many mansions. Were it not so, I should have told you, because I go to prepare a place for you. And if I go and prepare a place for you, I am coming again, and I will take you to myself; that where I am, there you also may be. And where I go you know, and the way you know."

Thomas said to him, "Lord, we do not know where thou art going, and how can we know the way?" Jesus said to him, "I am the way, and the truth, and the life. No one comes to the Father but through me. If you had known me, you would also have known my Father. And henceforth you do know him, and you have seen him."

Philip said to him, "Lord, show us the Father and it is enough for us." Jesus said to him, "Have I been so long a time with you, and you have not known me? Philip, he who sees me sees also the Father. How canst thou say, 'Show us the Father?' Dost thou not believe that I am in the Father and the Father in me? The words that I speak to you I speak not on my own authority. But the Father dwelling in me, it is he who does the works. Do you believe that I am in the Father and the Father in me? Otherwise believe because of the works themselves. Amen, amen, I say to you, he who believes in me, the works that I do he also shall do, and greater than these he shall do, because I am going to the Father. And whatever you ask in my name, that I will do, in order that the Father may be glorified in the Son. If you ask me anything in my name, I will do it. (John 14:1-14.)

The grace of a holy death must crown all other graces. There at the hour of death, we will leaf through the book of our life. As we see its various pages we shall anxiously look for our Guardian Angel's classification of those days—excellent day, good day, poor day, very poor day. . . . At least, may we then receive the grace to wash away our every sin in the blood of Jesus! May our Blessed Mother obtain for us a holy death.

In a short while, this earth will be exchanged for the glory of heaven. This miserable abode will presently give way to that eternal Jerusalem where God reigns and with Him His faithful children.

The prudent Christian proceeds through life distrusting himself and hoping in God. With confidence in Christ, he prays daily for the grace of final perseverance. We meditated on the agony and death of Jesus our Master on the cross. Jesus is the great model of the dying. To merit the grace of a holy death, let us devoutly recite the fifth sorrowful mystery of the Rosary and the prayer, "Soul of Christ." Moreover, reflecting that the happiest death after Christ's was His Blessed Mother's, let us say the "Hail Mary" well throughout our lives, and also the Fourth Glorious Mystery of the Rosary. In every "Hail Mary" we say, "Pray for us . . . at the hour of our death." Devotion to St. Joseph, too, the Patron of the dying, aims at obtaining for us a holy death in the arms of Jesus and Mary.

We may place the intention now that all the Hail Marys we recite shall be an urgent appeal to our Mother to come to assist us in our last agony. Some writers say—and St. Joseph Cafasso gives the explanation—that Our Lady comes visibly to those who are devoted to her to help them on their death-beds. The very edifying deaths of St. Aloysius, St. Stanislaus, St. John Berchmans, and St. Joseph Cafasso himself, and many other Saints are witness to this fact.

Often let us call on St. Joseph. If a soul expires in the arms of Jesus, Mary, and Joseph, he will remain for all eternity blissful in their embrace.

We conclude by saying the remaining parts of the chaplet to St. Joseph.

CHAPLET TO ST. JOSEPH

(Continued)

3. O St. Joseph, we venerate you as the model of workingmen, the friend of the poor, the consoler of the afflicted and exiled, the Saint of Providence. On earth you visibly represented the universal goodness and solicitude of the Heavenly Father. You were the carpenter of Nazareth and the teacher of work to the Son of God, Who became a humble laborer for us. At Nazareth, work was elevated to dignity as a means of sanctification and redemption. Aid with your prayers all who labor in intellectual, moral and material work. For the nations tormented by social problems, obtain legislation in conformity with the Gospel; for everyone, the spirit of Christian charity, for the world a social order based on the teachings of the Supreme Pontiff. St. Joseph, provide for us.   St. Joseph, pray for us.

4. O St. Joseph, foster-father of Jesus, I bless the Lord for your intimacy with Him during His infancy and youth in Bethlehem, Egypt, and Nazareth. You loved Him paternally and you were filially loved. Your faith made you adore

in Him the Incarnate Son of God, while He obeyed you, served you, and listened to you. You had sweet conversations with Him, and with Him you shared work, great trials and tender consolations. Grant us your joy and your power in heaven. Obtain for me the grace never to offend and lose Jesus through sin. Pray for me that I may always receive Holy Communion and confess myself well, attain to a great intimacy with Jesus and a tender and strong love for Him while on earth, and possess Him forever in Heaven. I ask you also for the grace which I desire most... St. Joseph, take care of it.   St. Joseph, pray for us.

5. O St. Joseph, pure spouse of Mary, we humbly ask you to obtain for us a true devotion to our most tender Mother, Teacher and Queen. By divine will, your mission was associated with that of Mary. You were the head of the Holy Family, the model of fathers, the guardian of vocations. With Mary you shared trials and joys; with her you entered into a holy competition in virtue, work and merit; and union of mind and heart. O St. Joseph, pray for the fathers and mothers of families; pray for the innocence of youth; pray for religious and priestly vocations. Obtain for us the grace to know the Blessed Virgin Mary as you knew her, to imitate her, to love her, to pray to her always. Draw many souls to her maternal Heart.

St. Joseph, pray for us.

6. O St. Joseph, protector of the dying, we pray to you for all the dying, and beg your assistance in the hour of our death. You merited a happy departure from a holy life, and in your last hours you had the ineffable consolation of being assisted by Jesus and Mary. Deliver us from a sudden death. Obtain for us the grace to imitate you in life, to detach our heart from all worldly things and daily to store up treasures for the moment of our death. Obtain for us the grace to receive the last Sacraments well, and together with

Mary, inspire us with sentiments of faith, hope, love and sorrow for sins, so that we may breathe forth our soul in peace.   St. Joseph, pray for us.

7. O St. Joseph, protector of the universal Church, look benignly upon the Pope, the Episcopate, the Clergy, the Religious and the laity. Pray for the sanctification of all. The Church is the fruit of the Blood of Jesus, your foster Son. We entrust to you our supplications for the extention, the liberty, and the exaltation of the Church. Defend her from errors, from evil and from the powers of hell, as you once saved the threatened life of Jesus from the hands of Herod. May Christ's desire come true: "That there be one fold under one shepherd." Obtain for us the grace to be living and active members of the Church militant, that we may eternally rejoice in the Church triumphant.

St. Joseph, pray for us.

THE PARTICULAR
JUDGMENT

VII

THE SOUL'S APPEARANCE BEFORE GOD

After meditating on death, it is useful to turn to the topic of the particular judgment. We shall consider it in three sections devoted to the soul's appearance before God, the examination, and the verdict.

"*It is appointed unto men to die once and after this comes the judgment*" (HEB. 9:27). *Death is not as terrifying for itself as for what follows it.*

It is up to us to win the favor of our blessed Savior. Before we meet His justice, let us take advantage of the mercy He offers us. Someday, Jesus Christ will be seated before us to judge us, but now in the Blessed Sacrament He is elevated on the altar before us to save us, to give us His merits and endow us with His graces. Let us bow our heads in His presence and adore Him with faith, hope, love and sorrow.

We shall appear before Christ, our all-wise Judge

"Then will the kingdom of heaven be like ten virgins who took their lamps and went forth to meet the bridegroom and the bride. Five of them were foolish and five wise. But the five foolish, when they took their lamps, took no oil with them, while the wise did take oil in their vessels with the lamps. Then as the bridegroom was long in coming, they all became drowsy and slept. And at midnight a cry arose, 'Behold, the bridegroom is coming, go forth to meet him!' Then all those virgins arose and trimmed their lamps. And the foolish said to the wise, 'Give us some of your oil, for our lamps are going out.' The wise answered, saying, 'Lest there may not be enough for us and for you, go rather to those who sell it, and buy some for yourselves.'

"Now while they were gone to buy it, the bridegroom came; and those who were ready went in with him to the marriage feast, and the door was shut. Finally there came also the other virgins, who said, 'Sir, sir, open the door for us!' But he answered and said, 'Amen I say to you, I do not know you.' Watch therefore, for you know neither the day nor the hour."   (Matt. 25:1-13.)

We shall die, and in the very room where we die, the judgment will take place. While our corpse is still warm, and our relatives are asking one an other whether we have expired, our soul, having left the body, will meet Jesus Christ. There shall the judgment-seat be erected, and we shall face i alone, accompanied only by our deeds, good or bad Christ has no need of witnesses, neither of the devil' accusations nor of the saints' defense of us. He knows all things; He is the all-wise Judge. He see our mind and the thoughts entertained there. He knows the whole story, in detail, from start to finish Christ knows every sentiment of our heart, from the lowest to the holiest. He knows these sentiment in all their particulars, in all their fine points, in al their intensity. Christ knows every word uttered from the first moment of our use of reason down to he last time our lips formed a word. Every word is written in the book of life–empty words, holy words, forgotten words. "The court was convened, and the books were opened" (Dan. 7:10).

Moreover, Christ knows all the works, all the movements of our hands, from those of the priest in distributing Holy Communion and lifting the Sacred Host for the adoration of the people, to the most material actions, the most common, and the worst. He knows how many letters have flowed from our pen and how much labor we accomplished. He knows every step we have taken, the studies we have pursued, our relationships and correspondence, our daily routine of home life. He is, in short, the all-wise Judge.

Furthermore, Our Lord knows how much should have been done, in correspondence to all His graces. He knows the degree of health a person had, the degree of intelligence, keenness of mind, memory, and ability; the amount of graces accompanying a priestly or religious vocation, the graces given in childhood, youth, and adulthood; the inspirations, promptings and occasions received.

A man says to himself: "I did that one night, locked in my room, protected by darkness. It was simply a sentiment of my heart, desire, hatred. . . .

No one ever knew, not even my confessor, for I covered it perfectly." Foolish reasoning! While he thought he was wrapped in the folds of darkness, an angel was beside him and a knowing hand was writing. For there is an eye that sees everything everywhere, always. There is an ear that hears everything, everywhere and always. There is a recording hand that misses nothing. They belong to God.

God sees me! And everything will show up in front of that divine, all-wise Judge. All things are reflected in Him as in a mirror. He keeps a record of everything. It is a characteristic of Divine Wisdom to have all things present at all times; for Him there is no past or future—everything is present.

What tremendous consolation for good souls! What consolation for us who now are meditating and praying! Christ, the most wise Judge will remember it. In our earliest years, our mother pointed the picture of Our Blessed Mother and the Crucifix out to us. We joined the hands of innocence and stammered, "Jesus, Mary." How many acts span the distance from that day to the last kiss of the Crucifix by dying lips! Yet Jesus remembers everything—those victories over our passions, those repressions of angry impulses, that diligence at work, those quick ejaculations. Some are so diligent, yet in such a hidden fashion, that no one suspects the worth of those souls. They receive no reward on this earth, but will it always be so? Thanks be to God, it will not, for our God is omniscient, all-knowing. The good done is written on the Heart of Christ, never to be erased! We shall take our good deeds with us, for they are the property of whoever performs them.

Jesus is all-wise! Therefore, let good souls rejoice! He knows all our holy desires, our efforts, and the love in our hearts, even when we do not succeed in human affairs. The wicked, on the other hand, ought to fear for their foolish hope that they are unseen and unheard when they sin secretly. "No one will ever know this," they say; "not even in confession will it be made known." Those who talk like this are guilty of two faults–the sin itself and the determination to hide it.

Psalm 109 shows us Christ our Judge triumphing over His enemies, after having drunk from the torrent of sorrow. Let us recite this Psalm and also the first two points of the Chaplet to the Guardian Angel, for the grace of obtaining a favorable judgment.

PSALM 109

The Messias: King, Priest, and Conqueror

The Lord said to my Lord: "Sit at my right hand till I make your enemies your footstool."

The scepter of your power the Lord will stretch forth from
    Sion:
"Rule in the midst of your enemies.
Yours is princely power in the day of your birth, in holy
    splendor;
before the daystar, like the dew, I have begotten you."
The Lord has sworn, and he will not repent:
"You are a priest forever, according to the order of
    Melchisedec."
The Lord is at your right hand;
he will crush kings on the day of his wrath.
He will do judgment on the nations, heaping up corpses;
he will crush heads over the wide earth.
From the brook by the wayside he will drink;
therefore will he lift up his head.

CHAPLET TO THE GUARDIAN ANGEL

1. My Guardian Angel, you are a pure spirit, always
close to me, and yet always immersed with the heavenly
hosts in the vision, love and joy of the Blessed Trinity. In
your intimacy with God, obtain for me lively faith, firm
hope and an ardent desire for heaven. Make me ever better
understand that I was created for God and that He is my
supreme and sole Good, my eternal happiness. Communicate
to me the supreme wisdom of seeking first the kingdom of
God and His justice in all things, certain that the rest will
be given me besides.

    Glory Be. Angel of God, etc.

2. My Guardian Angel, you are the minister of my
eternal salvation, destined always to enlighten, guard, rule
and guide me. I was entrusted to you by God in His mercy.
God elected you to bear me in your hands, so that I shall
not be caught in dangers to soul and body, and to forestall
the deceits of the world and overcome all obstacles, so that

my soul may keep free from stain in the midst of error and vice. Inspire me with the holy will of God, enlighten those who direct me, keep me on the right path, and present my prayers to God. Above all, defend me from the assaults of the enemy at the hour of my death, so that I may breathe forth my soul in peace.

Glory Be. Angel of God, etc.

Christ our Judge, is all-knowing

And he said also to his disciples, "There was a certain rich man who had a steward, who was reported to him as squandering his possessions. And he called him and said to him, 'What is this that I hear of thee? Make an accounting of thy stewardship, for thou canst be steward no longer.'

"And the steward said within himself, 'What shall I do, seeing that my master is taking away the stewardship from me? To dig I am not able; to beg I am ashamed. I know what I shall do, that when I am removed from my stewardship they may receive me into their houses.' And he summoned each of his master's debtors and said to the first, 'How much dost thou owe my master?' And he said, 'A hundred jars of oil.' He said to him, 'Take thy bond and sit down at once and write fifty.' Then he said to another, 'How much dost thou owe?' He said, 'A hundred kors of wheat.' He said to him, 'Take thy bond and write eighty.'

"And the master commended the unjust steward, in that he had acted prudently; for the children of this world, in relation to their own generation, are more prudent than the children of the light. And I say to you, make friends for yourselves with the mammon of wickedness, so that when you fail they may receive you into the everlasting dwellings."

(Luke 16:1-9)

On judgment day, the time of mercy will close. Jesus will then make His justice prevail and the power He received from His Father. The Father has given Him the authority to judge the good and the wicked. And Christ will justly reward all the good done and punish all evil.

Even the smallest good actions will bring their reward. A glass of water given for love of Christ will not go without its reward, and an abundant reward, too. How many good deeds are unrewarded on this earth! It might be said that a cloak of silence hides the greater number of duties performed in the home, the majority of the sacrifices we ask of our hearts, the best aspect of that love with which souls seek the Lord. But Christ weighs every act and bestows upon it a proportionate reward.

Figuring in every act are, first, the intention with which it is done; second, the state of the soul, whether it be in grace or not during the action; third, the degree of knowledge and awareness that precedes; fourth, the greater or lesser degree of intensity in the will's consent; fifth, the value of the work in itself—whether it be more or less good or bad; and sixth, the manner in which it is performed, that is, in how holy or unworthy a fashion. To acquire merit, the good act must be complete.

In this world, a deceptive scale is used, for judgment is made on the basis of appearances. God, instead, takes every element into account, and nothing escapes Him. With our lives, we render ourselves deserving of merit or of blame. The good done piles up, and it almost seems that God forgets it. But this is not so! It will all be there at our judgment. In certain souls, evil, too, accumulates. Here again, it seems as though God is silent, even when evil is obstinate and defiant. But the Lord is a good remunerator even when He delays.

Judgment will come. And what bliss will flood the faithful soul when it at last meets Jesus and can contemplate Him in all His goodness–when it sees the smile on the face of this Savior it has sought and loved! This will be the meeting of a son with a much-loved father whom he has yearned to see. It will be the long-awaited embrace of friend with Friend. It will be a moment of indescribable joy.

Judgment will come. For the sinner, it will be a terrible encounter with an angry Christ! Men have died of fear before facing certain human courts of justice. Unworthy sons who have caused the death of their mother by their crimes cannot bring themselves to face her on her deathbed. What then must it be like to appear before God?

Let us analyze our actions and never be content with a superficial look at appearances. The judgment of men should not hold our attention. What counts is the real nature of our acts. "He who judges me is the Lord" (I Cor. 4:4). Hypocrisy, which covers evil with the cloak of innocence, and false human respect, which omits to do good for fear of criticism, must be avoided. If our deeds are substantially good, we shall have our reward. But if they are amiss, what will happen to us? Let us do good, and do it in an upright way!

While we conclude with the recitation of Psalm 110, let us ponder on the words: "The fear of the Lord is the beginning of wisdom." Then we shall continue the Chaplet to the Guardian Angel.

PSALM 110

Praise of God for His Goodness

I will give thanks to the Lord with all my heart
in the company and assembly of the just.
Great are the works of the Lord,
exquisite in all their delights.
Majesty and glory are his work,
and his justice endures forever.
He has won renown for his wondrous deeds;
gracious and merciful is the Lord.
He has given food to those who fear him;
he will forever be mindful of his covenant.
He has made known to his people the power of his works,
giving them the inheritance of the nations.

The works of his hands are faithful and just;
sure are all his precepts,
Reliable forever and ever,
wrought in truth and equity.
He has sent deliverance to his people;
he has ratified his covenant forever;
holy and awesome is his name.
The fear of the Lord is the beginning of wisdom;
prudent are all who live by it.
His praise endures forever.

Glory Be.

CHAPLET TO THE GUARDIAN ANGEL

(Continued)

3. Angel of God, I thank you for having accepted and fulfilled until now the duty of guarding me, so unworthy, and of being with me throughout life. I also humbly ask your pardon for having often been deaf to your inspirations. Do not abandon me. It was only ignorance or weakness—or even malice, but for me your friendship is a great treasure. Rather, show yourself more attentive the more you see me weak and unhappy. Obtain these graces for me, from Jesus and Mary: a heart which is docile and receptive to your counsels; respect for your presence everywhere; lasting confidence in your solicitous protection; true devotion to you, to be one day your fellow-citizen in heaven.

Glory Be. Angel of God.

4. My Guardian Angel, faithful and strong in virtue, you are one of the Angels who, led by St. Michael, overcame Satan and his followers. That battle which one day took place in heaven is now being waged on earth. The prince of evil and his followers contend for souls against Jesus Christ living in the Church. Obtain for me perseverance in renouncing the devil and his works, and fidelity in

keeping the promises made in Baptism. Increase in me the strength to live united to Jesus Christ, Whose soldier I became in Confirmation. Look upon my weakness and the danger I run of losing myself. Give me also the true spirit of apostolate. The battle is against the devil. Reveal to me his snares, fight beside me, obtain for me final perseverance.

Glory Be. Angel of God.

Christ, our Judge, is all-powerful

"For it is like a man going abroad, who called his servants and handed over his goods to them. And to one he gave five talents, to another two, and to another one, to each according to his particular ability, and then he went on his journey. And he who had received the five talents went and traded with them, and gained five more. In like manner, he who had received the two gained two more. But he who had received the one went away and dug in the earth and hid his master's money.

"Then after a long time the master of those servants came and settled accounts with them. And he who had received the five talents came and brought five other talents, saying, 'Master, thou didst hand over to me five talents; behold, I have gained five others in addition.' His master said to him, 'Well done, good and faithful servant; because thou hast been faithful over a few things, I will set thee over many; enter into the joy of thy master.'

"And he also who had received the two talents came and said, 'Master, thou didst hand over to me two talents; behold, I have gained two more.'

His master said to him, 'Well done, good and faithful servant; because thou hast been faithful over a few things, I will set thee over many; enter into the joy of thy master.'

"But he who had received the one talent came and said, 'Master, I know that thou art a stern man; thou reapest where thou hast not sowed and gatherest where thou hast not winnowed: and as I was afraid, I went away and hid thy talent in the earth; behold, thou hast what is thine.' But his master answered and said to him, 'Wicked and slothful servant! thou didst know that I reap where I do not sow, and gather where I have not winnowed? Thou shouldst therefore have entrusted my money to the bankers, and on my return I should have got back my own with interest. Take away therefore the talent from him, and give it to him who has the ten talents. For to everyone who has shall be given, and he shall have abundance; but from him who does not have, even that which he seems to have shall be taken away. But as for the unprofitable servant, cast him forth into the darkness outside, where there will be the weeping, and the gnashing of teeth.'"   (Matt. 25:14-30.)

Jesus Christ is the all-powerful Judge. To those who have done well He will say, "Enter into the joy of your Lord." The good servant will rise, and the heavens will open above him. Notwithstanding the rage of Lucifer, he will enter into the kingdom of the blessed, borne there by the omnipotent word of Christ. With regard to the wicked servant, Christ will say to the angels: "Take him from here and banish him into the darkness." Immediately the wicked soul will be hurled down, and no pleas or tears will be of use. The almighty command of Christ will cast him into that dark pit, where there shall be the "weeping and gnashing of teeth."

On this earth, little thought is given to Christ. The Pharisees of old accused Him, Pilate scourged Him and condemned Him, the soldiers crucified Him and jeered at Him. Yes, little attention is paid to Christ. His Commandments are despised, His counsels and inspirations are neglected. He is freely offended, even in church. He is publicly blasphemed. And there are some unfortunates who go so far as to betray Christ by receiving Him in Communion with mortal sin on their souls! Yet, will the Lord remain silent forever? Is He unable to impose His authority, His Commandments, His counsels? No, He will not be quiet forever. The day will come when we shall be confronted by His omnipotence, like tiny tots before the giant Goliath.

What have we to gain by these reflections? We should resolve to be ready at all times, which means being faithful to the practice of examining our conscience. Whoever examines and condemns himself will not be questioned and condemned. The faults of which we accuse ourselves before God, for which we ask pardon, and for which we repent in Confession, will be cancelled. What blindness it is thoughtlessly to bury remorse of conscience and go to judgment with stained souls!

Examinations of conscience are to be made in the morning, during the day, in the evening, at the end of the week for Confession, at the end of the month, and once for the whole year. Our hearts must be probed well and everything pulled out for inspection. The more bad points we discover and detest now, the less we shall carry to the judgment.

Let us remember that at the judgment we shall be defenseless, but here on this earth we have a great means at our disposal: the possibility of examining ourselves, repenting, and being forgiven. Let us fear God. Realizing how little merit we have, let us work intensely and diligently to acquire it, begging Jesus Christ, meanwhile, to give us His own. Then we shall meet our Judge with peaceful hearts, for He will be our Rewarder, our Father, coming to lead us into our blessed home in heaven.

Let us now say the final part of the chaplet to the Guardian Angel, after reciting Psalm 31.

PSALM 31

Remission of Sin

Happy is he whose fault is taken away,
whose sin is covered.
Happy the man to whom the Lord imputes not guilt,

in whose spirit there is no guile.
As long as I would not speak, my bones wasted away
with my groaning all the day,
for day and night your hand was heavy upon me;
my strength was dried up as by the heat of summer.
Then I acknowledged my sin to
you, my guilt I covered not.
I said, "I confess my faults to the Lord,"
and you took away the guilt of my sin.
For this shall every faithful man pray to you
in time of stress.
Though deep waters overflow,
they shall not reach him.
You are my shelter; from distress you will preserve me;
with glad cries of freedom you will ring me round.
I will instruct you and show you the way you should walk;
I will counsel you, keeping my eye on you.
Be not senseless like horses or mules:
with bit and bridle their temper must be curbed,
else they will not come near you.
Many are the sorrows of the wicked,
but kindness surrounds him who trusts in the Lord.
Be glad in the Lord and rejoice you just;
exult, all you upright of heart.

Glory Be.

CHAPLET TO THE GUARDIAN ANGEL

(Continued)

5. O all you Angels of the Lord, you are called to pay noble homage, to give praise and incessantly bless the August Trinity, and to make reparation for our omissions. You are true lovers of God and of souls, continuing in your song of "Glory to God in the highest and peace on earth to men of good will." You form the heavenly army against the forces of hell, so that the Holy Name of God may be held

acred, the kingdom of Jesus Christ may come, and His will
e fulfilled on earth as it is in heaven. Supplicate the Immaculate Queen of the Apostles for the Church of Jesus
Christ. Keep watch over humanity, so that it may live in
peace and acknowledge its God and Eternal Judge. Extend
our protection over rulers, workers, and those who suffer.
Cast the devils into hell, save the world from their wiles,
n order that the reign of truth, of justice, and of love may
e established. Amen.

Glory Be. Angel of God.

VIII

THE EXAMINATION OF THE SOUL

We have already considered our appearance before Christ
our supreme Judge. Now we move on to a consideration of th
examination, the testimonies, and the proceedings of the judg
ment. It is true that God's judgment will take place in an in
stant, but we must consider it part by part for our greate
spiritual profit.

Let us be sincere with God

Fear of the Lord is glory and splendor, gladness and a festive crown. Fear of the Lord warms
the heart, giving gladness and joy and length of
days. He who fears the Lord will have a happy
end; even on the day of his death he will be
blessed. The beginning of wisdom is the fear of
the Lord, which is formed with the faithful in the
womb. With devoted men was she created from of
old, and with her children her beneficence abides.
Fullness of wisdom is fear of the Lord; she inebri-
ates men with her fruits. Her entire house she fills
with choice foods, her granaries with her harvest.
Wisdom's garland is fear of the Lord, with blos-
soms of peace and perfect health. Knowledge and
full understanding she showers down; she height-
ens the glory of those who possess her. The root of
wisdom is fear of the Lord; her branches are length
of days.

One cannot justify unjust anger; anger plunges
a man to his downfall. (Sirach 1:9-19.)

The fear of the Lord is the beginning of wisdom. "My flesh shudders with dread of you, and I fear Your ordinances" (Ps. 118:120). Lord, pierce me with a holy fear, for I want to fear Your judgments.

Our soul must appear before Christ, our supreme Judge. Let us lift up our eyes and see whether we can meet Him without trembling. Can we calmly look into the penetrating eyes of Christ? His gaze goes straight to the depths of our heart. And we shall have to give Him an account of all the good and evil we have done in life.

Everything is written in the book of life. Not a thing has been forgotten. Some souls have remained faithful to Jesus their whole lives through; others have turned from God and refused to obey Him. Our life is a trial. Have we given proof of fidelity to God? We shall be saved forever. Have we been unfaithful to God? Ah, how much we ought to fear the judgment! Every man is prone to evil. Yet there are those whose lives as a whole reflect fidelity to God, even though they may have erred once in a while. And, unfortunately, there are others who have been unfaithful to God for the most part, although they did some little good.

Let us examine ourselves mercilessly. Do we try to serve God, as the chief aim of our lives? As

a whole, is our life marked by fidelity to God's laws?
Or is it basically far from God? The fallen angels,
who gave proof of infidelity, were hurled into hell
despite their excuses and pretexts. The good angels
proved themselves faithful and were raised to the
Beatific Vision. Both Cain and Abel offered sacri
fices to the Lord, but their interior dispositions
were different. And we are well aware of the end
of each.

If the judgment were to take place now, could
we say that we have, for the most part, been faith
ful to God? A man can say that he is basically
faithful if he observes the Commandments, loves
and serves God, and avoids sin. If he should fall at
times, he rises again, does penance, and once more
goes ahead in faithful service to the Lord. The su
preme Judge, therefore, will declare that this soul
has done well. "Blessed is that servant whom his
master, when he comes, shall find doing his duty"
(Cf. Matt. 24:46). Instead, if a soul disobeys God,
transgresses His laws, seeks wealth and honors, and
does his duty only out of fear of what others will
say otherwise—this soul will have to admit that he
has been unfaithful to God. Everyone does a little
good, but we must scrutinize the substance and the
intention behind it. Was it done for God or for
ourselves?

The judgment of God will go very deep. "I will explore Jerusalem with lamps" (Soph. 1:12). How many mistakes will not be held against souls, because substantially they were seeking God! And on the other hand, how many apparently good works, when examined in God's light, will be seen to have been ruined by many defects and sins! Are we sincere with God? Do we seek the Lord wholeheartedly? And when we confess ourselves, especially, are we sincere?

There are souls who truly seek God and accuse themselves of their defects and sins as they are, in substance, together with the real root of their falls— self-love, for example, or pride, or envy, or laziness, or anger. On the other hand, not even in the confessional are some souls sincere. This is their real trouble; they hide, cover up, and pretend. In fact, some make it their program systematically to hide everything. But the only ones they deceive are themselves! God cannot be fooled. He scrutinizes intentions: "O searcher of heart and soul, O just God" (Ps. 7:10).

Let us recite the first joyful mystery, the Annunciation of the Archangel to Mary. We must rejoice at the thought that Jesus came down from heaven not as a judge, but rather as a savior. So we shall try to go to Him in sincerity of heart. Let us "make straight the ways of the Lord" and be honest with Him. There is no place for self-deception. Sincerity is required in life and in the confessional!

FIRST JOYFUL MYSTERY

The Archangel Gabriel announces to the most holy Virgin Mary the incarnation of Our Lord Jesus Christ, and her elevation to be the Mother of God. Mary accepts, declaring herself to be the handmaid of the Lord. Let us learn and ask for the virtue of humility.

Let us be sincere with our neighbor

A patient man need stand firm but for a time, and then contentment comes back to him. For a while he holds back his words, then the lips of many herald his wisdom. Among wisdom's treasures is the paragon of prudence; but fear of the Lord is an abomination to the sinner. If you desire wisdom, keep the commandments, and the Lord will bestow her upon you; for fear of the Lord is wisdom and culture; loyal humility is his delight. Be not faithless to the fear of the Lord, nor approach it with duplicity of heart. Play not the hypocrite before men; over your lips keep watch. Exalt not yourself lest you fall and bring upon you dishonor; for then the Lord will reveal your secrets and publicly cast you down, because you approached the fear of the Lord with your heart full of guile.

My son, when you come to serve the Lord, prepare yourself for trials. Be sincere of heart and steadfast, undisturbed in time of adversity. Cling to him, forsake him not; thus will your future be great. Accept whatever befalls you, in crushing misfortune be patient; for in fire gold is tested, and worthy men in the crucible of humiliation. Trust God and he will help you; make straight your ways and hope in him.

(Sirach 1:20-29; 2:1-6.)

All the sham fabricated by man with foolish human prudence will topple. At the judgment, it will all be revealed.

There shall be the accusation. Who will accuse the sinner before the judgment seat of God? And of what will he be accused? The angels will declare having seen him sin. They will tell of their efforts to draw him out of evil, but all in vain. The devils, too, will charge that the sinner succumbed to their temptations, and they will conclude by claiming him now for themselves. Even the walls wherein he sinned will cry out in accusation against the sinful soul.

His own conscience will become his accuser. Many times, remorse of conscience is silenced, or put off and overlooked. The Pharisees contented themselves with a mere external holiness, for the benefit of those who beheld them. They washed the cup on the outside only, so to speak. Whitened sepulchres, our Lord called them, and they have their modern counterparts in some who proclaim themselves perfect gentlemen. Man has his duties as a Christian and before that, as a creature—duties toward God and himself. It is certainly not sufficient for him to perform only part of these duties; he must discharge them all. Even when monuments have been erected in memory of a man, even when he has been raised to high posts and given special marks of distinction, let us not forget that the judgment will reveal him as he really is. The mask will be torn off, if mask there was—if he was not truly good, upright, and holy.

The upright man will be exalted at the judgment, first by the angels, faithful witnesses of his good works. Even the devils will pay him honor, showing their rage at not having been able to conquer him. What is more, the very rooms and localities wherein he did good will proclaim him. But above all, the just man will be praised by his conscience for having heeded its voice and faithfully followed it.

Let us be sincere with our fellow men! It is insincerity to be ruled by hypocrisy or to do good for the sole purpose of being seen. It is also insincerity to neglect doing good for fear of being laughed at. We must have a real love of God and profess our convictions, our faith, frankly and proudly. The judgment of men in this life is of little import. The one who will judge us is the Lord: "With me it is a very small matter to be judged by you or by man's tribunal. . . . he who judges me is the Lord" (1 Cor. 4:3-4).

In eternity, both the good and the wicked will testify to the virtue of the upright man, as they will also bear witness to the evil conscience of the sinner. This world is often concerned solely with the external, with appearances, and how often are we not in danger of following the viewpoints of the worldly, who gloss evil over!

Let us be honest with man, and we shall be praised by God.

To obtain this sincerity, let us say the second joyful mystery of the rosary.

SECOND JOYFUL MYSTERY

The Virgin Mary hastens to visit and assist St. Elizabeth. Let us admire Mary's neighborly love and ask for it.

Let us be sincere with ourselves

You who fear the Lord, wait for his mercy, turn not away lest you fall. You who fear the Lord, trust him, and your reward will not be lost. You who fear the Lord, hope for good things, for lasting joy and mercy. Study the generations long past and understand; has anyone hoped in the Lord and been disappointed? Has anyone persevered in his fear and been forsaken? has anyone called upon him and been rebuffed? Compassionate and merciful is the Lord; he forgives sins, he saves in time of trouble.

> Woe to craven hearts and drooping hands, to
> the sinner who treads a double path! Woe to the
> faint of heart who trust not, who therefore will
> have no shelter! Woe to you who have lost hope!
> what will you do at the visitation of the Lord?
> Those who fear the Lord disobey not his words;
> those who love him keep his ways. Those who fear
> the Lord seek to please him, those who love him
> are filled with his law. Those who fear the Lord
> prepare their hearts and humble themselves before
> him. Let us fall into the hands of the Lord and
> not into the hands of men, for equal to his majesty
> is the mercy that he shows.
>
> (Sirach 2:7-18.)

After the testimonies have been heard before
the judgment seat of God, the arguments will be
presented, the case will be stated.

What excuses can a sinner offer? Can he, perhaps, affirm that he did not receive sufficient grace?
The Lord will reply, "If you had prayed, graces
would have been given you." Perhaps the accused
might say he did not have sufficient time and that
he intended to give himself to God later on? The
Lord would reply, "Time was given you, but how
much you wasted! Others, with that same amount
of time, or even less, became saints." Again, the
sinner might protest, "But my friends acted no
differently. . . ." And Christ would reply that the
others will have to give an account of their deeds
as soon as they appear before the tribunal of God,

but meanwhile he, the sinner, is already being judged and must worry about himself. Perhaps the soul might say that his passions were too strong? The Lord would answer, "The Saints became Saints by doing violence to themselves. The kingdom of God belongs to the strong and the brave. On the other hand, prayer makes possible, through the grace of God, what would otherwise be impossible to men." At that the wicked would be silenced.

The faithful man will not attribute to himself the good he has done. He will declare that if he was faithful to God it was through the help he received from the Lord. He will say, "Lord, I must kiss the feet of the angels and Our Lady for the help they gave me. If I did not sin, it was through the grace of Holy Communion. If I picked myself up after a fall, it was through the help of my confessor." Continuing, he will express great gratitude: "Lord, You deigned to enrich my soul in baptism, in confirmation, at the altar, in Holy Mass—and my soul is full of gratitude to You! Your wounds, Jesus, are my merits. It is Your mercy that has saved me. O Lord, I want heaven not so much for myself as for Your glory, so that I may proclaim Your mercy for all eternity."

From every corner of heaven and earth, a universal testimony will rise in favor of this soul,

declaring it holy and worthy of heaven. The Lord
will then lead it into eternal bliss, for it will be beautiful and loaded with merit, and because Christ will
see in it His own image: "For those whom he has
foreknown, he has also predestined to become conformed to the image of his Son" (Rom. 8:29).

Let us be sincere with ourselves, and especially
with regard to the voice of conscience. Conscience
makes itself heard when it is a question of good to
be done. It is a strong urge to act courageously. It
makes its voice heard when faced with evil. In this
case, it is a powerful admonition. Let us listen to it!

Furthermore, conscience is satisfied after a good
act, whereas after evil has been committed, it gives
no peace. It must, therefore, be heeded. Conscience
calls for progress, for a daily ascent toward perfection, for an increase of merit. The just man walks
the straight path faithfully every day. And his
conscience will ask for its reward from the Supreme
Judge.

When we make our examination of conscience,
let us do so in all sincerity and honesty. Where conscience finds evil, no excuses are to be tempted, no
self-deception permitted. What conscience pro-
nounces good must be continued, without compro-
mise. Every day, the devil concocts new deceits and
excuses, but this is a diabolic art. The famous pagan

philosopher Cicero advised going into one's room at night, in the quiet dark, and putting every act of the day through an inspection, a merciless inspection—every act, every word, every sentiment, every place visited. . . . How few judge themselves dispassionately! Very few they are, indeed. All too often the voice of passion, the clever snares of the devil, and the tenets of the world deceive many souls.

Let us ask the Lord for the grace of being honest with ourselves. If truly we are seeking God, we need only go ahead resolutely and fearlessly! But if we realize that we are seeking self, we ought to be afraid, and change. The fear of God is wisdom.

Let us now recite the third joyful mystery to obtain the grace of being honest with ourselves.

THIRD JOYFUL MYSTERY

Born in the stable of Bethlehem, Jesus is laid in a manger, amid the most abject poverty. Let us begin to esteem the virtue of poverty and ask it of Jesus and Mary.

IX

SENTENCE IS PRONOUNCED
OVER THE SOUL

We have already considered our appearance before the tribunal of God, and the examination of our life. Now we must meditate on the verdict. Later we shall reflect on the general judgment, but at present we are concerned with the question: what will be the outcome of our particular judgment?

There are three verdicts which can be given at the particular judgment: a sentence to eternal punishment; a sentence to the pains of purgatory; or immediate admission into heaven.

We shall begin by considering the verdict Jesus will communicate to the elect soul, which passed into the next life clothed with grace and perfectly purified, without any debts left with the justice of God.

The judgment pronounced over the elect soul

And this do, understanding the time, for it is now the hour for us to rise from sleep, because now our salvation is nearer than when we came to believe. The night is far advanced; the day is at hand. Let us therefore lay aside the works of darkness, and put on the armor of light. Let us walk becomingly as in the day, not in revelry and drunkenness, not in debauchery and wantonness, not in strife and jealousy. But put on the Lord Jesus Christ, and as for the flesh, take no thought for its lusts.

But him who is weak in faith, receive, without disputes about opinions. For one believes that he may eat all things; but he who is weak, let him eat vegetables. Let not him who eats despise him who does not eat, and let not him who does not eat judge him who eats; for God has received him. Who art thou to judge another's servant? To his own lord he stands or falls; but he will stand, for God is able to make him stand. For one esteems one day above another; another esteems every day alike. Let everyone be convinced in his own mind. He who regards the day, regards it for the Lord; and he who eats, eats for the Lord, for he gives thanks to God. And he who does not eat, abstains for the Lord, and gives thanks to God. For none of us lives to himself, and none dies to himself; for if we live, we live to the Lord, or if we die, we die to the Lord. Therefore, whether we live or die, we are the Lord's. For to this end Christ died and rose again, that he might be Lord both of the dead and of the living. But thou, why dost thou judge thy brother? Or thou, why dost thou despise thy brother? For we shall all stand at the judgment-seat of God; for it is written, "As I live, says the Lord, to me every knee shall bend, and every tongue shall give praise to God."

Therefore every one of us will render an account for himself to God.

(Rom. 13:11-14; 14:1-12.)

Will our meeting with Jesus Christ be as tender and as full of love as was Magdalen's after the resurrection?

St. Aloysius asked his confessor if there are
souls who go straight to heaven without passing
through purgatory, and the reply he received was,
"Yes, there are." This marvelous judgment falls to
those souls who leave this earth after cancelling all
debts contracted with the Lord, to those souls who
have loved God with their whole mind, will, and
heart, as the holy Gospel says.

How did such souls live? They purified their
minds from every worldly or distracting thought,
fixing their gaze on God and on His will. They had
no preferences, for their guiding rule was always
what would please God. They loved the Lord so
much that the most delightful hours of their days,
weeks, and years were the hours spent with Him before the Tabernacle. Truly they loved God with
their whole mind, will and heart.

Such a soul will leave this earth in grace, un-
stained. God will rest His gaze on it, take pleasure in
the sight, and invite it with the words: "Come,
spouse of Christ, receive your crown." "You who
have loved your God alone, who have sought nothing but His will, who have had no other aim in all
you did but to serve your heavenly Father better,
come! Come, spouse of Christ, take possession of
the great crown prepared for you." Thus, the soul
will go straight from this land of exile to its heaven-

home. In this case, judgment will be simply
recognition on the part of the Lord, with one in-
stantaneous gaze, of the soul's beauty, innocence
and grace.

"Come, O truly blessed of My Father! You
sought the Lord only and He will be yours forever.
Your desire will be forever satisfied: 'Blessed are
they who hunger and thirst for justice, for they shall
be satisfied' (Matt. 5:6). Let the heavenly gates
open wide and let this soul enter into the possession
of the kingdom it earned!"

At the burial of children, the ceremony is a
triumphant celebration for a soul gone to join the
angels. So there is, indeed, rejoicing both in
heaven and on earth. And we shall now recite the
Psalm which the Church puts on our lips for the
blessed celebration of the entrance of children into
heaven. Let us imagine ourselves accompanying
one of these fortunate souls who has passed from
among us like a white dove, without a stain; or,
even better, one of those religious souls who bring
to heaven a double crown of merit: innocence and
love, the lily and the rose.

After we recite Psalm 112, we shall say the first
two points of the Chaplet to the Sacred Heart.

PSALM 112

Praise of the Lord for His Care of the Lowly

Praise, you servants of the Lord,
praise the name of the Lord.
Blessed be the name of the Lord
both now and forever.
From the rising to the setting of the sun
is the name of the Lord to be praised.
High above all nations is the Lord;
above the heavens is his glory.
Who is like the Lord, our God, who is enthroned on high
and looks upon the heavens and the earth below?
He raises up the lowly from the dust;
from the dunghill he lifts up the poor
To seat them with princes,
with the princes of his own people.
He establishes in her home the barren wife
as the joyful mother of children.

Glory Be.

CHAPLET TO THE SACRED HEART

O Jesus, our Master, I, an unworthy sinner, prostrate
before You, adore Your Heart, which has so greatly loved
mankind and has not spared anything for it. I believe in
Your infinite love for us. I thank You for the great gift
which You gave to mankind, especially the Gospel, the
Holy Eucharist, the Church, the Priesthood, the religious
state, Mary as our Mother and Your very life.

1. O Jesus, Divine Master, I thank and bless Your most
generous Heart for the great gift of the Gospel. You have
said: "I was sent to evangelize the poor." Your words bear
eternal life. In the Gospel, You have revealed divine mysteries, taught the way of God with truthfulness, and offered
the means of salvation. Grant me the grace to preserve

our Gospel with veneration, to listen to it and to read it
according to the spirit of the Church and to spread it with
the love with which You preached it. May it be known,
honored, and received by all! May the world conform to its
life, laws, customs, and doctrines. May the fire You brought
upon the earth inflame, enlighten, and give warmth to all.

*Sweet Heart of my Jesus, make me love You more and
more.*

2. O Jesus, Divine Master, I thank and bless Your most
amiable Heart for the great gift of the Holy Eucharist.
Your love makes You dwell in our tabernacles, renew Your
passion and death in the Mass, and make Yourself food of
our souls in Holy Communion. May I know You, O hidden
God! May I draw salutary waters from the font of Your
Heart. Grant me the grace to visit You every day in this
Sacrament, to understand and assist devoutly at Holy Mass,
to receive Holy Communion often and with the right dispositions. May all mankind heed Your invitation: "Come to
Me, all of you."

Sweet Heart of my Jesus, etc.

The sentence given the soul
stained with venial sin

Therefore let us no longer judge one another,
but rather judge this, that you should not put a
stumbling-block or a hindrance in your brother's
way. I know and am confident in the Lord Jesus
that nothing is of itself unclean; but to him who
regards anything as unclean, to him it is unclean.
If, then, thy brother is grieved because of thy food,
no longer dost thou walk according to charity. Do
not with thy food destroy him for whom Christ

died. Let not, then, our good be reviled. For the kingdom of God does not consist in food and drink, but in justice and peace and joy in the Holy Spirit; for he who in his way serves Christ pleases God and is approved by men. Let us, then, follow after the things that make for peace, and let us safeguard the things that make for mutual edification. Do not for the sake of food destory the work of God! All things indeed are clean; but a thing is evil for the man who eats through scandal. It is good not to eat meat and not to drink wine, nor to do anything by which thy brother is offended or scandalized or weakened. Thou hast faith. Keep it to thyself before God. Blessed is he who does not condemn himself by what he approves. But he who hesitates, if he eats, is condemned, because it is not from faith; for all that is not from faith is sin.

(Rom. 14:13-23.)

A different sentence awaits the soul who leaves this life without having fully purified itself after sinning. This person loved God, but not with his whole mind. In that mind there were thoughts which were not wholly supernatural.

He loved the Lord with his will, but not with his whole will, for there were often desires, words and actions not completely holy. He loved his God but not with his whole heart. He prayed without fervor, was often indifferent concerning his friendship with God, and neglectful about acquiring merit

To this soul, Christ will say: You are saved and you are My friend, but unfortunately I still see stains in you. I still behold imperfections, worldly thoughts and earthly sentiments. How different you yet are from the angels who stand before My throne in heaven! Therefore, those thoughts must be purified in the flames; those desires refined by longing; that will of yours rooted wholly in your God, the Supreme Good. Go down into purgatory. I shall await you, but not until you have paid to the last iota–through the suffrages of the faithful or through the intensity of those flames–can you be admitted to My sight.

The soul will realize that it is stained and will feel the need to bury itself in the flames, because it will love God's honor and beauty more than itself.

Now, what does our conscience tell us? Have our thoughts been totally supernatural? our desires? Are our words and actions completely good and pure? Are our prayers wholly fervent and devout? Or will we have to descend after death into that fire to yearn–who knows how long?–for the vision, the possession, the joy of heaven? May our love of God be such that we can say to the Lord: "I love You with all my heart above all things." Perhaps when we examine our conscience, we come up with a long list of imperfections and failings, but God has a far more perceptive eye. Therefore, let us ask forgiveness also for what we do not know. With good reason, then, does the Church offer suffrage for adults, in the form of Masses, indulgences and exercises of devotion.

Let us now recite The Song of Zachary, the "Benedictus," and then continue the Chaplet to the Sacred Heart.

CANTICLE OF ZACHARY

Blessed be the Lord, the God of Israel, because he has visited and wrought redemption for his people, and has raised up a horn of salvation for us, in the house of David his servant, as he promised through the mouth of his holy ones, the prophets from of old; salvation from our enemies, and from the hand of all who hate us, to show mercy to our forefathers and to be mindful of his holy covenant, of the oath that he swore to Abraham our father, that he would grant us, that delivered from the hand of our enemies, we should serve him without fear, in holiness and justice before him all our days. And thou, child, shalt be called the prophet of the Most High, for thou shalt go before the face of the Lord to prepare his ways, to give to his people knowledge of salvation through forgiveness of their sins, because of the loving-kindness of our God, wherewith the Orient from on high has visited us, to shine on those who sit in darkness and in the shadow of death, to guide our feet into the way of peace.

❖

I am the resurrection and the life: he who believes in Me although he be dead shall live; and everyone who lives, and believes in Me, shall not die forever.

❖

Have mercy, O Lord, we beseech You, on Your servant, so that he, who always sought to fulfill Your will, may not suffer Your punishments; but as the bond of faith united him to the faithful on earth, so may he by Your mercy, be united to the choirs of Angels. Through Christ our Lord. Amen.

CHAPLET TO THE SACRED HEART

(Continued)

3. O Jesus, Divine Master, I bless and thank Your most sweet Heart for the great gift of the Church. She is the Mother who instructs us in the truth, guides us on the way to heaven, and communicates supernatural life to us. She continues Your mission of salvation here on earth as Your Mystical Body. She is the ark of salvation. She is infallible, indefectible, catholic. Grant us the grace to love her as You loved and sanctified her in Your Blood. May the world know her; may all enter Your fold; may everyone humbly cooperate in Your reign.

Sweet Heart of my Jesus, etc.

4. O Jesus, Divine Master, I bless and thank Your most loving Heart for the institution of the priesthood. Priests are sent by You, as You were sent by the Father. To them You have committed the treasures of Your doctrine, Your law, and Your grace, and souls themselves. Grant me the grace to love them, to listen to them, and to let them guide me in Your ways. Send good laborers into Your vineyard, O Jesus. May Priests be the purifying and preserving salt of the earth; may they be the light of the world; may they be the city placed on the mountaintop; may they be according to Your own Heart; and may they have one day in heaven, as their crown and joy, a multitude of souls conquered for Christ.   *Sweet Heart of my Jesus, etc.*

5. O Jesus, Divine Master, I thank and bless Your most holy Heart for the institution of the religious state. Through it, You have called many to evangelical perfection. You have

made Yourself their model, their help, and their reward. O Divine Heart, multiply religious vocations. Sustain them in the faithful observance of evangelical counsels. May they be the Church's most fragrant gardens. May they be prayerful souls who console You and work for Your honor in every form of apostolate.   *Sweet Heart of my Jesus, etc.*

The sentence of the damned soul

Remember your Creator in the days of your youth, before the evil days come and the years approach of which you say, I have no pleasure in them; before the sun is darkened, and the light, and the moon, and the stars, while the clouds return after the rain; when the guardians of the house tremble, and the strong men are bent, and the grinders are idle because they are few, and they who look through the windows grow blind; when the doors to the street are shut, and the sound of the mill is low; when one waits for the chirp of a bird, but all the daughters of song are suppressed; and one fears heights, and perils in the street; when the almond tree blooms, and the locust grows sluggish and the caper berry is destroyed, because man goes to his lasting home, and mourners go about the streets; before the silver cord is snapped and the golden bowl is broken, and the pitcher is shattered at the spring, and the broken pulley falls into the well, and the dust returns to the earth as it once was, and the life-breath returns to God who gave it. Vanity of vanities, says Coheleth, all things are vanity!

Besides being wise, Coheleth taught the people knowledge, and weighed, scrutinized and arranged many proverbs. Coheleth sought to find pleasing sayings, and to write down true sayings with precision. The sayings of the wise are like goads; like fixed pegs are the topics given by one collector. As to more than these, my son, beware. Of the making of many books there is no end, and in much study there is weariness for the flesh.

The last word, when all is heard: Fear God and keep his commandments, for this is man's all; because God will bring to judgment every work, with all its hidden qualities, whether good or bad.
(Eccl. 12:1-14.)

Behold the great conclusion reached by Ecclesiastes after much experience: all our works will be brought to judgment—the good to be rewarded, for God is a just rewarder, and the bad to be punished, for He is a just judge.

Turning to the sinful soul, Our Lord, Who showed it mercy during its earthly life, will now present Himself as a severe, rigorously just judge, pronouncing sentence: "Go down into eternal fire, prepared for the devil and his followers."

"Soul, I invited you to heaven and you scorned My call. I died on the cross for you, and you made My passion useless. I warned you about hell, and you turned a deaf ear to My threat. Now, since you refused My blessing, take My curse. Go! Be off to the eternal fire!"

This, then, is the horrible end of a life stubbornly rooted in evil. We must not think that salvation or perdition depend solely on the last instant of life. Often it depends on one moment, but generally, on the habitual tenor of life. Who is it that is contented at his last moment? The soul who has led a good life. But if we take the wrong road, especially in our youth, what will happen to us? "Wide is the gate and broad is the way that leads to destruction" (Matt. 7:13); "Strive to enter by the narrow gate" (Luke 13:24).

We read: "Fear God and keep his commandments" (Eccl. 12:13). This is everything. All our works will be brought to judgment. Everything we do that does not enter into the service of God is vanity. Everything we do in the service of God is merit, salvation and eternal joy: "Fear God and keep his commandments."

Let us now recite the "Miserere," Psalm 50, so that the Lord may keep us deeply impressed by the thought of the judgment: "Happy the man who is always on his guard" (Prov. 28:14). "Fear God and observe his commandments"–everything else is vanity and affliction of spirit. May the fear of God convert us as it has converted many souls, who then became outstanding for the holiness of their lives. The fear of the Lord occupies a very important place in the gifts of the Holy Spirit because the way of purgation comes first, followed by the way of illumination, which, in turn leads to the way of union. Let us ask this gift of God. Then let us say the last two points of the chaplet to the Sacred Heart.

PSALM 50

The Miserere: Prayer of Repentance

Have mercy on me, O God, in your goodness;
in the greatness of your compassion wipe out my offense.
Thoroughly wash me from my guilt
and of my sin cleanse me.
For I acknowledge my offense,
and my sin is before me always:
"Against you only have I sinned, and done what is evil in
    your sight"—
That you may be justified in your sentence,
vindicated when you condemn.
Indeed, in guilt was I born,
and in sin my mother conceived me;
Behold, you are pleased with sincerity of heart,
and in my inmost being you teach me wisdom.
Cleanse me of sin with hyssop, that I may be purified;
wash me, and I shall be whiter than snow.
Let me hear the sounds of joy and gladness;
the bones you have crushed shall rejoice.
Turn away your face from my sins,
and blot out all my guilt.
A clean heart create for me, O God,
and a steadfast spirit renew within me.
Cast me not out from your presence,
and your holy spirit take not from me.
Give me back the joy of your salvation,
and a willing spirit sustain in me.
I will teach transgressors your ways,
and sinners shall return to you.
Free me from blood guilt, O God, my saving God;

then my tongue shall revel in your justice.
O Lord, open my lips,
and my mouth shall proclaim your praise.
For you are not pleased with sacrifices;
should I offer a holocaust, you would not accept it.
My sacrifice, O God, is a contrite spirit;
a heart contrite and humbled, O God, you will not spurn.
Be bountiful, O Lord, to Sion in your kindness
by rebuilding the walls of Jerusalem;
Then shall you be pleased with due sacrifices,
burnt offerings and holocausts;
Then they shall offer up bullocks on your altar.

CHAPLET TO THE SACRED HEART

(Continued)

6. O Jesus, Divine Master, I thank and bless Your most merciful Heart for having given us Mary as our mother, teacher, and queen. On the Cross You placed us all in her hands, You gave her a big heart, and great wisdom and power. May all men know her, love her, and pray to her! May all permit themselves to be led by her to You, the Savior of mankind. I place myself in her hands, as You did. May I be with Mary Most Holy now, in the hour of my death, and for all eternity. *Sweet Heart of my Jesus, etc.*

7. O Jesus, Divine Master, I thank and bless Your most meek Heart, which led You to give Your life for me. Your blood, Your wounds, the scourges, the thorns, the cross, and Your bowed head speak to my heart: no one loves more than he who gives his life for the loved one. The Shepherd died to give life to the sheep. I, too, want to spend my life for You. Grant that You may always, in all things and everywhere dispose of me for Your greater glory. May I always say: "Thy will be done." Inflame my heart with a holy love for souls, so that I may love them even to the greatest sacrifice. *Sweet Heart of my Jesus, etc.*

PURGATORY

PURGATORY

X

THE NATURE OF PURGATORY

Let us ask three graces of Jesus, our Divine Master: to avoid purgatory, to learn from purgatory, and to empty purgatory.

After the particular judgment, the soul will receive its sentence. Either it will be admitted at once into heaven, condemned immediately to hell, or sent to purify itself in the flames of purgatory.

The nature of purgatory

And seeing the crowds he went up to the mountain. And when he was seated, his disciples came to him. And opening his mouth he taught them, saying,

"Blessed are the poor in spirit, for theirs is the kingdom of heaven.

Blessed are the meek, for they shall possess the earth.

Blessed are they who mourn, for they shall be comforted.

Blessed are they who hunger and thirst for justice, for they shall be satisfied.

Blessed are the merciful, for they shall obtain mercy.

Blessed are the clean of heart, for they shall see God.

Blessed are the peacemakers, for they shall be called children of God.

Blessed are they who suffer persecution for justice' sake, for theirs is the kingdom of heaven.

> Blessed are you when men reproach you, and persecute you, and, speaking falsely, say all manner of evil against you, for my sake.
>
> Rejoice and exult, because your reward is great in heaven; for so did they persecute the prophets who were before you."
>
> (Matt. 5:1-12.)

The Church of Jesus Christ has three branches. There is the Church militant, composed of the faithful struggling on earth against the spirit of evil. Then there is the Church triumphant, in heaven, where Christ reigns with all His elect. Finally, there is the Church suffering, which is a kind of half-way state, a temporary state preparatory to entrance into heaven. They who leave this earth in God's grace but are not worthy to enter at once into the vision and enjoyment of God, are retained in a place of suffering, purgatory.

This is a state of purification by means of which the soul concludes the total detachment of his affections from earthly things in order to ground them once and for all in God.

It is a place for making satisfaction, where souls who have debts with the justice of God finish paying them.

Purgatory is, moreover, a state of painful love. There the tepid soul, who passed out of life without that fervor needed for entrance into heaven, completes the refinement of his desires. With his ardent yearning, he finally merits to enter heaven.

Purgatory is both a blessed and a painful place. Why blessed? Because those souls are all saved! St. Francis de Sales says that if they were given a choice between returning to this world or remaining in that fire, they would prefer to stay there. They are already sure of going to heaven! Here on earth, instead, we live in great uncertainty. Yet, at the same time, purgatory is painful, for there are many physical and moral sufferings in that prison of fire. The souls held captive there are burning with thirst for God, longing to be able to drink from the refreshing Fountain, trying with their sighs to hasten the vision of the Lord! What a price they pay for entrance into heaven!

Do many souls go to purgatory? Our Faith has nothing to say on this subject; it is content with teaching us that purgatory exists and that the souls suffering there can be helped by us, by our suffrages, particularly by the Holy Sacrifice of the Mass. But if we follow the sentiments of the saints, to the question as to whether many go to purgatory, we must reply about like this:

The greater part of mankind is not so wicked or so obstinate in wrongdoing as to deserve hell. Most people sin out of weakness and repent as soon as they commit the sin. At least before dying, most have some sentiments of sorrow and hope. Will they then be condemned to hell? This would not be compatible with the justice of God since only they who die in mortal sin, definitely committed and definitely not forgiven, are condemned to hell. Moreover, the Lord is all-merciful–to save us, He died on the cross!

Yet the majority of men are not so holy that they can enter heaven at once. Some vain thoughts, some angry sentiments, some indulgence toward our body or our heart, some thoughtless words–how many miseries prevent the gates of heaven from opening wide at once! On the other hand, we ourselves would not dare, with certain stains, to enter heaven, where all is holy and perfect. The soul itself, having beheld God's infinite sanctity at the judgment, would at no cost enter heaven before being thoroughly cleansed and purged. These souls, then, who do not deserve hell and are not yet worthy of heaven, go to be completely purified in purgatory. There they finish paying their debts to God's justice. It might be called a vestibule, where souls cleanse themselves and put on the wedding garment to be admitted to the real presence of God.

Let us conclude with a prayer to avoid purgatory.

PRAYER TO AVOID PURGATORY

Most merciful Jesus, for Your dolorous Passion and for the love You bore me, I pray You to forgive me the punishments I have merited with my sins. Grant me, therefore, the spirit of penance, delicacy of conscience, avoidance of every deliberate venial sin, and the dispositions necessary to earn indulgences. I promise to offer suffrages as much as I can to the souls in purgatory, and, as soon as my soul is freed from the bonds of my body, do You, O infinite Goodness, admit it to the Eternal Vision and joy of heaven.

Our Father, Hail Mary, Eternal Rest.

Why souls are sent to purgatory

"You are the salt of the earth; but if the salt loses its strength, what shall it be salted with? It is no longer of any use but to be thrown out and trodden underfoot by men.

"You are the light of the world. A city set on a mountain cannot be hidden. Neither do men light a lamp and put it under the measure, but upon the lamp-stand, so as to give light to all in the house. Even so let your light shine before men, in order that they may see your good works and give glory to your Father in heaven." (Matt. 5:13-16.)

There are three causes for the sentence to purgatory: 1) punishment for past sins for which full atonement has not been made; 2) venial sin; and 3) tepidity.

Let us first consider **punishment for past sin.** When we go to confession, the sin and the eternal punishment are taken away, but the temporal punishment is not always completely cancelled. This depends on the sorrow, the dispositions we bring to the Sacrament of Penance. Ordinarily debts with divine justice remain, but they are temporal. They can be discharged in this life or in the next. Here on earth, they can be cancelled by mortification and by gaining indulgences. However, if we go into eternity without having made full satisfaction, God will require us to pay through the sufferings of purgatory. Sin is a great evil, for it offends God, hurts us and our neighbor, too–at least indirectly. Ordinarily, the penance given by the confessor is not sufficient fully to repair the harm done by sin.

Coming now to **venial sin,** the second cause, we note that on this earth, lukewarm souls give little importance to it. Venial sins are committed very frequently. Worldly, proud, or foolish thoughts; sentiments that are far from being elevated; dangerous attachments or animosities; inconsiderate words; excessive curiosity; wasteful daydreaming; laziness; bursts of anger; acts of pride, of stinginess, of gluttony–and so the list goes. When we look closely at ourselves, we certainly feel a need to lower our heads before Christ in deep shame. Some people live in such a distracted fashion that when they take a minute out in the evening to look over the day, they discover a great many of these defects sprinkled throughout it. These failings are quite readily dismissed as trifles or confessed almost without sorrow. Yet in reality they are piling up debts with the justice of God.

The third cause for punishment in purgatory is **lukewarmness,** and it is the most common. A soul who was not very fervent in the service of God, had no spiritual warmth or generosity, cannot possibly go from this life straight into the heavenly light, into intimate union with God. It must remain in that vestibule of heaven to cleanse and purify itself, and to desire heaven.

The lukewarmness of a soul shows itself in the way he examines his conscience, says rosaries, practises devotion to the Blessed Mother, to the Guardian Angel and the saints—and worse yet, with regard to Holy Mass, Holy Communion, and Confession.

Duties, too, are performed with the same lack of fervor.

O Divine Master! How ashamed we feel in Your sight! Lord, You Who see everything in our hearts, have mercy on us! Give us a period of time between our past life of lukewarmness (and perhaps worse than lukewarmness!) and death, a period of time in which to come to our senses, do penance, and live fervently!

Following the recitation of the Beatitudes, we shall say the first glorious mystery of the Rosary, that we may rise to a new life.

THE BEATITUDES

Blessed are the poor in spirit, for theirs is the kingdom of Heaven.

Blessed are the meek, for they shall possess the earth.

Blessed are they who mourn, for they shall be comforted.

Blessed are they who hunger and thirst for justice, for they shall be satisfied.

Blessed are the merciful, for they shall obtain mercy.

Blessed are the pure of heart, for they shall see God.

Blessed are the peacemakers, for they shall be called children of God.

Blessed are they who suffer persecution for justice' sake, for theirs is the kingdom of heaven.

FIRST GLORIOUS MYSTERY

Jesus Christ rises gloriously from the sepulchre. This resurrection represents our own resurrection from the grave of sins and defects. Let us ask of the Blessed Virgin this spiritual revival.

The way to avoid purgatory

"Do not think that I have come to destroy the Law or the Prophets. I have not come to destroy, but to fulfill. For amen I say to you, till heaven and earth pass away, not one jot or one tittle shall be lost from the Law till all things have been accomplished. Therefore whoever does away with one of these least commandments, and so teaches men, shall be called least in the kingdom of heaven; but whoever carries them out and teaches them, he shall be called great in the kingdom of heaven. For I say to you that unless your justice exceeds that of the Scribes and Pharisees, you shall not enter the kingdom of heaven.

"You have heard that it was said to the ancients, 'Thou shalt not kill'; and that whoever shall kill shall be liable to judgment. But I say to you that everyone who is angry with his brother shall be liable to judgment; and whoever says to his brother, 'Raca,' shall be liable to the Sanhedrin; and whoever says, 'Thou fool!', shall be liable to the fire of Gehenna."   (Matt. 5:17-22.)

There are three means of avoiding purgatory. The first is to **do penance.** Christ our Master strongly urged us to do it. St. Augustine, St. Mary Magdalen, St. Margaret of Cortona and many other converted sinners fervently applied themselves to the practice of penance. He who imposes checks on his mind does penance for the sins of thought he has committed. Mortification of the imagination atones for sins of imagination. Control of the heart is reparation for sins of affection and attachment. Restraint in speech is penance for sins of the tongue. Mortification in eating is atonement for sins committed in satisfying the palate. In general, then, penance consists of doing the opposite of sin. On this earth, works of penance have a threefold value: impetratory (obtaining favors and graces), satisfactory (atoning for sins), and meritorious (increasing our grace and glory in heaven). In the next life, instead, the sufferings of purgatory have only a satisfactory value.

A second means is to **avoid deliberate venial sin.** People who say: "Oh, this isn't anything serious; you won't go to hell for it," manifest lukewarmness and lack of knowledge. They show that they do not understand what purgatory is.

The reader has undoubtedly heard of the man who begged a priest to say Mass for him as soon as he died. Immediately following his death, the priest only took care of the most urgent matters pertaining to the care of the body before going at once to celebrate Mass for him. In all, not more than an hour had passed. When he finished Mass, he went into the sacristy, and there the deceased appeared before him.

"I have been freed from purgatory through your Mass," he said, "but why did you forget about me for such a long time?"

"How can you say that, when it is only about an hour since you died?" exclaimed the priest.

"Only an hour! Only an hour! Ah, you really do not know, then, what it means to stay one hour in purgatory!"

We do not know! If we did, certain viewpoints would be changed forever!

Thirdly, we ought to **stir up fervor** if we desire to avoid purgatory. Let us be fervent in reading the Holy Bible, in receiving Holy Communion, in assisting at Holy Mass, in examining our conscience, and in offering prayers and good works for the holy souls in purgatory. We must never grow weary of cleansing and re-cleansing this soul of ours, and beautifying it with ejaculations and devotion to the Blessed Mother.

Whoever purifies his heart, making it as pure as the angels in heaven, will render himself worthy of going straight from this earth to the vision of God. Such a man lives in God here below; his thought is fixed on God; his heart longs for God. Blessed are they who hunger and thirst for the justice of God, for they shall be satisfied!

Let us say the Litany of the Sacred Heart to obtain the grace of paying all the debts we have contracted with divine justice, before we leave this earth. Then we shall say the second glorious mystery to be able to detach ourselves from everything, meritoriously, while still in this life.

THE LITANY OF THE SACRED HEART

Lord, have mercy on us.
Christ, have mercy on us.
Lord, have mercy on us.
Christ, hear us.
Christ, graciously hear us.

God the Father of Heaven,
God the Son, Redeemer of the world,
God the Holy Ghost,
Holy Trinity, one God,
Heart of Jesus, Son of the Eternal Father,
Heart of Jesus, formed by the Holy Ghost in the womb of
    the Virgin Mother,
Heart of Jesus, substantially united to the Word of God,
Heart of Jesus, of Infinite Majesty,
Heart of Jesus, Sacred Temple of God,
Heart of Jesus, Tabernacle of the Most High,
Heart of Jesus, House of God and Gate of Heaven,
Heart of Jesus, burning furnace of charity,
Heart of Jesus, abode of justice and love,
Heart of Jesus, full of goodness and love,
Heart of Jesus, abyss of all virtues,
Heart of Jesus, most worthy of all praise,
Heart of Jesus, king and center of all hearts,
Heart of Jesus, in whom are all the treasures of wisdom
    and knowledge,
Heart of Jesus, in whom dwells the fullness of divinity,
Heart of Jesus, in whom the Father was well pleased,
Heart of Jesus, of whose fullness we have all received,
Heart of Jesus, desire of the everlasting hills,
Heart of Jesus, patient and most merciful,
Heart of Jesus, enriching all who invoke Thee,
Heart of Jesus, fountain of life and holiness,
Heart of Jesus, propitiation for our sins,
Heart of Jesus, loaded down with opprobrium,
Heart of Jesus, bruised for our offenses,
Heart of Jesus, obedient unto death,
Heart of Jesus, pierced with a lance,
Heart of Jesus, source of all consolation,
Heart of Jesus, our life and resurrection,

have mercy on us.

Heart of Jesus, our peace and reconciliation,

Heart of Jesus, victim for sin,

Heart of Jesus, salvation of those who trust in Thee,

Heart of Jesus, hope of those who die in Thee,

Heart of Jesus, delight of all the Saints,

have mercy on us.

Lamb of God, who takest away the sins of the world, Spare us, O Lord.

Lamb of God, who takest away the sins of the world, Graciously hear us, O Lord.

Lamb of God, who takest away the sins of the world, Have mercy on us.

v) Jesus, meek and humble of heart.

ʀ) Make our hearts like unto Thine.

Let us Pray

O Almighty and eternal God, vouchsafe to regard the Heart of Thy dearly beloved Son, and the praises and satisfaction He offers Thee in the name of sinners; and appeased thereby, grant pardon to them who seek Your mercy. We beg it of Thee in the name of the same Jesus Christ, Thy Son, who liveth and reigneth God, with Thee, in the unity of the Holy Spirit, world without end. Amen.

SECOND GLORIOUS MYSTERY

Jesus ascends into heaven in wondrous glory and triumph. Let us ask for detachment from the honors, goods, and pleasures of this world, and for a desire to have only the joys, glory and goods of heaven.

XI

THE SUFFERINGS OF PURGATORY

Through the infinite merits of the Cross, we hope that with the forgiveness of our sins we shall also have our purgatory shortened. We hope further to obtain for the suffering souls, freedom and relief, and for ourselves, the grace to do penance for our sins in this life.

The pain of loss

Behold, I tell you a mystery: we shall all indeed rise, but we shall not all be changed—in a moment, in the twinkling of an eye, at the last trumpet. For the trumpet shall sound, and the dead shall rise incorruptible and we shall be changed. For this corruptible body must put on incorruption, and this mortal body must put on immortality. But when this mortal body puts on immortality, then shall come to pass the word that is written, "Death is swallowed up in victory! O death, where is thy victory? O death, where is thy sting?"

Now the sting of death is sin, and the power of sin is the Law. But thanks be to God who has given us the victory through our Lord Jesus Christ.

(I Cor. 15:51-57.)

Purgatory is the temporary privation of the vision of God. This suffering is called the pain of loss.

The better to understand it, let us reflect that after death, all the desires of the soul will be centered in one desire only: the longing to be with God. The soul will feel itself powerfully drawn by the beauty and holiness of God. It will burn with thirst for eternal happiness, its whole will bent on seeking God. Spurred on by this desire, it would want to lift itself up and wing its way to the Lord, but the divine hand will hold it back: "You are not yet pure enough. You must purify yourself."

St. Benedict beheld the soul of his sister, St. Scholastica, soaring toward heaven in the form of a white dove. To rise like that, a soul must be all white. St. Catherine of Genoa, who had many visions on purgatory, says: Suppose there were only one loaf of bread on this earth and mankind was half-starved. Suppose there were only one source of water and men were parched with thirst. You would see men stretching their hands toward that bread, begging for that refreshing water. They would all be crying, "I'm hungry! I'm starving to death! I'm thirsty, I'm dying of thirst!" Now, then, after this life, God is the only bread capable of nourishing us, the only water that will quench our thirst: "I am the bread that has come down from heaven"; "He who drinks of the water that I will give him shall never thirst; but the water that I will give him shall become in him a fountain of water, springing up unto life everlasting" (John 6:41; 4:13-14.) The souls in purgatory strain toward God and God rejects them. They are racked with hunger pangs and receive no food. They are tormented by thirst and may have to pant for water a long time!

On fire with love of God, St. Teresa was afflicted by a holy sadness at not seeing her end in sight. "I die because I am not dying!" she would exclaim. "I die with the desire of going to God." What must this desire not be, then, for those souls no longer enveloped by the body, tending toward God alone? After Absalom had been banished forever from his father's sight, he sent word that he preferred death: either he should be admitted to King David's presence, he said, or he should be put to death. Those desolate souls sigh for their heavenly Father from the solitude of purgatory.

An impressive story is told of a missionary to a remote region of Alaska who spent almost thirty years in near total solitude. After about twenty-eight years, he was close to a state of shock for sorrow at not viewing the face of another human being. But who could describe the desolation of the poor souls in purgatory waiting to see the face of God? "When shall I go and behold the face of my God?" (Ps. 41:3.) they anxiously ask the Guardian Angels who come down to console them. When shall

we see the face of God our Father, Mary our
Mother, the Angels and the holy souls of heaven,
our brothers?

Let us recite the words of the hymn, "May the
Angels Accompany You to Paradise." Oh, may the
angels lead these souls to heaven! Then we shall
say the third glorious mystery of the Rosary, that
the Holy Spirit may grant us purification and grace.

May the Angels accompany you to Paradise; at Your arrival may the Martyrs receive you and lead you into the holy
city of Jerusalem. May the choir of Angels receive you, and
may you find eternal rest with Lazarus, who was once poor.

THIRD GLORIOUS MYSTERY

The Holy Spirit descends upon the Apostles to enlighten, comfort and sanctify them. Let us ask for the gifts
of the Holy Spirit, especially wisdom, fortitude and zeal.

The pain of sense

And making a gathering, he sent twelve
thousand drachmas of silver to Jerusalem for sacrifice to be offered for the sins of the dead, thinking well and religiously concerning the resurrection. (For if he had not hoped that they that were
slain should rise again, it would have seemed super-
fluous and vain to pray for the dead.) And because
he considered that they who had fallen asleep with
godliness, had great grace laid up for them, it is

therefore a holy and wholesome thought to pray
for the dead, that they may be loosed from sins.
(2 Mach. 12:43-46.)

Besides the privation of the vision of God,
souls in purgatory undergo the sufferings common-
ly called the pains of sense. "A man is punished by
the very things through which he sins" (Wis. 11:16).
The same human faculties which served sin must
submit to the torment of purification—senses, powers of the soul, sentiments of the body. The suffering is the same as in hell with the one difference
that the pains of hell will never end, whereas the
pains of purgatory must come to an end; the pains
of hell serve only to punish, but those of purgatory
serve to satisfy for sin and to free the soul.

The soul will suffer in its intelligence. In that
prison it will understand that it could very easily
have become much holier, and acquired more merit
while on earth. It will think of all the graces received, all the opportunities offered, and all the
circumstances in which it could have given much
greater glory to God, done much more good for itself, and been of much greater help to its fellowmen.

It will suffer in its memory. It will recall that
on earth others with fewer occasions of merit, perhaps less graces, less instruction and a lower position, merited more with God. Bitterly it will think
of relatives, devout young men and women, good-

living people who reached high sanctity, whereas it remained far behind. It will reflect that with a little penance, these flames could easily have been avoided; a little more diligence in gaining indulgences could have freed it from that suffering. But it waited and put matters off. Acknowledging its fault, it will have to bow humbly, saying, "God is just and His sentence is just. I deserved this through my fault; through my fault, through my most grievous fault!"

The soul will suffer in the will, too, for this will, enflamed by the desire to see. God, will feel rejected by Him. This will be punishment for coldness in Communion, indifference in matters of piety, and reluctance to perform works of zeal. Everywhere it wandered about distractedly, without love, without a heart. It will have to admit then, "I am here in purgatory because I wanted to be."

Bodily senses will suffer—eyesight, hearing, tongue, palate, heart, and touch. Yes, every illicit satisfaction, no matter how small, if voluntary, must be paid for in that terrible fire. God forbids us to do evil; if we sin, reparation is required, either by penance here or punishment there, down to the last iota.

If we cannot meditate directly on this, let us reflect on the words of St. Thomas: All the sufferings of this earth taken together would not equal the smallest pain of purgatory. Thus, if we put together all the sufferings of the martyrs, who were fed to wild beasts, buried alive, beheaded, burned at the stake and even covered with oil to be burned in public gardens, all these would never measure up to the least sufferings of purgatory. It is all natural pain, but in purgatory, God's mercy and justice join to multiply our sufferings. His justice demands satisfaction; His mercy desires to see this satisfaction completed quickly so that the soul may soon enter heaven.

After reciting the following prayer from the Mass of the Dead, let us say the fourth glorious mystery to obtain the grace of a holy death by the intercession of Our Lady assumed into heaven.

PRAYER

O Lord Jesus Christ, King of glory, deliver the souls of all the faithful departed from the pains of hell and from the deep pit; deliver them from the lion's mouth, that hell may not engulf them, and that they may not fall into darkness; but may Saint Michael, the standard bearer, take them into the holy light; * which Thou didst promise to Abraham and to his seed. ℣. We offer Thee, O Lord, sacrifices and prayers of praise; do Thou accept them in behalf of those souls whom we commemorate this day; grant them, O Lord, to pass from death to life: * Which Thou didst promise to Abraham and to his seed.

FOURTH GLORIOUS MYSTERY

The Most Holy Virgin expires through pure love of God and is taken up into Heaven with marvellous glory. Let us ask for a holy life, so as to die in God's holy love.

The fire

And I heard a voice from heaven, saying, "Write: Blessed are the dead who die in the Lord henceforth. Yes, says the Spirit, let them rest from their labors, for their works follow them."

(Apoc. 14:13.)

Of all the sufferings of purgatory, one of the most painful to the senses is the fire. It is a material fire which burns those souls to purify them, but does not consume them. The fire of purgatory is lit by the justice of God. It is not the fire we know on this earth. St. Augustine and St. Thomas tell us that it is the very fire of hell, the only difference being that the fire of hell is an eternal revenger whereas the fire of purgatory is a temporary purifier.

Can we picture that prison of fire wherein souls burn day and night, resignedly awaiting, although in agony, the hour of liberation? We cannot keep our hand on a hot stove or on an iron; in fact, we cannot even stand a match flame on a finger! What must it be, then, to remain in purgatory?

"I am in purgatory!" declared a soul who appeared after death. "And to give you a taste of the sufferings therein, I want you to stretch out your hand." Her friend did so, and the vision let one drop of her burning perspiration fall upon it. That drop was enough to burn a hole in her flesh, causing excruciating pain.

Often our hearts are hard. There are friends of ours in purgatory crying: "Pity me, pity me, O you my friends!" (Job 19:21). Perhaps you have a mother or father there, who was too indulgent with your failings! You say you have a sensitive heart, yet you do not think of them, not even once a week, say little of once a day! And certainly we all have brothers and sisters in Christ there, souls for whom He gave His blood and His life. At least, when you retire for the night, think: I shall spend the night peacefully, enjoying a well-earned rest after a day of hard work, but those souls are in a bed of fire. The heat they suffer is of far greater intensity than the blazing gridiron on which St. Lawrence was martyred! Before taking our repose, let us send a thought to them, an "Eternal Rest." We need to become more tender-hearted. Insensitive hearts leave insensitive people behind them.

How often have I been a witness to this fact! I have seen people attending the funerals of their friends with such indifference. They chattered and looked around to the right and the left. But then I saw that when the time came for these very people to be carried to the cemetery, they received the same treatment. At their funerals, too, there was idle chatter, laughs, and even joking.

The measure we use with others will be used with us. This is the law of the Gospel. Let us see to it that our measure is the same as the Sacred Heart's—infinitely merciful. Let us share His desire to see the souls in purgatory united to Him as soon as possible and joined in His embrace in heaven. We shall pray with our whole heart in union with that divine Heart: "In Him, with Him, and through Him."

Let us now recite the "Dies Irae" and then the fifth glorious mystery to ask the Blessed Mother to bring us as soon as possible to enjoy her glory in heaven.

THE DIES IRAE

Lo the day, that day of ire,
When the world shall end by fire,
Warned by Sibyl and David's lyre.
Then men's hearts with fear shall tremble,
As the Judge will all assemble,
To sift for souls who Him resemble.
Loudly shall the trumpet sound,
Piercing tombs in the earth profound,
Calling souls His throne to surround.
Nature and death are stupified,
As the sepulchres open wide,
Bodies hie to the Judge's side.
Then before Him shall be placed,
The book wherein all deeds are traced,
The verdict from thence shall be based.

When the Judge for His seat shall make,
Nothing then shall remain opaque,
No sin His judgment will forsake.

Wretched me, what can I then plead?
Whom shall I ask to intercede,
When the holy much mercy need?

King of tremendous majesty,
Who saves e'en gratuitously,
Save me too, O Font of mercy.

Good Jesus, t'was my salvation,
Caused Thy wondrous Incarnation,
Leave me not now to damnation.

To seek me Thou didst not distain,
And on the Cross died with much pain,
Let not such anguish be in vain.

Just Judge seeking vindication,
Grant me the gift of remission,
Ere the day of retribution.

Guilty now my heart is moaning,
And my shame with anguish owning,
O God, spare this sinner groaning.

Thou who Mary's soul absolvest,
And the thief to Heaven invitest,
Now to me a hope vouchsafest.

My prayers and sighs in vain ascend,
But Thou, good Lord, will condescend,
Save from fires that never end.

Place amid Thy sheep accord,
Keep me from the guilty horde,
Set me on Thy right, O Lord.

The wicked, sighing are condemned,
Where for them there is no amend;
Among Thy saints do Thou me send.

Prostrate, sorrowing I implore,
Heart like ashes to the core,
Dying, save me evermore.
   Day of tears and mournful sighs,
When from earth shall man arise,
Stained with guilt, his doom he will know,
   O Lord, mercy on him bestow.
O sweet Jesus, from pain release,
Grant all souls Thy eternal peace. Amen.

FIFTH GLORIOUS MYSTERY

Mary is crowned Queen of heaven and earth, dispenser of all graces and our most lovable Mother. Let us resolve to be devoted to the Most Holy Virgin and ask the gift of perseverance.

XII

DUTIES TOWARD THE SOULS IN PURGATORY

Having considered what purgatory is and the sufferings therein, it remains for us to consider our duty to help the poor souls, the possibility of so doing, and continuity of suffrages.

Our obligation to help the poor souls

"Amen, amen, I say to you, the hour is coming and now is here, when the dead shall hear the voice of the Son of God, and those who hear shall live. For as the Father has life in Himself, even so he has given to the Son also to have life in himself; and he has granted him power to render judgment, because he is Son of Man. Do not wonder at this, for the hour is coming in which all who are in the tombs shall hear the voice of the Son of God. And they who have done good shall come forth unto resurrection of life; but they who have done evil unto resurrection of judgment. (John 5:25-29)

Are we obliged to help the souls in purgatory? Certainly. In fact, at times this obligation may be a duty of justice, especially when there are souls there for whom we were responsible, to whom we gave bad example or who did good to us, materially or spiritually.

Let us speak first of all of our duty with regard to those toward whom we had responsibility–either as parents, teachers, priests and confessors, or simply as friends. We must lower our heads and strike our breasts for not having fully performed our duty toward them with prayer, example, words, exhortations, vigilance, and correction. All those whom I assisted in death, especially in the early years of my priesthood, are always present to me at the altar, every morning. How can we forget those with whom we have come in contact during our lives? Who knows if they may not be suffering because of our negligence?

Next, we have obligations if there are souls in purgatory whom we have scandalized or made cold and indifferent by our bad example, our lukewarmness or our own indifference. If they are now suffering through our fault, the duty of justice requires that we procure for them what we caused to be delayed for them–the sight of God, the beatific vision.

Finally, we owe suffrages as evidence of gratitude to all who have cared for us–parents, teachers, confessors, preachers, pastors, spiritual benefactors, material benefactors. We assisted at that priest's Mass, received absolution from that other priest, benefited from the guidance and patient explanations provided by teachers. Let us now give back what we received. Kindness is repaid by kindness. Those souls can no longer help themselves and they reach out appealingly to us.

Very often we are bound by filial piety. Perhaps we have a father or mother, sisters or brothers, grandparents, aunts or uncles in purgatory. Certainly some of our ancestors are there. Let us, then, preserve affection for our own blood! And should we not fear—as we said before—that someone may be there because his over-indulgence toward us displeased the Lord somewhat? In any case, must we not always remember that we are obliged to love those who so loved us? If we received our natural life from them, or intellectual and moral life, let us now give them eternal life with our prayers.

We may also be obliged to pray for some in purgatory because we promised we would, since they were close friends. Promises made at a death-bed are among the most sacred.

Furthermore, we are obliged by love of God. Jesus Christ gave His blood for those souls and with what desire He waits for them in heaven! The Lord thirsts for these souls, and we can quench that divine thirst by our suffrages.

Then there is the duty arising from love of neighbor. When one of our fellowmen is suffering and we can relieve him without much effort, we are strictly obliged to do so. So if we are generous with material help, how much more charity we ought to practice with indulgences, prayers, and Masses for the souls in purgatory!

Lastly, we owe it to ourselves. Let us think that perhaps before very long we ourselves will have need of the same mercy. Who can be sure of paying all his debts to God on this earth and leaving this life fully purified? The mercy we used with others will be used with us. Blessed are the merciful, for they shall find mercy.

Even on this earth, this is true. Whoever prays for the poor souls in purgatory finds it easier to avoid venial sin, to atone for his sins, to acquire a delicate conscience, and to obtain graces. One good man used to say, "In my needs and in my greatest worries, I always have recourse to the holy souls in purgatory." Those souls are suffering, too, so, to our way of thinking, they can better understand our needs and have pity on us. When we help them, in their deep gratitude, they pray for us. And when they go to heaven, they will never stop recommending us to God until they see us with them in heaven.

Let us now offer three prayers for the souls in purgatory.

FOR THE SOULS IN PURGATORY

O Lord, my Creator and Redeemer, I believe that in Your justice, You established purgatory for those souls who pass into eternity before having totally satisfied for their debts of guilt and punishment. I also believe that in Your mercy You accept suffrages, particularly the Holy Sacrifice of the Mass, for their relief and freedom. Stir up faith in me and infuse in my heart sentiments of pity towards these dear suffering brethren.

O Lord Jesus Christ, King of glory, through the intercession of Mary and all the saints, free the souls of the faithful departed from the punishments of purgatory. St. Michael, standard-bearer of the heavenly army, guide them to the holy light promised by the Lord to Abraham and to his descendants. I offer You, O Lord, sacrifice and prayers of praise. Accept them for the souls that we remember this day, and admit these souls into eternal light and glory.

O Jesus, my good Master, I beseech You on behalf of the souls towards whom I have more serious duties of gratitude, justice, charity, and family relationship: my parents, my spiritual and temporal benefactors, and my loved ones. I recommend to you the persons who have greater responsibilities on earth: priests, rulers, religious superiors, brothers, sisters, and teachers. I beseech You also for forgotten souls, and for those who were more devoted to the Holy Eucharist and the Blessed Virgin. O Lord, deign to admit them soon into eternal happiness.

Eternal rest grant unto them, O Lord, and let perpetual light shine upon them. May they rest in peace. Amen.

(Three times.)

Ways of helping the souls in purgatory

"All that the Father gives to me shall come to me, and him who comes to me I will not cast out. For I have come down from heaven, not to do my own will, but the will of him who sent me. Now

> this is the will of him who sent me, the Father,
> that I should lose nothing of what he has given
> me, but that I should raise it up on the last day.
> For this is the will of my Father who sent me, that
> whoever beholds the Son, and believes in him,
> shall have everlasting life, and I will raise him up
> on the last day."
>
> (John 6:37-40.)

The God Who confined souls to the prison of fire that they might be beautified did so because He loves them. And because of this same love, He has given us the key to open the gates of heaven to them. It is a teaching of faith that the souls in purgatory can be helped by the suffrages of the faithful, especially by the holy sacrifice of the Mass. Moreover, we have other means at our disposition. Holy Communion is one of these. It is a great act of love between man and God, because love tends towards union. Many people have the habit of receiving Communion every Tuesday, or at least the first Tuesday of the month, for the faithful departed.

Another means is the visit to the Blessed Sacrament. In these visits we have recourse to the Heart of Jesus, asking Him to have compassion at the sight of the great suffering of those poor souls.

In particular we have Holy Mass with which to help the poor souls. In this case, it is not just us praying. It is the Son of God showing His wounds to His Heavenly Father. We pray the Mass with Jesus, and He is always heard by reason of His infinite merits. Consequently the Church praises, approves and encourages the practice of having Mass celebrated for the dead and assisting at it for them. Moreover, in every Mass, the priest remembers the faithful departed.

There are still other means—the rosary, for one. The rosary invokes the motherly tenderness of Mary Most Holy for the souls in purgatory. It is highly enriched with indulgences, too. Then, there are the Stations of the Cross, which are a remembrance of the passion of our Lord. In making the Way of the Cross, we accompany our Savior to Calvary, there to be moved at the sight of His sufferings and to pray through His merits and His holy wounds.

We can gain indulgences for the poor souls. Most of the prayers we say are indulgenced—Acts of Faith, Hope and Charity, the Angelus, the Sign of the Cross, ejaculations, and so forth. We gain the indulgences if we have the intention of doing so, and most of these are applicable to the souls in purgatory. Good works, apostolic endeavors, penance, practice of charity to the poor are still other means of winning relief for the holy souls.

Thus, we are capable of helping them. If, then, we can help them, the natural conclusion is that we

must help them. Who is exempt from the obligation of loving his neighbor? Who can be excused from helping, if he can, when there is a grave need? Hence, anyone with a heart, anyone with faith and love for Christ, will be moved at the thought of the souls in purgatory and will pray for them–starting now!

Let say part of Psalm 143, "Blessed be the Lord my rock," and try to keep the following suggested intentions in our prayers.

PSALM 143

Prayer for Victory and Prosperity

Blessed be the Lord, my rock,
who trains my hands for battle, my fingers for war;
My refuge and my fortress, my stronghold, my deliverer,
My shield, in whom I trust, who subdues people under me.
Lord, what is man, that you notice him;
the son of man, that you take thought of him?
Man is like a breath;
his days, like a passing shadow.
Incline your heavens, O Lord, and come down;
touch the mountains, and they shall smoke;
Flash forth lightening, and put them to flight,
shoot your arrows, and rout them;
Reach out your hand from on high–
Deliver me and rescue me from many waters,
from the hands of aliens,
Whose mouths swear false promises
while their right hands are raised in perjury.

Glory Be.

INTENTIONS

Let us pray for:

1. The next soul about to enter heaven.

2. The one with the greatest sufferings.

3. The one whose liberation would bring the greatest glory to God.

4. The most abandoned soul.

5. The one who has been longest in purgatory.

6. The one who would have to stay there the longest.

7. The last one to enter.

8. The one who lived the longest on earth.

9. The one with the shortest earthly life.

10. The soul whom Jesus and Mary desire to see freed more quickly.

11. The one most devoted to Our Lord.

12. The most devoted to our Blessed Mother.

13. The most devoted to St. Joseph.

14. The most devoted to the saints.

15. The most devoted to St. Anne.

16. The one who prayed the most for sinners.

17. The one who prayed the most for the lukewarm.

18. The one who prayed the most for the sick.

19. The one who prayed the most for the dying.

20. The one who prayed the most for the deceased.

21. The one who prayed the most for our separated brethren.

22. The one who prayed the most for unbelievers.

23. The one who prayed the most for the Pope.

24. The one who prayed the most for bishops.

25. The one who prayed the most for missionaries.

26. The one who prayed the most for priests.

27. The one who prayed the most for his parents and friends.

28. The one who prayed the most for religious.

29. The one who prayed the most for rulers.

30. The one who prayed the most for officials and soldiers.

31. The one who prayed the most for his enemies.

32. The one who prayed the most for the poor and the rich.

33. The soul for whom I am most obliged to pray.

34. Those who were my partners in sin.

35. Those to whom I was an occasion of sin.

36. The one who did me the most good spiritually.

37. The one who did me the most good materially.

38. The most outstanding in the love of God.

39. The most outstanding in the love of neighbor.

40. The most outstanding in humility.

41. The most outstanding in kindness.

42. The most outstanding in patience.

43. The most outstanding in resignation.

44. The most outstanding in temperance.

45. The most outstanding in compassion.

46. The most outstanding in faith.

47. The most outstanding in hope.

48. The one who sinned the most because of pride.

49. The one who sinned the most because of anger.

50. The one who sinned the most because of envy or jealousy.

51. The one who sinned the most because of revenge or bitter hatred.

52. The one who sinned the most because of vanity.

53. The one who sinned the most because of immodesty.

54. The one who sinned the most because of injurious words.

55. The one who sinned the most because of useless words.

56. The one who sinned the most because of oaths or curses.

57. The one who sinned the most because of laziness.

Let us give unceasing help to the poor souls so as to live a life of charity

"I am the living bread that has come down from heaven. If anyone eat of this bread he shall live forever; and the bread that I will give is my flesh for the life of the world."

The Jews on that account argued with one another, saying, "How can this man give us his flesh to eat?"

Jesus therefore said to them, "Amen, amen, I say to you, unless you eat the flesh of the Son of Man, and drink his blood, you shall not have life in you. He who eats my flesh and drinks my blood has life everlasting and I will raise him up on the last day."

(John 6:51-56.)

The thought of purgatory is salutary. In fact, it induces us to fear venial sin and detest it, to desire to be fervent, and to feel compassion. This thought of purgatory is also beneficial because it arouses zeal for our neighbor's welfare. It is a holy practice to teach and write about purgatory every time the occasion presents itself.

All during our lives, therefore, it would be well to read and write about purgatory, act with it in mind, and constantly offer our prayers.

With regard to the first practice, books and sermons which recall the faithful departed and the sufferings of purgatory do good always. Secondly, our patient toil, our diligent performance of daily duties, our mental labors, and our daily sacrifices are means of emptying purgatory and avoiding it ourselves. If our confessor permits, we might also proceed to an act of greater benefit to the holy souls, of more profound and continual charity–the heroic act of charity. By this act, one gives up, in favor of the holy souls, all the satisfactory value of his good deeds, prayers, and sacrifices, and even the suffrages which will come to him after death from charitable souls. Someone might protest, "If I give everything to others, what will be left for me?" The answer is that we shall have not just that little good which we had of ourselves, but a great amount multiplied by charity, by the exchange of prayers from the grateful souls in purgatory, and by the application of the merits of Jesus Christ.

In the third place, let us offer prayers regularly. Sometimes we feel more inclined toward compassion; at other times, less. But the man of true piety is superior to these changing feelings. He establishes certain practices and is faithful to them. They might be the following: every day, the "De Profundis" and the "Eternal rest" each time he prays; every week some special prayer on Tuesday, and especially Holy Communion; every month, the first Tuesday dedicated to the poor souls; every year, the month of November sanctified for their benefit.

Let us willingly wear the brown scapular of Our Lady of Mount Carmel and join purgatorial societies. We can make an agreement with good brethren for after death: the one left behind will offer suffrages, and the one freed from purgatory will strive to draw the other to salvation.

Never must we forget that those who practice charity will find charity, and those who are merciful will receive mercy. Charity and mercy are not synonymous with weak sentimentalism; they consist of actions. Whoever saves a soul assures his own salvation. Whoever frees a soul from purgatory will find a host of friendly souls surrounding him on his deathbed. "Happy is he who has regard for the lowly and the poor; in the day of misfortune the Lord will deliver him" (Ps. 40:2). In fact, a band of those who have already reached heaven will come to meet him as he enters eternal bliss.

If we pray, we shall find prayers; if we offer suffrages, we shall find them; if we free others, we shall ourselves be freed.

Now let us say three short prayers for the holy souls.

FOR ALL THE FAITHFUL DEPARTED

My Jesus, by the sorrows You suffered in Your agony in the Garden, in Your scourging and crowning with thorns, on the way to Calvary, in Your crucifixion and death, have mercy on the souls in purgatory, and especially on those

that are most forsaken. Deliver them from the dire torments
they endure. Call them and admit them to Your tender
embrace in heaven.

Our Father, Hail Mary, Eternal Rest.

O God, the Creator and Redeemer of all the faithful,
grant to the souls of Your servants and handmaids the remission
of all their sins, that through our devout supplications,
they may obtain the pardon they have always desired.

Our Father, Hail Mary, Eternal Rest.

May our suppliant prayer, we pray You, O Lord, profit
the souls of Your servants and handmaids, that You may
free them from all sins, and make them sharers in Your
Redemption.

Our Father, Hail Mary, Eternal Rest.

HEAVEN

XIII

THE NATURE OF HEAVEN

Our special intentions in this meditation will be the following: to obtain from Our Lord the grace to think much more frequently of heaven, to feel attracted toward it, to augment our desire for it so that we shall continuously aspire to it, to grow constantly in fervor to the point of undergoing all the major sacrifices demanded by daily living—for the great bliss that awaits us. "So great is the happiness that is coming to me that every suffering seems a delight!"

We already long for heaven and it is for this reason that we make sacrifices and go without even lawful pleasures in view of a greater good. But the more we reflect on heaven, the more it will attract us and stir up our fervor.

Often let us say the Hail, Holy Queen. *This is the song of the exiled yearning for his homeland, the prayer of those who lift their thoughts from this valley of tears to the supreme happiness of heaven, and beg Our Lady. ". . . after this our exile, show unto us the blessed fruit of thy womb, Jesus."*

Let heaven be our ruling thought

And while eating with them, he (Jesus) charged them not to depart from Jerusalem, but to wait for the promise of the Father, "of which you have heard," said he, "by my mouth; for John indeed baptized with water, but you shall be baptized with the Holy Spirit not many days hence."

They therefore who had come together began to ask him, saying, "Lord, wilt thou at this time restore the kingdom to Israel?"

But he said to them, "It is not for you to know the times or dates which the Father has fixed by his own authority; but you shall receive power when the Holy Spirit comes upon you, and you shall be witnesses for me in Jerusalem and in all Judea and Samaria and even to the very ends of the earth."

And when he had said this, he was lifted up before their eyes, and a cloud took him out of their sight. And while they were gazing up to heaven as he went, behold, two men stood by them in white garments, and said to them, "Men of Galilee, why do you stand looking up to heaven? This Jesus who has been taken up from you into heaven, shall come in the same way as you have seen him going up to heaven." (Acts 1:4-11.)

Seeing Christ ascending into heaven, the Apostles felt something similar to what we feel at times when we reflect on the heaven that awaits us and on the earth on which we now move. We feel a desire to follow Christ at once on His heavenward ascent, to rise with Him into the heavenly regions. "I desire to depart and to be with Christ" (Phil. 1:23). The Angels have to shake us out of this sweet contemplation and remind us that heaven has to be earned.

Heaven, you are ours! You are the one and only lasting good! On these two truths we shall pause to reflect now.

Heaven is ours. Everything else, of this world—these homes, these clothes, these goods of every kind–are merely loaned to us for a little while. They are to be used to reach heaven. But heaven itself is a good which will never be taken away. God created it for us, and us for it. "You made us for Yourself, O Lord," said St. Augustine. God created us to know Him, to love Him, and to serve Him in this life, to possess Him forever in heaven.

This life is in reality a short trip. When travelling by train, no one would dream of considering the train or the car he is in as his own! Nor do passengers pay much attention to the cities through which they pass on the way to their destination. We are travelling toward the Lord; we are on a trip in this life. Let each of us, then, fix his eyes on his goal, his home up above. Everything passes, as the days pass. Everything surrounding us is ours only on loan. Heaven is our country, our family home, our own. We are exiles aiming for home, sons anxious to behold their Heavenly Father: "Here we have no permanent city" (Heb. 13:14).

On a trip, we experience only in desire the joys we shall find when we reach our destination. "I rejoiced because they said to me, 'We will go up to the house of the Lord'" (Ps. 121:1). This miserable life so often hands us bitter days! Will things always be this way? No, indeed! Look up–there is a place prepared up there for each one of us. . . . Let me stress that: for each one of us there is a throne–for me, for you, for all who labor and suffer and hope in this life: "Until my relief should come" (Job 14:14).

Heaven is a lasting good, a permanent one. This life is short. The days and the years fly by unbelievably fast, and they seem to grow shorter as we grow older. But heaven will never end; it is eternal. Our homeland is heaven. It will be a day without a sunset, youth without old age, joy undisturbed by the fear of suffering. How unfair we are to ourselves if we do not think of heaven, the one and only true treasure, and ours forever! We shall have more courage if we think of it. We shall rejoice and forge ahead enthusiastically. The virtue we now practice with great effort will then seem the best and most precious thing imaginable.

Ah, to what a home God is inviting us! To heaven! What cause for rejoicing! Let us recite Psalm 121: "I rejoiced because they said to me, 'We will go up to the house of the Lord.' " And let us ask God for the grace often to lift our hearts from the misery of this earth to heaven, which we hope to reach, and where we hope to be all together again. After the psalm, we shall say the third joyful mystery, that our hearts may be detached from everything. Thus we will be free to ascend more quickly to heaven.

PSALM 121

The Pilgrim's Greetings to Jerusalem

I rejoiced because they said to me,
"We will go up to the house of the Lord."
And now we have set foot
within your gates, O Jerusalem—
Jerusalem, built as a city
with compact unity.
To it tribes go up,
the tribes of the Lord,
According to the decree for Israel,
to give thanks to the name of the Lord.
In it are set up judgment seats,
seats for the house of David.
Pray for the peace of Jerusalem!
May those who love you prosper!
May peace be within your walls,
prosperity in your buildings.
Because of my relatives and friends
I will say, "Peace be within you!"
Because of the house of the Lord, our God,
I will pray for your good.
Glory Be.

THIRD JOYFUL MYSTERY

Born in the stable of Bethlehem, Jesus is laid in a manger in the most abject poverty. Let us esteem the virtue of poverty and ask it of Jesus and Mary.

Heaven is our greatest desire

"The kingdom of heaven is like a treasure hidden in a field; he who finds it hides it, and in his joy goes and sells all that he has and buys that field.

"Again, the kingdom of heaven is like a merchant in search of fine pearls. When he finds a single pearl of great price, he goes and sells all that he has and buys it.

"Again, the kingdom of heaven is like a net cast into the sea that gathered in fish of every kind. When it was filled, they hauled it out, and sitting down on the beach, they gathered the good fish into vessels, but threw away the bad. So will it be at the end of the world. The angels will go out and separate the wicked from among the just, and will cast them into the furnace of fire, where there will be the weeping, and the gnashing of teeth.

"Have you understood all these things?" They said to him, "Yes." And he said to them, "So then, every Scribe instructed in the kingdom of heaven is like a householder who brings forth from his storeroom things new and old."

(Matt. 13:44-52.)

Christ further said: "Seek first the kingdom of God and His justice, and all these things shall be given you besides" (Matt. 6:33).

To seek first the kingdom of God means to let heaven lead the list of all our desires. "Seek first the kingdom of God." This is the highest good. On earth there are many types of good things, but none are really worth desiring. They are only to be used. The wealth of this earth passes, but those who did not cling to it and used it only in a holy way, will have treasure in heaven. The admiration of our fellow men disappear. As a last token of esteem, they will accompany our coffin to the cemetery. However, the soul who did not look for esteem and used the high opinion others had of him only to do good, will receive praise and acclaim from God. Studies end, little satisfactions are soon over, our very body dies. Let us seek treasures that do not end with death. "Lay up for yourselves treasures in heaven, where neither rust nor moth consumes" (Matt. 6:20). If you wish to be rich, seek true wealth. The martyrs courageously suffered the cruelest torments because they kept their gaze on heaven. The first martyr, St. Stephen, who was stoned to death, cried out: "Behold, I see the heavens opened, and the Son of Man standing at the right hand of God" (Acts 7:55). With these heavenly visions, we might almost say that the martyrs did not feel the earthly torments they underwent.

Why have virgins bid farewell to all the pleasures of the world to consecrate themselves entirely to God? For heaven. They desire to prepare a beautiful eternity for themselves: "Five of the virgins were wise." Why do so many young men leave every comfort and convenience at home to go off in search of a soul, drawn by a high ideal? To win a soul for heaven and then die. Ah, heaven! The more we look at it, the more the earth loses its attraction. Echoing

across the centuries comes the ecstatic cry of
St. Philip Neri: "Heaven! Heaven!"

Why, then, are we yet so attached to this earth?
Why does it take such effort to remember heaven?
Why must we almost force ourselves to desire it?
Why are we so lazy when it comes to gaining merit?
The answer is that we do not understand what
heaven is, or rather, we do not let the desire for it
permeate us.

Let us try to fix the thought of heaven firmly
in our minds and stir up a burning desire for it,
praying with the angels and saints. May they who
are already experiencing it allow us to feel something of the joy that floods their spirit.

Now we shall say the "Angel of God" nine
times, to the nine choirs of angels, that they may obtain for us an attraction for heaven. We shall conclude with the fourth joyful mystery of the Rosary,
asking to merit the heavenly reward by the constant
practice of virtue.

PRAYER TO THE GUARDIAN ANGEL

Angel of God, my guardian dear
To whom God's love entrusts me here,
Ever this day, be at my side
To light and guard, to rule and guide.
(Nine times.)

FOURTH JOYFUL MYSTERY

Mary, although not in duty bound, presents Jesus in the temple and perfectly fulfills what was prescribed for her purification. Let us consider and ask for the obedience of the Blessed Virgin.

Heaven is the greatest grace
for which to pray

> Now one of those robbers who were hanged was abusing him, saying, "If thou art the Christ, save thyself and us!" But the other in answer rebuked him and said, "Dost not even thou fear God, seeing that thou art under the same sentence? And we indeed justly, for we are receiving what our deeds deserved; but this man has done nothing wrong." And he said to Jesus, "Lord, remember me when thou comest into thy kingdom." And Jesus said to him, "Amen I say to thee, this day thou shalt be with me in paradise."
>
> (Luke 23:39-43.)

In the Gospel, Our Lord tells us: "The kingdom of heaven is like a merchant in search of fine pearls. When he finds a single pearl of great price, he goes and sells all that he has and buys it" (Matt. 13:45-46).

Heaven is worth giving up everything to gain. Let us relinquish everything to gain everything. Our "everything" however, is very little, and that which we gain by relinquishing it is the greatest good,

supreme happiness. While we are on this earth, we
must ask the Lord for many graces. We must ask
to grow in virtue and to conquer our chief fault;
we must ask for the spirit of prayer and recollection,
for a love for the obligations we have taken on, and
also, for earthly goods, in due proportion. Graces
and favors for ourselves and others—we do, indeed
need to ask for them. But above all these graces, we
must ask for final perseverance, for the salvation
of our soul, for heaven.

Let us never forget that our prayers should
conclude with the closing words of the "Anima
Christi": "In the hour of my death call me; bid me
come to You on high, that with Your saints I may
praise You." We pray that we may attain to eternal
happiness and with the angels chant the praises
of the Lord.

> "Whom else have I in heaven? And when I am
> with you, the earth delights me not. Though my
> flesh and my heart waste away, God is the rock
> of my heart and my portion forever. But for me, to
> be near God is my good; to make the Lord God my
> refuge. I shall declare all your works in the gates
> of the daughter of Sion."
>
> (Ps. 72:25-26, 28.)

There are many psalms, but all of them are
directed to obtain for us the grace of forever singing,
"Glory be to the Father, and to the Son, and to the
Holy Spirit," in heaven.

We have many forms of piety–Holy Communion, Holy Mass, the Sacraments, rosary, etc. And there are many special devotions, many churches, many ceremonies, many sacred duties. To obtain eternal salvation, in all these functions, in all these Sacraments, in every Mass, in every rosary, we implicitly say, "This is to save my soul."

There are those who do not pray and they arouse great pity, for one who does not pray loses his soul. Others, instead, do pray, and they are a source of consolation, for he who prays will be saved. Still others pray but yet imperfectly, for their requests are for the things of this earth! The first thing to ask for is heaven! All the rest will be given besides. Say: I ask nothing earthly of You, Lord. Only one thing I ask, one thing I seek: "One thing I ask of the Lord; this I seek: to dwell in the house of the Lord all the days of my life" (Ps. 26:4). May I have the grace of living forever in God's home, as His son: "If we are sons, we are heirs also: heirs indeed of God and joint heirs with Christ" (Rom. 8:17).

Why, then, should we ask for what pertains to this earth? Ask for heaven! Heaven is always a bargain, no matter what it costs. Our days are valuable in proportion to what they earn for eternity. In the evening, let us bless God for having let us work one more day for Him, and thus to have increased our reward with every hour. Heaven must figure into every prayer, as we pray for perseverance to the end.

We ought to read the "Beatitudes" often to impress upon our minds the principal grace for which to ask. The Beatitudes speak of the virtues which bring contentment in this life and eternal happiness in heaven. And when we say the fifth glorious mystery, we should pause to consider the glory enjoyed by our Blessed Mother and the saints. With a holy envy, let us long for that which is meant to be ours, too; it awaits us and we, on our part, want to attain to it.

Now we shall say the fifth joyful mystery, for the grace to be faithful to our vocation in life.

FIFTH JOYFUL MYSTERY

The Boy Jesus remains for three days among the learned men in the temple, listening to them and asking them questions. Let us pray for the grace to know and follow our vocation.

XIV

HEAVEN IS GLORY

Let us continue our reflections on heaven, desiring to attain to it and asking for this grace. First, we shall consider the glory our body will enjoy in heaven; second, the special glory of certain groups of the blessed, and third, the difference between the glory of those with greater merit and those with less.

The glory of the body in heaven

"Then will the kingdom of heaven be like ten virgins who took their lamps and went forth to meet the bridegroom and the bride. Five of them were foolish and five wise. But the five foolish, when they took their lamps, took no oil with them, while the wise did take oil in their vessels with the lamps. Then as the bridegroom was long in coming, they all became drowsy and slept. And at midnight a cry arose, 'Behold, the bridegroom is coming, go forth to meet him!' Then all those virgins arose and trimmed their lamps. And the foolish said to the wise, 'Give us some of your oil, for our lamps are going out.' The wise answered, saying, 'Lest there may not be enough for us and for you, go rather to those who sell it, and buy some for yourselves.'

"Now while they were gone to buy it, the bridegroom came; and those who were ready went in with him to the marriage feast, and the door was shut. Finally there came also the other virgins, who said, 'Sir, sir, open the door for us!' But he answered and said, 'Amen I say to you, I do not know you.' Watch therefore, for you know neither the day nor the hour."

(Matt. 25:1-13.)

"Let your loins be girt about and your lamps burning, and you yourselves like men waiting for their Master's return from the wedding"

(Luke 12:35).

The lighted lamps signify the upright intention which should be behind our actions. The oil is the supply of good deeds. The "loins girt about" of those waiting for the bridegroom recall the sacredness of the body. This body, if holy, will share the soul's glory, just as it shared its merit on earth.

The foolish virgins, though unprepared to meet the master, grew drowsy and slept. They were lazy. Often, the body is pampered, and the result is sins of gluttony, sensuality and sloth. Such behavior is in reality hatred of the body, for it will bring ruin upon it.

We must not forget that for the body, too, there is heaven. It will have to suffer annihilation in the grave when death performs its work, but at the general resurrection, the voice of the Angel will command the dead to arise: "So also with the resurrection of the dead. What is sown in corruption rises in incorruption; what is sown in dishonor rises in glory; what is sown in weakness rises in power; what is sown a natural body rises a spiritual body" (I Cor. 17:42-44). On the day of the general judgment, with the soul, the body will enter heaven endowed with subtlety, impassibility, immortality, agility, and splendor. It will have its own beatitude, for all the senses will have to receive their reward—especially those which were of greater service in knowing, loving and serving God.

The body of Jesus Christ arose glorious; the body of the Blessed Virgin, His Mother, was assumed into heaven. Those who have tried to imitate them will also be glorified in body at the resurrection. The eyes that often looked at good and inspiring things, the ears that readily took in the word of God, the tongue that spoke well and charitably, the heart that beat for Christ—these will not remain forever in the grave. Those eyes will gaze in rapture on the Blessed Trinity and the Mother of God; those ears will thrill to the melodies of heaven; that tongue will sing the glories of the Lord in harmony with the angels and the saints; that heart will be overwhelmed in a torrent of joy and happiness. The entire body, now impassible, immortal, and adorned with radiant splendor, will exchange earth for heaven, the land of exile for the homeland, humiliation for eternal bliss.

Blessed are they who are wise enough to use their health and senses well in this life! "I am saving my eyes to behold the face of Mary most holy in heaven," a saint used to say. Blessed are they who listen to the word of God, for they shall hear the music of heaven. Blessed are they who spend their time on earth in penance, fatiguing toil and mortifications for the Lord. Some day these wearisome labors will be rewarded with eternal rest. Blessed are virginal bodies. Blessed are the hands that are never idle and always bring blessings. Blessed are the feet of those who go about spreading the word of God, the holy Gospel: "How beautiful are the feet of those who preach the gospel of peace; of those who bring glad tidings of good things!" (Rom. 10:15). Blessed are the tongues which share the message of Christ with their neighbors. What a reward they will reap one day! This, then, is true love of the body–to deprive it of satisfactions on this earth and subject it to fatiguing labor, so that it will enjoy an eternity of bliss.

The second glorious mystery, "Christ's ascension into heaven," reminds us that like Christ's, our bodies, too, will rise to heaven. Now let us say the prayer, "Soul of Christ," that our body and tongue, especially, may be sanctified by contact with the Body and Blood of Jesus, and that through this contact, our heart may be cleansed and sanctified, too. Then we shall offer a fervent prayer to Mary Immaculate.

SOUL OF CHRIST

Soul of Christ, sanctify me.
Body of Christ, save me.
Blood of Christ, inebriate me.
Water from the side of Christ, wash me.
Passion of Christ, strengthen me.
O good Jesus, hear me.
Within Your wounds, hide me.
Permit me not to be separated from You.
From the malignant enemy, defend me.
In the hour of my death, call me.
And bid me come to You.
For ever and ever.
Amen.

PRAYER

O most holy Virgin, we beg you to visit our home, and keep far from it the snares of the devil. Live with us, Mary, our Mother, Teacher, and Queen. And may the holy Angels preserve us in peace.

My dear and sweet Mother Mary, keep me in your holy protection. Guard my mind, my heart and my senses, that I may not be stained by sin.

Sanctify my thoughts, desires, words and actions, so that I may please you and your Jesus, my God, and gain a holy paradise with you. Jesus and Mary, give me your most holy blessing. (Bow the head) In the name of the Father, and of the Son, and of the Holy Ghost. Amen.

The aureole of certain saints

"A little while and you shall see me no longer; and again a little while and you shall see me, because I go to the Father."

Some of his disciples therefore said to one another, "What is this he says to us, 'A little while and you shall not see me, and again a little while and you shall see me'; and, 'I go to the Father?'". They kept saying therefore, "What is this 'little while' of which he speaks? We do not know what he is saying."

But Jesus knew that they wanted to ask him, and he said to them, "You inquire about this among yourselves because I said, 'A little while and you shall not see me, and again a little while and you shall see me.' Amen, amen, I say to you, that you shall weep and lament, but the world shall rejoice; and you shall be sorrowful, but your sorrow shall be turned into joy. A woman about to give birth has sorrow, because her hour has come. But when she has brought forth the child, she no longer remembers the anguish for her joy that a man is born into the world. And you therefore have sorrow now; but I will see you again, and your heart shall rejoice, and your joy no one shall take from you.   (John 16:16-22.)

Although the good often have to suffer on this earth, God will see to it that they have their reward. Those who work the hardest will have a special reward in heaven. Heaven is called a "crown," and all the blessed will receive their crown: "There is laid up for me a crown of justice," wrote St. Paul. Some saints however, will have a second crown called an aureole, a kind of special radiance reserved to them alone. There are three of these: for virgins, for martyrs, and for doctors.

The aureole of virgins is the distinguishing reward of those who have loved only the Lord on this earth: "They were singing as it were a new song. . .; and no one could learn the song except those hundred and forty-four thousand, who have been purchased from the earth. These are they who were not defiled with women; for they are virgins" (Apoc. 14:3-4). Virgins! Near Christ is their place of honor; in their hands they hold their lily and about their heads shines the special aureole of virgins. Well do they merit this distinction in heaven for having understood and carried out Christ's words: "Not all can accept this teaching; but those to whom it has been given" (Matt. 19:11).

Next, there is the aureole of martyrs who underwent sufferings, torments, and persecution for the name of Christ. In their hands they carry the palm indicative of the glory they earned with their sufferings. St. Stephen, St. Lawrence, St. Agnes and many, many other glorious names come to our minds when we think of martyrs. "These who are clothed in white robes, who are they? And whence have they come? . . . These are they who have come out of the great tribulation, and have washed their robes and made them white in the blood of the Lamb" (Apoc. 7:13-14). And about their heads shines their particular crown–the aureole of martyrs.

Finally, the doctors and great preachers receive a special aureole, for besides having conquered themselves and loved the Lord, they drove the devil from the hearts of their fellow men and led them to love God, too. Therefore, it is fitting that in addition to the glory they earned for themselves, they should be rewarded also for the merits they induced others to earn. "The wise shall shine brightly like the splendor of the firmament, and those who lead the many to justice shall be like the stars forever" (Dan. 12:3). Thus, like the virgins and martyrs, the doctors, too, will be honored in heaven with a second aureole.

Among all the saints, the greatest glory is reserved for the Blessed Mother, because she enjoys the total glory of all the saints taken together. Moreover, she possesses a still higher dignity, special to her alone: "The holy Mother of God is exalted above the choirs of angels in the heavenly kingdom." To her belongs the lily of virgins—"Virgin of virgins;" the crown of doctors, for she is the "Seat of wisdom"; and the palm of martyrs, because she is the Queen of Martyrs.

What glory can we expect? There are martyrs of charity, of patience, of faith, of community life. . . . There are dedicated writers, famous preachers, teachers, catechists, and zealous apostles in the

home. And the aureoule of purity can be earned
by anyone who wants it and prays.

Let us now say the Litany of the Saints.

THE LITANY OF THE SAINTS

Lord, have mercy on us.
Christ, have mercy on us.
Lord, have mercy on us.
Christ, hear us.
Christ, graciously hear us.
God, the Father of Heaven, have mercy on us.
God, the Son, Redeemer of the world, have mercy on us.
God, the Holy Spirit, have mercy on us.
Holy Trinity, one God, have mercy on us.
Holy Mary,
Holy Mother of God,
Holy Virgin of Virgins,
St. Michael,
St. Gabriel,
St. Raphael,
All you holy Angels and Archangels,
All you holy orders of blessed Spirits,
St. John the Baptist,
St. Joseph,
Al you holy Patriarchs and Prophets,
St. Peter,
St. Paul,
St. Andrew,
St. James,
St. John,
St. Thomas,
St. James,
St. Philip,

pray for us.

St. Bartholomew,
St. Matthew,
St. Simon,
St. Thaddeus,
St. Matthias,
St. Barnabas,
St. Luke,
St. Mark,
All you holy Apostles and Evangelists,
All you holy Disciples of the Lord,
All you holy Innocents,

St. Stephen,
St. Lawrence,
St. Vincent,
SS. Fabian and Sebastian,
SS. John and Paul,
SS. Cosmas and Damian,
SS. Gervase and Protase,
All you holy Martyrs,
St. Sylvester,
St. Gregory,
St. Ambrose,
St. Augustine,
St. Jerome,
St. Martin,
St. Nicholas,
All you holy Bishops and Confessors,
All you holy Doctors,

St. Anthony,
St. Benedict,
St. Bernard,
St. Dominic,
St. Francis,
All you holy Priests and Levites,
All you holy Monks and Hermits,

pray for us.

St. Mary Magdalene,
St. Agatha,
St. Lucy,
St. Agnes,
St. Cecilia,
St. Catherine,
St. Anastasia,

pray for us.

All you holy Virgins and Widows,
All you holy men and women, Saints of God, make inter-
          cession for us.
Be merciful, spare us, O Lord.
Be merciful, graciously hear us, O Lord.
From all evil,
From all sin,
From Your wrath,
From sudden and unprovided death,
From the snares of the devil,
From anger and hatred and every evil will,
From the spirit of fornication,
From lightning and tempest,
From the scourge of earthquake,
From plague, famine and war,
From everlasting death,
Through the mystery of Your holy Incarnation,
Through Your coming,
Through Your birth,
Through Your Baptism and holy fasting,
Through Your Cross and Passion,
Through Your death and burial,
Through Your holy Resurrection,
Through Your admirable Ascension,
Through the coming of the Holy Ghost,
          the Paraclete,
In the day of judgment,

O Lord, deliver us.

We sinners,   We beseech You, hear us.
That You would spare us,   "

That You would bring us to true repentance,

That You would vouchsafe to govern and preserve Your holy Church,

That You would vouchsafe to preserve our Apostolic Prelate, and all orders of the Church, in holy religion,

That You would vouchsafe to give peace and true concord to Christian kings and princes,

That You would vouchsafe to grant peace and unity to all Christian people,

That You would vouchsafe to confirm and preserve us in Your holy service,

That You would bring back all the erring to the unity of the Church, and lead all infidels to the light of the Gospel.

That You would lift up our minds to heavenly desires,

That You would render eternal blessings to all our benefactors,

That You would deliver our souls, the souls of our brethren, relations and benefactors, from eternal damnation,

That You would vouchsafe to give and preserve the fruits of the earth,

That You would vouchsafe to grant eternal rest to all the faithful departed,

That You would vouchsafe to graciously hear us,

Son of God,

Lamb of God, Who takest away the sins of the world, spare us, O Lord.

Lamb of God, Who takest away the sins of the world, graciously hear us, O Lord.

Lamb of God, Who takest away the sins of the world, have mercy on us.

Christ, hear us.   Christ, graciously hear us.

Lord, have mercy.   Christ, have mercy.

Lord have mercy.

Our Father, etc.

Differences in glory among the blessed

"For it is like a man going abroad, who called his servants and handed over his goods to them. And to one he gave five talents, to another two, and to another one, to each according to his particular ability, and then he went on his journey. And he who had received the five talents went and traded with them, and gained five more. In like manner, he who had received the two gained two more. But he who had received the one went away and dug in the earth and hid his master's money.

"Then after a long time the master of those servants came and settled accounts with them. And he who had received the five talents came and brought five other talents, saying, 'Master, thou didst hand over to me five talents; behold, I have gained five others in addition.' His master said to him, 'Well done, good and faithful servant; because thou hast been faithful over a few things, I will set thee over many; enter into the joy of thy master.'

"And he also who had received the two talents came and said, 'Master, thou didst hand over to me two talents; behold, I have gained two more.' His master said to him, 'Well done, good and faithful servant; because thou hast been faithful over a few things, I will set thee over many; enter into the joy of thy master.'"

(Matt. 25:14-23.)

Whoever uses his talents well will receive his due reward in heaven. They who worked harder for God and loved Him with greater fervor will receive a greater recompense. Indeed, Sacred Scripture assures us that everyone is rewarded according to what he has done. It is only natural that the servant who has worked the most should receive the most pay. There must be quite a differnce between the reward given to one who has worked only a few hours, a few days or a few years, as compared to that given another who has toiled twenty, thirty, fifty years for the Lord. Can we guess at the glory enjoyed by the great Apostle Paul?–"I have labored more than any of them" (1 Cor. 15:10). Can we imagine the reward given St. Alphonse de Liguori, who lived until he was ninety and spent his long life in every kind of labor? "Star differs from star in glory" (1 Cor 15:41). Every star shines, but some are especially bright. Likewise, the blessed in heaven enjoy a vision proportionate to their fidelity to God on earth, to their efforts to know Him and to make others know Him.

We must bolster our courage. It is neither wise nor prudent to try to do as little as possible. The truly wise are indefatigable workers: they are always thinking up some ingenious way of furthering good and holy causes. It is no sign of cleverness always to put things off–"I'll turn over a new leaf soon; I'll begin to work for sanctity later on; someday I'll get around to converting myself. . . ." He is far more prudent who declares, "Today I shall begin–and right now!"

There are different categories of saved souls: the lukewarm, who just barely make it, and enter heaven only after a long purgatory, perhaps; the fervent, who ascend to the highest regions; and the saints, whose glory is much higher and more perfect!

Of what practical value for our lives are these reflections? Let us recall the promises of the Sacred Heart of Jesus. He has said that sinners will find a refuge in His heart; that lukewarm souls will draw fervor from devotion to this Heart; and that fervent souls will find in this Heart great perfection and sanctity. Whatever be our present state, then, let us have recourse to the Eucharistic Heart of Jesus and ask Him to shake us out of tepidity, to lead us from lukewarmness to fervor, and from fervor to sanctity. The toil lasts but little, and the reward is eternal.

To obtain this grace, let us now recite the prayer to the Queen of Apostles.

TO THE QUEEN OF THE APOSTLES

O Immaculate Mary, Co-redemptrix of the human race, behold men redeemed by the blood of your Divine Son, yet still immersed in the darkness of error and the mire of vice.

The harvest is always great, but the laborers are still very few. Have pity, O Mary, upon your children whom the dying Christ entrusted to you from the cross. Increase religious and priestly vocations. Give us new apostles full of wisdom and fervor. Sustain with your maternal care those souls who consecrate their lives for the good of their neighbor. Recall your care for Jesus and the Apostle John. Remember your sweet petitions to our Lord to obtain the Holy Spirit for the Apostles. You were the counselor of the first Apostles, and of the Apostles of all times. By your powerful intercession, renew again the Divine Pentecost upon those called to the apostolate. Sanctify them and inflame them with holy zeal, for the glory of God and the salvation of souls. Guide them in all their efforts. Guard them with your graces. Sustain them in moments of discouragement. Crown their zeal with success.

Grant our prayer, O Mary, that all men may receive the Divine Master, Way, Truth and Life. May they all become docile children of the Catholic Church, and may the whole world resound with your praises, and honor you as Mother, Teacher and Queen. Thus we may all attain to eternal happiness in Heaven. Amen.

Hail Mary.
Queen of Apostles, pray for us.

XV

IN HEAVEN, WE SHALL CONTEMPLATE GOD, SUPREME TRUTH

Now is the time to ask the Lord for a living faith in heaven, for the grace to know Him well in this life—were we not created to know Him?— and for the grace to make Him known to men, because they who teach and act well will be great in heaven: "Whoever does away with one of these least commandments and so teaches men, shall be called least in the kingdom of heaven; but whoever carries them out and teaches them, he shall be called great in the kingdom of heaven" (Matt. 5:19). These latter will not be confined to the lowest places. On the contrary, they will be called near Jesus, near His throne—as the clergy take their places in church, in the sanctuary near the altar.

The Beatific Vision

Now after six days Jesus took Peter, James and his brother John, and led them up a high mountain by themselves, and was transfigured before them. And his face shone as the sun, and his garments became white as snow. And behold, there appeared to them Moses and Elias talking together with him. Then Peter addressed Jesus, saying, "Lord, it is good for us to be here. If thou wilt, let us set up three tents here, one for thee, one for Moses, and one for Elias." As he was still speaking, behold, a bright cloud overshadowed them, and behold, a voice out of the cloud said, "This is my beloved Son, in whom I am well pleased; hear him." And on hearing it the disciples fell on their faces and were exceedingly afraid. And Jesus came near and touched them, and said to them, "Arise, and do not be afraid." But lifting up their eyes, they saw no one but Jesus only.

And as they were coming down from the mountain, Jesus cautioned them, saying, "Tell the vision to no one, till the Son of Man has risen from the dead."

(Matt. 17:1-9.)

Here was a foretaste of the beatific vision to which we are called.

What does 'beatific vision' mean? It means seeing God face to face, as He is, in a direct manner. On this earth, we do not see God with our bodily eyes. We only know Him a little through His creatures, that is, we behold the world, the work of His hands, and come to know God the Creator of these works. The world exists and manifests both order and beauty. Hence, the Lord, Who created it from nothing, must be an all-wise, all-beautiful Being. We also know God, in this life, as He is revealed to us in Holy Scripture. This knowledge comes from God Himself, Who even revealed mysteries to us, such as the mystery of the Blessed Trinity. However, neither the knowledge we have through reasoning nor the knowledge of mysteries which we receive from faith is the vision of God. Both of these are external, so to speak.

Instead, upon our entrance into heaven, we shall see God, just as we see our own father when we come home at night. In heaven we shall know the Lord not only by sight, as we know things now; we shall know Him by the light of glory.

St. Peter beheld the person of Christ the God-Man, and gazed on His face as He spoke, admiring His beauty and unfailing goodness. But when he climbed Mt. Thabor and there beheld Christ trans-figured before him, Peter had a foretaste of the heavenly vision, because he saw Our Lord in glory and he saw Him by means of a vision. The impor-tant point is that on this earth, knowledge of God, either by reason or by faith, does not render us fully blessed; it only makes us contented. Once our soul has been freed from our body, however, and later, when the resurrected body enters heaven, the soul will enjoy the vision of God to the fullest.

Just as the palate delights in sweets, so the in-tellect is made for the truth and for the Lord. God made us for Himself. And this intellect of ours, which now sees little difference between being in error and being in the truth, will rejoice and exult at knowing the Lord and His beauty. It will be in-comparably happier than is a lover of good foods when tasting specialties! In fact, in heaven our in-telligence will know a bliss similar to what the angels experience, for although our body will be satisfied, the satisfaction of the soul at knowing God, Truth and Goodness itself, will be immensely superior.

It is no longer simply a matter of mastering human learning. Do we not at times envy the learning of St. Thomas Aquinas, who produced works so marvellous and so clear? Do we not feel somewhat envious of those scholars who knew nature so well and were almost rapt out of themselves in contemplating its beauties? Take, then, all the learning of the greatest literary figures and linguists, the record of the whole of world history, the knowledge of natural sciences, the highest attainable wisdom in the fields of law, sociology, philosophy, letters, science, history and anything else real or imaginable—all this knowledge taken together concerns merely the work of God and is, therefore, infinitely inferior to the knowledge of God. What, then, must it be to know the great Author of everything, God Himself, and in Him, all natural learning? To know the Lord, Who is the Author of all knowledge, and Truth itself?

You who love to study and to learn, seek the kingdom of God and His justice; you shall see God and shall have all human knowledge besides.

Heaven, heaven! How beautiful, how desirable you are! Jesus Christ Himself is the lamp of heaven: "The city has no need of the sun or the moon to shine upon it. For the glory of God lights it up, and the Lamb is the lamp thereof" (Apoc. 21:23).

Now, then, let us recite Psalm 147, "Glorify the Lord, O Jerusalem." Let the heavenly Jerusalem praise the Lord! In heaven, the angels and saints see Him and adore Him. There dwells the Father, the divine Word–the Wisdom of the Father–and the Holy Spirit. What a brilliant light shines into the eyes of the blessed, so to speak! In fact, it is God Himself entering into them. The blessed become one with God, not by nature, but by union of knowledge.

Let us lift ourselves to heaven. When we adore the Blessed Sacrament on the altar, our eyes behold only the Eucharistic species, but one day Christ will reveal Himself to us. We shall see Him "face to face," (1 Cor. 13:12.)–as He is.

After the Psalm, we shall say the Acts of Faith, Hope and Charity, reflecting on heaven as we pray.

PSALM 147

Glorify the Lord, O Jerusalem;
praise your God, O Sion.
For he has strengthened the bars of your gates,
he has blessed your children within you.
He has granted peace in your borders;
with the best of wheat he fills you.
He sends forth his command to the earth;
swiftly runs his word!

He spreads snow like wool;
frost he strews like ashes.
He scatters his hail like crumbs;
before his cold the waters freeze.
He sends his word and melts them;
he lets his breeze blow and the waters run.
He has proclaimed his word to Jacob,
his statutes and his ordinances to Israel.
He has not done thus for any other nation;
his ordinances he has not made known to them.
Alleluia.
Glory Be.

ACT OF FAITH

O my God, I firmly believe that You are one God in three Divine Persons, Father, Son and Holy Ghost. I believe that Your Divine Son became man and died for our sins, and that He will come to judge the living and the dead. I believe these and all the truths which the Holy Catholic Church teaches, because You have revealed them, Who can neither deceive nor be deceived.

ACT OF HOPE

O my God, relying on Your infinite goodness and promises, I hope to obtain pardon of my sins, the help of Your grace, and life everlasting, through the merits of Jesus Christ, my Lord and Redeemer.

ACT OF LOVE

O my God, I love You above all things, with my whole heart and soul, because You are all good and worthy of all love. I love my neighbor as myself for the love of You. I forgive all who have injured me and I ask pardon of all whom I have injured.

In heaven, mysteries will be revealed to us

And behold a certain man came to him and said, "Good Master, what good work shall I do to have eternal life?" He said to him, "Why dost thou ask me about what is good? One there is who is good, and he is God. But if thou wilt enter into life, keep the commandments." He said to him, "Which?" And Jesus said, "Thou shalt not kill. Thou shalt not commit adultery. Thou shalt not steal. Thou shalt not bear false witness. Honor thy father and mother. And, thou shalt love thy neighbor as thyself." The young man said to him, "All these I have kept; what is yet wanting to me?" Jesus said to him, "If thou wilt be perfect, go, sell what thou hast, and give to the poor, and thou shalt have treasure in heaven; and come, follow me." But when the young man heard the saying, he went away sad, for he had great possessions.

But Jesus said to his disciples, "Amen I say to you, with difficulty will a rich man enter the kingdom of heaven. And further I say to you, it is easier for a camel to pass through the eye of a needle, than for a rich man to enter the kingdom of heaven." The disciples, hearing this, were exceedingly astonished, and said, "Who then can be saved?" And looking upon them, Jesus said to them, "With men this is impossible, but with God all things are possible."

Then Peter addressed him, saying, "Behold, we have left all and followed thee; what then shall we have?" And Jesus said to them, "Amen I say to you that you who have followed me, in the regeneration when the Son of Man shall sit on the throne of his glory, shall also sit on twelve thrones, judging the twelve tribes of Israel. And everyone who has left house, or brothers, or sisters, or father, or mother, or wife, or children, or lands, for my name's sake, shall receive a hundredfold, and shall possess life everlasting. But many who are first now will be last, and many who are last now will be first."

(Matt. 19:16-30.)

Let us ponder those words of Christ: "Amen I say to you, with difficulty will a rich man enter the kingdom of heaven," and: "Many who are first now will be last, and many who are last now will be first."

Heaven is promised to those who love God not in words but in deeds, i.e., in observance of His commandments. In fact, an immense reward is destined for souls who show their love by observing not only the commandments but also the counsels. Fortunate are they who follow the counsels Christ gave that young man. The Apostles had followed them: "We have left all and followed thee!" And Jesus said to them, "You . . . shall possess life everlasting" (Matt. 19:27-29).

In heaven we shall behold in God all natural knowledge and every external work of God, but more than that, we shall behold even mysteries in God. Natural wonders thrill us no end, but revealed truths are far greater. Now we barely manage to recite these truths, without understanding them, yet by saying and believing them, we gain merit for the

next life. Some of these truths were revealed by
Our Lord, the Divine Master, such as the mystery
of the Holy Eucharist–the fact that the Eucharist is
the Body, Blood, Soul and Divinity of Jesus Christ.
Our eyes see only the appearances, but our faith
believes in the Real Presence. The Heart of Christ,
living and true is there; the Son of God Himself is
there. Still other mysteries are the Incarnation, the
Resurrection of Christ, and the mystery of mysteries,
the Blessed Trinity. One God in three Persons–this
mystery so deep, so sublime, so vast, excites our
hearts to a great desire to behold the Lord. St. Paul
cried out: "Oh, the depth of the riches of the wisdom and of the knowledge of God!" (Rom. 11:32).

The science of theology, when studied with
good will, arouses great enthusiasm, as do studies
of ascetical doctrine under such teachers and doctors as St. Bernard and St. Francis de Sales; the
study of the highest mysticism, taught by St. Teresa
and St. Bonaventure; the study of dogmatic theology, with St. Augustine as the teacher; moral theology under St. Alphonsus; and pastoral theology,
with St. Gregory the Great.

Going further, what do we feel when reading
of St. Gemma Galgani's ecstasies? What does the
priest feel as he recites the passages of his breviary
concerning the stigmata of St. Francis of Assisi?

What do we experience when reading the revelations of St. Margaret Mary Alacoque who, from the foot of the altar, saw the Tabernacle open and Christ present Himself to her, opening His side to show her His Heart? And what feelings flood our soul when we think of St. Paul, who learned the Gospel "by a revelation of Jesus Christ" (Gal. 1:12), and who was taken up into the third heaven to contemplate indescribable beauties not seen on earth, and to hear words not heard on earth: "He was caught up into paradise and heard secret words that man may not repeat" (2 Cor. 12:4).

Lifting our minds in the thought of these things, off in the distance we see a faint ray of heaven, just as at dawn the first streaks of light in the East tell us that the sun is about to rise. While pondering on heavenly things, on these visions of the Saints, we desire heaven and we begin to see just how desirable it is. We understand how happy those blessed possessors of the vision of God must be, immersed in Him and constantly penetrating mysteries without ever being satiated, always eager for more and yet always satisfied!

God is an abyss of light! An abyss of love!

"Thou hast made us for Thyself, O Lord," cried St. Augustine, "and our hearts are restless until they rest in Thee!"

Let us have recourse to St. Ambrose, St. Augustine, St. Paul, St. Bonaventure, and St. Francis of Assisi, all of whom used to put off their hour of repose in order to prolong their meditation on heaven. It almost seems as if they wanted to experience that heavenly vision beforehand. And what passionate sighs for heaven escaped from those hearts!

How ashamed must we be at our lowness, at our preoccupation with the miserable and passing things of this earth! Although children of God, we are still children of Adam. Hence we must take heart and conquer whatever there is in us of Adam, of "the old man," and become truly similar to Christ, the "new man."

While He walked this earth, Jesus enjoyed the Beatific Vision and beheld His Father even in the Garden of Gethsemani.

"Sursum corda!" Sons of men, lift up your hearts!

After reciting St. Bernard's "Memorare," let us say the "Angel of God" three times to ask the angels to take pity on us and remind us often during the day of our destiny, of our homeland, especially when we are discouraged or when we must do violence to self and courageously follow the difficult path of virtue. May these angels then murmur words of comfort in our ear: "Heaven is beautiful and it is for you! God awaits you there!"

THE MEMORARE

Remember, most gracious Virgin Mary, that never was it known that anyone who fled to your protection, implored your help or sought your intercession, was left unaided. Inspired with this confidence, I fly to you, O Virgin of virgins, my Mother: To you I come, before you I stand, sinful and sorrowful. O Mother of the Word Incarnate! Despise not my petitions, but in your mercy, hear and answer me. Amen.

Angel of God (three times).

How to prepare for the Beatific Vision

"But when the Son of Man shall come in his majesty, and all the angels with him, then he will sit on the throne of his glory; and before him will be gathered all the nations, and he will separate them one from another, as the shepherd separates the sheep from the goats; and he will set the sheep on his right hand, but the goats on the left.

"Then the king will say to those on his right hand, 'Come, blessed of my Father, take possession of the kingdom prepared for you from the foundation of the world; for I was hungry and you gave me to eat; I was thirsty and you gave me to drink; I was a stranger and you took me in; naked and you covered me; sick and you visited me; I was in prison and you came to me.' Then the just will answer him, saying, 'Lord, where did we see thee hungry, and feed thee; or thirsty, and give thee drink? And when did we see thee a stranger, and take thee in; or naked and clothe thee? Or when did we see thee sick, or in prison, and come to

thee?' And answering the king will say to them,
'Amen I say to you, as long as you did it for one of
these, the least of my brethren, you did it for me.'

"Then he will say to those on his left hand,
'Depart from me, accursed ones, into the everlasting fire which was prepared for the devil and his
angels. For I was hungry, and you did not give me
to eat; I was thirsty and you gave me no drink;
I was a stranger and you did not take me in; naked,
and you did not clothe me; sick, and in prison, and
you did not visit me.' Then they also will answer and
say, 'Lord, when did we see thee hungry, or thirsty,
or a stranger, or naked, or sick, or in prison, and
did not minister to thee?' Then he will answer
them saying, 'Amen, I say to you, as long as you did
not do it for one of these least ones, you did not do
it for me.' And these will go into everlasting punishment, but the just into everlasing life."

(Matt. 25:31-46.)

We shall go into everlasting life–so ends the
Creed. After the time of faith comes the vision.
Faith disappears in heaven because God is seen.
Hope, too, ceases because its object is attained.
Only charity remains, which is life everlasting. Now,
then, if we want to attain to the vision of God, we
must prepare ourselves. The present life is the
preparation for heaven.

First of all, we have to rid our mind of everything earthly. Bad or vain thoughts, wrong intentions, empty, uncharitable thoughts or those against
faith–all these must be banished. Moreover, we have

to ask God's forgiveness if in the past we allowed our minds to be soiled by something evil, some thought that was not good. This might well be, for it is much harder to control the mind than to control the tongue or the hands. Therefore, we ask pardon for sins of thought, and for reading what was not worthwhile. In this way, we can shorten our purgatory and, if possible, avoid it altogether.

Secondly, we must live our faith and gain a good understanding of our religion, of its truths, both natural and supernatural. We must put our faith into practice, by making acts of faith and believing firmly. Every morning, let us say the Act of Faith, and always end with: Increase my faith, O Lord. "I do believe; help my unbelief" (Mark 9:23). Let us never forget that faith is the foundation of all justification and sanctity. "He who is just lives by faith" (Gal. 3:11). In order to do good, our inner faith must be profound.

Thirdly, we have to spread our faith, spread knowledge of God. How? By our example, by preserving purity of heart, by living a good life–this is a continual sermon to everyone, a sermon which generally makes a greater impression than a preached one. We can also preach by praying that God may be known, that the Gospel may reach souls everywhere, that Christ's kingdom may be spread throughout the world. We can preach by utilizing the press, producing good books and articles and seeing to it that they are widely circulated. We can use the motion picture, trying to provide films with a moral tone for many viewers, and the same type of radio and television program. The more we make the Lord known on this earth, the more brightly God's truth will shine for us in heaven.

Once again let us recall what we said in the beginning, "Whoever does away with one of these least commandments, and so teaches men, shall be called least in the kingdom of heaven; but whoever carries them out and teaches them, he shall be called great in the kingdom of heaven" (Matt. 5:19).

We will conclude with Pope Pius XII's prayer to Mary our Queen.

POPE PIUS XII'S PRAYER TO MARY, QUEEN

From the depths of this vale of tears where sorrowing humanity makes weary progress—through the surges of this sea of ours endlessly buffeted by the winds of passions—we raise our eyes to you, O most beloved Mother Mary, to be comforted by the contemplation of your glory and to hail you as Queen of heaven and earth, Queen of mankind.

With legitimate filial pride, we wish to exalt your Queenship and to recognize it as due to the sovereign excellence of your whole being, O dearest one, truly Mother of Him who is King by right, by inheritance and by conquest.

Reign, O Mother and Queen, by showing us the path of holiness and by guiding and assisting us that we may never stray from it.

In the heights of heaven you exercise your primacy over the choirs of angels who acclaim you as their Sovereign, and over the legions of saints who delight in beholding your dazzling beauty. So, too, reign over the entire human race, above all by opening the path of faith to those who do not yet know your Divine Son.

Reign over the Church, which acknowledges and extols your gentle dominion and has recourse to you as a safe refuge amid the calamities of our day. Reign especially over that part of the Church which is persecuted and oppressed; give it strength to bear adversity, constancy never to yield under unjust compulsion, light to avoid falling into the snares of the enemy, firmness to resist overt attack, and at every moment unwavering faithfulness to your kingdom.

Reign over men's minds, that they may seek only what is true; over their wills; that they may follow solely what is good; over their hearts, that they may love nothing but what you yourself love.

Reign over individuals and over families, as well as over societies and nations; over the assemblies of the powerful, the counsels of the wise, as over the simple aspirations of the humble.

Reign in the streets and in the squares, in the cities and the villages, in the valleys and in the mountains, in the air, on land and on sea; and hear the pious prayer of all those who recognize that yours is a reign of mercy, in which every petition is heard, every sorrow comforted, every misfortune relieved, every infirmity healed, and in which, at a gesture from your gentle hands, from death itself there arises smiling life.

Obtain for us that all who now in every corner of the world acclaim and hail you Queen and Lady may one day in heaven enjoy the fullness of your kingdom in the vision of your Divine Son, who with the Father and the Holy Spirit lives and reigns for ever and ever. Amen.

XVI

IN HEAVEN WE SHALL SEE GOD, THE HIGHEST GOOD

In the previous meditation on heaven, we considered the fact that our mind will be able to know and contemplate God, the Supreme Truth, Who will manifest Himself to us. Now we shall reflect on the fact that we will possess the Supreme Good in heaven. We shall meditate on the complete satisfaction to be enjoyed by our will.

In heaven we shall have every good in God

And I saw a great white throne and the one who sat upon it; from his face the earth and heaven fled away, and there was found no place for them. And I saw the dead, the great and the small, standing before the throne, and scrolls were opened. And another scroll was opened, which is the book of life; and the dead were judged out of those things that were written in the scrolls, according to their works. And the sea gave up the dead that were in it, and death and hell gave up the dead that were in them; and they were judged each one, according to their works.

And hell and death were cast into the pool of fire. This is the second death, the pool of fire. And if anyone was not found written in the book of life, he was cast into the pool of fire.

And I saw a new heaven and a new earth. For the first heaven and the first earth passed away, and the sea is no more. And I saw the holy city, New Jerusalem, coming down out of heaven from God, made ready as a bride adorned for her husband. And I heard a loud voice from the throne saying, "Behold the dwelling of God with men, and he will dwell with them. And they will be his people, and God himself will be with them as their God. And God will wipe away every tear from their eyes. And death shall be no more; neither shall there be mourning, nor crying, nor pain any more, for the former things have passed away."

And he who was sitting on the throne said, "Behold, I make all things new!" And he said, "Write, for these words are trustworthy and true." And he said to me, "It is done! I am the Alpha and the Omega, the beginning and the end. To him who thirsts I will give of the fountain of the water of life freely. He who overcomes shall possess these things, and I will be his God, and he shall be my son. But as for the cowardly and unbelieving, and abominable and murderers, and fornicators and sorcerers, and idolaters and all liars, their portion shall be in the pool that burns with fire and brimstone, which is the second death."

(Apoc. 20:11-15; 21:1-8.)

It is beautiful—marvelously so, in fact, to meditate on the last chapters of the Apocalypse, the description of the joys that await us in that blessed eternity, in the holy city of God. There the will knows full satisfaction and we shall have none of the evils that cause us fear in this life. We will have

God and in Him, every delight we can desire on this earth, plus many more of which we cannot even dream here below.

No evils in heaven! How wonderful to think that there will be an end to mourning and tears, pain, sorrow and death! In heaven, we shall never again suffer physically. How many ailments we have to endure in this life! Any one of innumerable diseases may strike without warning. Every part of the human body is subject to many afflictions. The biting cold of winter, the suffocating heat of summer and especially the inevitability of our last illness are ever with us, threatening and painful. The thought of death brings a shudder of apprehension to everyone. The only comfort comes in remembering that even in this we shall be doing God's will.

Moral sufferings are even more numerous. Disillusionment, sorrows, acts of ingratitude, temptations, doubts, remorse, anxiety, and in particular, the fear of devout souls that they have fallen, or may fall into sin—who can describe these sufferings?

This earth is truly a land of exile, and we are, indeed, "mourning and weeping in this valley of tears." But in heaven, there will be no more physical or spiritual suffering, and not even the fear or worry lest the happiness come to an end. If it were possible to eliminate every trouble from this life, would that be heaven? No, but it would be something. Add every possible desirable good–knowledge, sanctity, peace, grace, and the certainty of happiness. Not even this would be heaven. But add the Supreme Good, and you have heaven.

We are not made for this world's wealth. Is happiness found among those who count up thousand dollar bills? They might better be called the "troubled class," or rather, "those who afflict themselves." We are not made for human glory, which is all vanity and passes like smoke, accompanied by great jealousy and envy and leaving in its wake more discontentment than before. We are not made for the pleasures and satisfactions of the flesh, which disappear before they are yet savored and make room for remorse, suffering and dejection. For what, then, **are** we made? For the true Good, God, the highest and the infinite good. Let us ponder on these words: God, the highest Good, infinite and true, will satisfy us for all eternity. Our will, after death, will be wholly and entirely intent on one goal–to possess God. And to the soul God will say: "Enter into the joy of your Master. . . I shall be your very great reward" (cf. Matt. 25:21, and Gen. 15:1). The Lord will be ours and we shall be His for all eternity.

Choose, human soul, between earth and heaven, **between the goods of this life or the delights of heav-**

en. Which choice is the wisest, the most prudent? Let us beg the Holy Spirit for His gifts of knowledge and wisdom, understanding and counsel.

In this life, the happiness of the just man who seeks God alone is often derided. The world admires the cunning of the man who knows how to get what he wants. The fact is, however, that his cleverness will catch up with him and bury him in ruin. Only he who possesses God will possess everything forever.

Heaven! Give me heaven! Such is the yearning of great souls. Who cares about this earth, about pleasures and wealth and honor—give me heaven!

Wise indeed was St. Thomas More's reply to his wife, who was urging him to save his life by acting against his conscience. "For twenty or thirty more years of earthly happiness," he said, "do you want me to give up an eternity of bliss, give up the one Good, the Supreme Good?"

Let us now offer the following prayer to Our Lady that she may lift our desires heavenward and with our desires, elevate our whole will, too.

PRAYER TO OUR LADY

Most lovable Queen of heaven and earth, beloved Daughter of the Father, sublime Mother of the Divine Son, illustrious Spouse of the Holy Spirit, I venerate and praise that privilege, unique in the world, whereby, pleasing God in your humility and conserving your spotless virginity, you became the great Mother of the Divine Savior, our Master, true Light of the world, uncreated Wisdom, source of all truths and first Apostle of truth. For the indescribable joy you felt and for that sublime privilege, I bless the august Trinity and I ask you to obtain for me the grace of heavenly wisdom, to be a humble and fervent disciple of Jesus, a devoted child of the Church, and a pillar of truth. Make the light of the Gospel shine to the farthest bounds of the earth, overcome errors, gather all men round the See of Peter. Enlighten preachers and writers, O Mother of Good Counsel, O Seat of Wisdom, O Queen of all Saints.

Hail Mary. Queen of Apostles, pray for us.

There is no doubt about the possession of God

And there came one of the seven angels who had the bowls full of the seven last plagues; and he spoke with me, saying, "Come, I will show thee the bride, the spouse of the Lamb." And he took me up in spirit to a mountain, great and high, and showed me the holy city of Jerusalem, coming down out of heaven from God, having the glory of God. Its light was like to a precious stone, as it were a jasper-stone, clear as crystal. And it had a wall great and high with twelve gates, and at the gates twelve angels, and names written on them, which are the names of the twelve tribes of the children of Israel. On the east are three gates, and on the north three gates, and on the south three gates, and on the west three gates. And the wall of the city has twelve foundation stones, and on them twelve names of the twelve apostles of the Lamb.

And he who spoke with me had a measure, a golden reed, to measure the city and the gates thereof and the wall. And the city stands foursquare, and its length is as great as its breadth; and he measured the city with the reed, to twelve thousand stadia: the length and the breadth and the height of it are equal. And he measured its wall, of a hundred and forty-four cubits, man's measure, that is, angel's measure. And the material of its wall was jasper; but the city itself was pure gold, like pure glass. And the foundations of the wall of the city were adorned with every precious stone. The first foundation, jasper; the second, sapphire; the third, agate; the fourth, emerald; the fifth, sardonyx; the sixth, sardius; the seventh, chrysolite; the eighth, beryl; the ninth, topaz; the tenth, chrysoprase; the eleventh, jacinth; the twelfth, amethyst. And the twelve gates were twelve pearls; that is, each gate was of a single pearl. And the street of the city was pure gold, as it were transparent glass.

And I saw no temple therein. For the Lord God almighty and the Lamb are the temple thereof. And the city has no need of the sun or the moon to shine upon it. For the glory of God lights it up, and the Lamb is the lamp thereof. And the nations shall walk by the light thereof; and the kings of the earth shall bring their glory and honor into it. And its gates shall not be shut by day; for there shall be no night there. And they shall bring the glory and the honor of nations into it. And there shall not enter into it anything defiled, nor he who practises abomination and falsehood, but those only who are written in the book of life of the Lamb.   (Apoc. 21:9-27.)

So entrancing is the description of this heavenly city that we are filled with a desire to see it now. What place on earth could resemble a city whose ruler is God, whose light is Christ, and whose inhabitants are angels, whose dwellings and streets are all of priceless gems? O heavenly Jerusalem, blessed vision of peace, we long for you!

What will really make us happy is the possession of God. To possess God! Every good thing we hope for on this earth is uncertain. Although one desires a long life, he does not know when death will come. He is not sure to what degree of knowledge he will attain. He is uncertain whether he will be able to earn and hold on to the wealth he desires. The lover of good times can never be sure if he will drain the cup of pleasure. The proud man cannot say for certain whether he will win the admiration to which he aspires—and so it goes. But the eternal good, God, is in no way doubtful. Whoever truly wants Him will possess Him. Such is God that in the very act of desiring Him, He is given, i.e., He is acquired by desiring. Any soul who repents of his sin and turns to God will not be disillusioned; his desire will not be in vain. God will be his! And those who are constant in their love of God during life will have Him!

By the stream of Babylon
we sat and wept

When we remembered Sion.
On the aspens of that land
we hung up our harps,
Though there our captors asked of us
the lyrics of our songs,
And our despoilers urged us to be joyous:
"Sing for us the songs of Sion!"
How could we sing a song of the Lord
in a foreign land?
If I forget you, Jerusalem,
may my right hand be forgotten!
May my tongue cleave to my palate
If I remember you not,
If I place not Jerusalem
ahead of my joy.
Remember, O Lord, against the children of Edom,
the day of Jerusalem,
When they said, "Raze it, raze it down to its founda-
    tions!"
O daughter of Babylon, you destroyer,
happy the man who shall repay you
the evil you have done us!
Happy the man who shall seize and smash
your little ones against the rock!

(Ps. 136.)

What joy this God will bring to the soul! Let
us recall the descriptions we have read of the joy
certain souls felt after Communion, when they wept
for happiness. We think of the bliss of St. Aloysius
and St. John Berchmans after Holy Communion.
We think of the joy of St. Stanislaus Kostka when
he received Our Lord from angels and then had
the added happiness of a vision of the Blessed

Mother giving him the Child Jesus. And what of the delight of St. Teresa at meeting the Divine Child beneath the portals of the convent, or the bliss of St. Anthony of Padua who, by his virginal purity, merited the grace of beholding the Infant Christ, and even enjoying himself with Him!

All such graces are rays from heaven, but in heaven itself, God is possessed wholly and entirely, eternally, and happily. If these joys of the fortunate souls we have mentioned were to be prolonged for years, or centuries if that were possible, who would not envy them? Now then, at the present, we imagine heaven to be somehow this bliss in order to have an idea, but this is only a faint notion of the reality, for we are, unfortunately, still on earth. Certain Saints received a foretaste of the joys of heaven to the point where there were moments when it seemed as though they already possessed heaven while still on earth. Heaven, however, is far greater than that. Up there it is no longer the mind reasoning to it; rather the heart is experiencing it.

Therefore, let us long for heaven. Some do desire it, but rather half-heartedly, for they never resolve to win it. They are weak-willed individuals. Others, instead, fervently desire it, and they are men of good will. How is our will? Does it resemble the determination of virgins who left all to gain all?

Is it the will of the martyrs who gave their lives to possess Life? When faced with trying days, let us remember that what must impart courage is the reward: "Each will receive his own reward according to his labors" (1 Cor. 3:8).

We conclude with a prayer to Our Lady: "O Mary, Queen of Angels."

PRAYER TO MARY, QUEEN OF ANGELS

O Mary, Queen of all the Angels, full of grace, conceived without sin, blessed among creatures, living tabernacle of God, remember the painful and solemn moment in which your dying Jesus from the cross gave you John as your son, and in him all men, and especially all the Apostles. What a tender love overflowed your heart at that moment for souls consecrated to the Apostolate, to the following of the Cross, to the love of Jesus. For your ineffable sufferings and those of your Divine Son, for your motherly heart, O Mary, increase the glorious phalanx of Apostles, of Missionaries, of Priests, of Virgins. May these souls shine for sanctity of life, integrity of morals, solid piety, profound humility, firm faith, and most ardent charity. May they all be saints and purifying salt of the earth, O Teacher of the Saints, O Mother of the Great High Priest and yourself Victim and Altar.

Hail Mary. Queen of Apostles, pray for us.

Heaven will bring full happiness to our will

And he showed me a river of the water of life, clear as crystal, coming forth from the throne of God and of the Lamb. In the midst of the city street, on both sides of the river, was the tree of life, bearing twelve fruits, yielding its fruit according to each month, and the leaves for the healing of the nations.

And there shall be no more any accursed thing; but the throne of God and the Lamb shall be in it, and his servants shall serve him. And they shall see his face and his name shall be on their foreheads. And the night shall be no more, and they shall have no need of lamp, or light of sun, for the Lord God will shed light upon them; and they shall reign forever and ever.

And he said to me, "These words are trustworthy and true; and the Lord, the God of the spirits of the prophets, sent his angel to show to his servants what must shortly come to pass. And behold, I come quickly! Blessed is he who keeps the words of the prophecy of this book." And I, John, am he who heard and saw these things. And when I heard and saw, I fell down to worship at the feet of the angel who showed me these things. And he said to me, "Thou must not do that. I am a fellow-servant of thine and of thy brethren the prophets, and of those who keep the words of this book. Worship God!"

And he said to me, "Do not seal up the words of the prophecy of this book; for the time is at hand. He who does wrong, let him do wrong still; and he who is filthy, let him be filthy still; and he who is just, let him be just still; and he who is holy, let him be hallowed still. Behold, I come quickly! And my reward is with me, to render to each one according to his works. I am the Alpha and the Omega, the the first and the last, the beginning and the end!" Blessed are they who wash their robes that they may have the right to the tree of life, and that by the gates they may enter into the city. Outside are the dogs, and the sorcerers, and the fornicators, and the murderers and the idolaters, and everyone who loves and practises falsehood.

"I, Jesus, have sent my angel to testify to you these things concerning the churches. I am the root and the offspring of David, the bright morning star." And the Spirit and the bride say, "Come!" And let him who hears say, "Come!" And let him who thirsts come; and he who wishes, let him receive the water of life freely. I testify to everyone who hears the words of the prophecy of this book. If anyone shall add to them, God will add unto him the plagues that are written in this book. And if anyone shall take away from the words of the book of this prophecy, God will take away his portion from the tree of life, and from the holy city, and from the things that are written in this book. He who testifies to these things says, "It is true, I come quickly!" Amen! Come, O Lord Jesus! The grace of our Lord Jesus be with all. Amen.

(Apoc. 22:1-21.)

Hence, blessed are they who wash their clothes in the Blood of the Lamb, Jesus. Who will reach that holy city, enriched with every good thing and without the slightest shadow of evil? Whoever observes the commandments of God with his whole will: "If thou wilt enter into life, keep the commandments" (Matt. 19:17). And those who practice the evangelical counsels, as well as the commandments, will attain to the possession of the most beautiful thrones in that city.

Happy shall we be in Heaven if we faithfully observe the commandments of God and of the Church. The Lord has given us two great means of arriving at this supernatural bliss—faith and good works. They form the stairway to heaven.

When the young man came to Christ to ask what he should do to be saved and was told to observe the commandments, he asked the same question we would ask now: "Which?" In reply, Christ named them, and we know them. We must first of all look at the negative aspect of every commandment, that is, the sins against it. And if we find, after following the explanation given by the catechism for the various sacraments, that our life, unfortunately, contains some dark points—some moments when we turned our back on God, when we disobeyed Him—let us weep over our faults, as Magdalen did, at the feet of the Divine Master. However, the commandments have a positive side, too; for example, the first commandment obliges us especially, to pray, the second, to have respect for and trust in the name of the Lord, and so forth. Have we done what these commandments order?

Furthermore, if we want to be perfect, there are the counsels, too. These are for the more gen-

erous, for those who are after a more beautiful
heaven. Christ told the young man to leave everything and give himself completely to the Lord: "Go,
sell whatever thou hast, and give to the poor, and
thou shalt have treasure in heaven; and come, follow me" (Mark 10:21). Underline those words, "a
treasure in heaven." The generous give Him proof
that they do want that treasure.

Let those more firmly rooted in virtue, those
desirous of being more generous with the Lord,
persevere with constancy in doing good to the very
end, as did St. Paul.

Now let us conclude with the prayer, "O Virgin
most pure."

PRAYER TO THE BLESSED VIRGIN

O Virgin most pure, august Queen of Martyrs, Morning Star, secure Refuge of sinners, rejoice for the days in
which you were teacher, comforter and mother of the Apostles in the cenacle, to invoke and receive the Divine Para-
clete, the Spirit with the seven gifts, Love of the Father and
of the Son, transformer of the Apostles. By your humble and
irresistible prayers, which always move God's Heart, obtain
for me the grace to understand the value of the souls which
Jesus Christ ransomed from hell with His Most Precious
Blood. May each one of us be filled with zeal for the beauty
of the Christian Apostolate. May the charity of Christ urge
us on. May the spiritual misery of poor mankind move us.
Let us feel in our hearts the needs of childhood, of adoles-
cence, of manhood, and of old age. May immense Africa,

vast Asia, promising Oceania, troubled Europe, and the two Americas exercise a powerful spell on our souls. May the apostolate of example and of the spoken word, of prayer and of the press, of motion pictures, radio and television, and the apostolate of the souls in purgatory win many generous souls, even to the point of undergoing the most painful sacrifices. O Queen of the Apostles, O Mother of mercy, our Advocate, to you we sigh, mourning in this valley of tears.

Hail Mary. Queen of Apostles, pray for us.

XVII

HEAVEN IS BLISS

Our soul aspires to happiness, to joy without end. It can find this happiness and joy only in heaven.

Hence we shall reflect on the fact that heaven is bliss, and that there the soul lives of God. Lastly, we shall consider how to prepare for it.

Heaven is joy in the Holy Spirit

And I saw, and behold, the Lamb was standing upon Mount Sion, and with him a hundred and forty-four thousand having his name and the name of his Father written on their foreheads. And I heard a voice from heaven like a voice of many waters, and like a voice of loud thunder; and the voice that I heard was as of harpers playing on their harps. And they were singing as it were a new song before the throne, and before the four living creatures and the elders; and no one could learn the song except those hundred and forty-four thousand, who have been purchased from the earth. These are they who were not defiled with women; for they are virgins. These follow the Lamb wherever he goes. These were purchased from among men, first-fruits unto God and unto the Lamb, and in their mouth there was found no lie; they are without blemish.

The state of grace makes us members of Jesus Christ. Since the members are part of the same body and are one with the head, they share the joy of the head. For this reason, the blessed will know the very happiness of Jesus Christ, the Son of God. And Christ, as the Son of God, enjoys the same glory and bliss as His Eternal Father. It is not another joy that the soul knows; it is one and the same happiness, although in different proportion: "Enter into the joy of your Master" (Matt. 25:21).

Man tends toward happiness. To satisfy his longing fully, this happiness must be the maximum, full, and eternal. Only God can fill the heart. Wealth cannot, for it is something external, and hence cannot quench the heart's thirst. Would we try to put water in a thirsty man's pocket? Pleasures cannot fill our hearts, either, for ours is a spiritual thirst, a thirst of the soul, and to try to satisfy us with sensual pleasures is like bathing our eyes in cool, refreshing water while our throat is parched. Neither can the esteem we enjoy in the minds of others satisfy us, for it remains in them, whereas we are looking for something of our own. Would we give a drink of water to a neighbor to quench our own thirst? Not even virtue or knowledge are enough, for they are only means, not the end. To say that they are the ultimate in satisfaction would be equivalent to affirming that sacrifice is happiness and that giving is the same as getting. Virtue, in the case of the martyrs, for example, was a great means of attaining to eternal bliss.

Only God is our eternal happiness, for He is the highest good, our spiritual, incomparable good. Even the saints find rest only in heaven. This earth is a trial; eternal rest is to be found in heaven, together with everlasting bliss. Christ prayed: "Father, I will that where I am, they also whom thou hast given me may be with me" (John 17:24). And He ascended victoriously into heaven. But when? After Calvary; after being condemned by Pilate, Herod, and Caiphas; after being abandoned and betrayed, after Gethsemane, Nazareth, exile into Egypt, and Bethlehem.

Before beginning His Passion, Our Lord prayed thus to His Father: "Now I am coming to thee; and these things I speak in the world in order that they may have my joy made full in themselves. . . . I do not pray that thou take them out of the world, but that thou keep them from evil. . . . Sanctify them in the truth. Thy word is truth. . . . Yet not for these only do I pray, but for those also who through their word are to believe in me; that all may be one, even as thou, Father, in me and I in thee. . . . And the glory that thou hast given me, I have given to them, that they may be one, even as we are one. . . . Father, I will that where I am, they also whom thou hast given me may be with me; in order that they may behold my glory, which thou hast given me, because thou hast loved me before the creation of the world" (John 17:13-24).

Now let us say the ejaculation, "Virgin Mary, Mother of Jesus, make us saints," fifty times, using our rosary beads, and reciting a "Glory Be" at the end of each decade.

In heaven, the soul lives of God, its light, strength, and joy

After this I saw a great multitude which no man could number, out of all nations and tribes and peoples and tongues, standing before the throne and before the Lamb, clothed in white robes, with palms in their hands. And they cried with a loud voice, saying, "Salvation belongs to our God who sits upon the throne, and to the Lamb." And all the angels were standing round about the throne, and the elders and the four living creatures; and they fell on their faces before the throne and worshipped God, saying, "Amen. Blessing and glory and wisdom and thanksgiving and honor and power and strength to our God forever and ever. Amen."

And one of the elders spoke and said to me, "These who are clothed in white robes, who are they? and whence have they come?" And I said to him, "My lord, thou knowest." And he said to me, "These are they who have come out of the great tribulation, and have washed their robes and made them white in the blood of the Lamb. Therefore they are before the throne of God, and serve him day and night in his temple, and he who sits upon the throne will dwell with them. They shall neither hunger nor thirst any more, neither shall the sun strike them nor any heat. For the Lamb who is in the midst of the throne will shepherd them, and will guide them to the fountains of the waters of life, and God will wipe away every tear from their eyes."

(Apoc. 7:9-17.)

The joy of heaven will be so great that our hearts would burst were they not sustained by a divine strength. While still on this earth, St. Francis Xavier used to cry out, seeking relief from the overwhelming joy of God's love: "Enough, O Lord, enough! No more! My heart cannot take any more!"

The joy of heaven will be caused by a threefold love, the very love Christ has for His Father.

There will be the love of benevolence, that is, the desire to see God loved and glorified. The Son was happy to seek and procure the glory of the Father: "I honor my father. . . . I do not seek my own glory" (John 8:49-50). He sought to promote the greater glory of His Father. The blessed will find great pleasure in giving God glory with their hymns of praise, their prayers and thanksgiving, just as Christ took delight in seeking the greater glory of His Father. In their earthly life, the saints lived by this motto–"To the greater glory of God"–and they sacrificed everything for it.

Then there is the love of complacence. The soul will be delighted by the infinite greatness, wisdom, power, and love of the eternal God. Before this infinite God, his joy will be ecstatic, far surpassing anything in human experience. It will be much more than the ecstasies of love into which St. Catherine of Siena fell, much more than the pleasure a father finds in a very devoted son, much more than the joyful emotion experienced by those who assist at a solemn canonization in St. Peter's. Heaven will bring a delight in love far, far superior to all this! The Angel whose beauty so stunned St. John that he wanted to adore him told the Apostle: "Thou must not do that, I am a fellow-servant of thine" (Apoc. 19:10). The soul will be immersed in God. With a love both tender and powerful he will cling to Him.

Lastly, there is the love of gratitude, the joy of being thankful to the Lord for creating, redeeming, and sanctifying us. The works of power, especially the creation, are attributed to the Father. To Him, Who is the beginning of all created things, visible and invisible; to Him Who is the king of glory and of the ages; to Him Who is the only true treasure, we shall sing, with overflowing gratitude for having created us: "To God alone, honor and glory".

To God the Son we owe our Redemption and the Holy Gospel. We will kiss the wounds in His hands, feet, and side. We shall rejoice over His Resurrection and Ascension, and over the Holy Eucharist, as over so many victories of love, because all this was done for us. We shall feel an ineffable happiness because of His Gospel, His Church, and His reward of the just: "In Him, and with Him, and through Him."

To the Holy Spirit–we owe our sanctification in love. We shall love Him for our adoption as children and heirs of God, for the priestly and religious vocation He gives; for His distribution of grace–both actual and sanctifying; for perseverance, for our resurrection, and for the beatific vision.

Let us begin here and now to gain experience in this threefold love of benevolence, complacence, and gratitude. Our true life is in heaven; on this earth we prepare ourselves and learn to know, serve and pray to God as His faithful children.

We shall conclude with a prayer to Jesus our Master.

TO JESUS OUR MASTER

O Jesus Christ, our Master, You are the Way, the Truth, and the Life. Grant that we may learn the most eminent wisdom of Your charity in the spirit of St. Paul the Apostle and of the Catholic Church. Send Your Holy Spirit to teach us and suggest to us what you taught with the consent of the Father.

Enlighten our minds; render our wills docile; teach us to pray devoutly.

O Lord, may I know You, love You, live in You, and enjoy You for all eternity.

Jesus Master, Way, Truth and Life, have mercy on us.

How to prepare for heaven

And the seventh angel sounded the trumpet; and there were loud voices in heaven saying, "The kingdom of this world has become the kingdom of our Lord and of his Christ, and he shall reign forever and ever." And the twenty-four elders who sit upon their thrones before God fell on their faces and worshipped God, saying, "We give thee thanks, O Lord God almighty, who art, and who wast, because thou hast taken thy great power and hast begun thy reign. And the nations were angered, but thy wrath came and the time for the dead to be judged, and for giving the reward to thy servants—the prophets, and the saints, and those who fear thy name, the small and the great—and for destroying those who corrupted the earth." And the temple of God in heaven was opened, and there was seen the ark of his covenant in his temple, and there came flashes of lightning, and peals of thunder, and an earthquake, and great hail.

(Apoc. 11:15-19.)

How can we prepare for the ineffable bliss of heaven? By keeping close to the Lord: "Our citizenship is in heaven" (Phil. 3:20). Through the Sacraments, the sacramentals and prayer, we must become incorporated in Christ. The Sacraments, especially the Eucharist, graft us into Jesus Christ. They confer new grace if they are Sacraments of the dead, or increase grace, if they are Sacraments of the living. And Holy Mass and Communion more directly increase grace within us. In fact, here we have the very Source and Author of grace.

The Sacramentals confer grace according to the dispositions of the recipient. Blessings, Bible reading, preaching, the sign of the cross, processions, the rites and ceremonies of the liturgy in general—these are all Sacramentals.

Prayer is, in itself, true love of God. We show we value God's company when we engage in intimate conversation with Him. A loving son very willingly spends time with his father. He listens to him, confides in him, asks his advice and help. In short, he lives on very intimate terms with him. Here we might make reference to those two little classics of St. Alphonse de Liguori: "The Great Means of Prayer" and "How to Converse Continually and Familiarly with God." In fact, prayer is, in a general sense, "a lifting of the mind and heart to God." Prayer includes meditation, spiritual reading, examination of conscience, the Rosary, morning and evening prayers, etc.

Every form of devotion is prayer—devotion to the Blessed Mother, to St. Joseph, to St. Paul, to the

Guardian Angels, to the Holy Souls in Purgatory, and to all the saints.

Conversation with God during this life demands victory over the imagination and over the human, earthly tendencies of our nature. This is why it brings a great reward in heaven. Indeed, even on this earth, after much effort and practice in prayer and contemplation, the saints reached the point of enjoying God. At least now, let us begin to become more and more attached to prayer. The love of God is shown by desiring and contemplating God, by keeping close to Him. The greater our intimacy and elevation in prayer, the less purgatory we shall have— perhaps, none at all. Moreover, our love for God and our joy in Christ Jesus will be much more intense.

Let us now offer the following prayer to St. Joseph.

TO ST. JOSEPH

O St. Joseph, father and guardian of virgins, into your keeping Jesus Christ, Innocence Itself, and Mary, the Virgin of virgins, were entrusted. Through that dear double pledge, Jesus and Mary, I pray and beseech you to preserve me from all impurity, and with undefiled mind, pure heart and chaste body, make me most chastely serve Jesus and Mary. Amen.

XVIII

THE GLORY OF THE BLESSED

Let us ask Christ for three favors as we make this medita-tion: 1) the zeal of the Apostles; 2) the fortitude of the martyrs; and 3) the virtue of the confessors.

They are the blessed citizens of that heavenly Jerusalem to which we are all called. "Therefore, you are now no longer strangers and foreigners, but you are citizens with the saints and members of God's household: you are built upon the founda-tion of the apostles and prophets with Christ Jesus himself as the chief cornerstone" (Eph. 2:19-20). We must consider the citizens of heaven as souls who have preceded us. There are, however, many thrones yet empty in that city, many palaces still vacant—these are ready for us. "I go to prepare a place for you" (John 14:2). "In my Father's house there are many mansions" (John 14:2). In these we are to dwell forever. Hence let us consider those who went before us: they preceded us in labor and merit, and ultimately in glory. Centering our attention on the glory they now enjoy in heaven, we take heart in our daily toil. "If this one and that one could do it, why not I?" exclaimed St. Augustine. We ask them to sustain us in our labors, save us from dangers, and lead us into their own glory.

The glory of the apostles

Therefore shall they receive the splendid crown, the beauteous diadem, from the hand of the Lord—for he shall shelter them with his right hand, and protect them with his arm. He shall take his zeal for armor and he shall arm creation to

257

requite the enemy; he shall don justice for a
breastplate and shall wear sure judgment for a
helmet; he shall take invincible rectitude as a
shield and whet his sudden anger for a sword, and
the universe shall war with him against the fool-
hardy. Well-aimed shafts of lightnings shall go
forth and from the clouds as from a well-drawn
bow shall leap to the mark; and as from his sling,
wrathful hailstones shall be hurled. The water of
the sea shall be enraged against them and the
streams shall abruptly overflow; a mighty wind
shall come against them and winnow them out like
the tempest; thus lawlessness shall lay the whole
earth waste and evildoing overturn the thrones
of potentates.   (Wisdom 5:16-23.)

Happy the rich man found without fault,
who turns not aside after gain! Who is he, that we
may praise him? He, of all his kindred has done
wonders, for he has been tested by gold and come
off safe, and this remains his glory; he could have
sinned but did not, he could have done evil but
would not, so that his possessions are secure, and
the assembly recounts his praises.

(Sirach 31:8-11.)

What great glory awaits the just man! On the
great day, everyone will receive from the just Judge
the praise coming to him. It is foolish to look for
human acclaim, when only praise from God is true
and lasting.

What are the virtues of the Apostles? Apostles
must possess knowledge and sanctity, but their most

characteristic virtue is zeal. However, zeal divorced from knowledge and sanctity cannot save souls.

Whoever on this earth couples his virtue and learning with zeal for the salvation of souls, thus becoming health for the world and the salt of the earth, will receive a double reward. Why? Because his recompense is twofold: "Whoever does away with one of these least commandments, and so teaches men, shall be called least in the kingdom of heaven; but whoever carries them out and teaches them, he shall be called great in the kingdom of heaven" (Matt. 5:19). The Apostles shall receive one reward for having done well and another for having taught others to do good; one reward for having been wise and possessed knowledge of God, and another for having communicated this knowledge. They are flames which not only shine but also give off light to guide men to heaven. Hence the apostolic souls will be doubly rewarded in heaven. Twofold honor is reserved for them: the glory they will receive from God and the glory they will receive from saved souls. St. Paul used to say, You whom I have saved are my crown and my glory.

Lift your eyes to heaven, all you who long for souls, you who are good and possess great faith and generosity, you who want to conquer the world–not with the sword, like Alexander the Great, but with

the cross, with charity, radiating light and love. Take
heart, for your ideal is a great one: "Give me the
people; keep the goods for yourself" (Gen. 14:21).
Immense is the reward that awaits you, for those
who both did and taught will be great in God's heavenly kingdom.

Let us ask Our Lady to watch over us so that
we may attain to heaven with her. We shall say
the Hail Holy Queen.

The glory of the martyrs

Then shall the just one with great assurance
stand before his oppressors who set at nought his
labors. Seeing this, they shall be shaken with
dreadful fear, and amazed at the unlooked-for
salvation. They shall say among themselves, rueful
and groaning through anguish of spirit: "This is
he whom we once held as a laughingstock and as a
type for mockery, fools that we were! His life we
deemed madness, and his death dishonored. See
how he is accounted among the sons of God; how
his lot is with the saints! We, then, have strayed
from the way of truth, and the light of justice did
not shine for us, and the sun did not rise for us.
We had our fill of the ways of mischief and of
ruin; we journeyed through impassable deserts,
but the way of the Lord we knew not. What did
our pride avail us? What have wealth and its boastfulness afforded us? All of them passed like a
shadow and like a fleeting rumor; like a ship
traversing the heaving water, of which, when it

has passed, no trace can be found, no path of its keel in the waves. Or like a bird flying through the air; no evidence of its course is to be found—but the fluid air, lashed by the beat of pinions, and cleft by the rushing force of speeding wings, is traversed: and afterward no mark of passage can be found in it. Or as, when an arrow has been shot at a mark, the parted air straightway flows together again so that none discerns the way it went through—even so we, once born, abruptly came to nought and had no sign of virtue to display, but were consumed in our wickedness." Yes, the hope of the wicked is like thistledown borne on the wind, and like fine, tempest-driven foam; like smoke scattered by the wind, and like the passing memory of the nomad camping for a single day. (Wisdom 5:1-14.)

Let us dwell for a while on the glory enjoyed by the martyrs. The Church counts her martyrs by the glorious thousands. Many authors, in fact, calculate the number to be in the millions. However, those who have given their lives for the faith are not the only martyrs. They, too, are martyrs who have given their lives for chastity, or sacrificed their very existence for charity, or immolated their entire being for obedience or some other virtue. Every virtue has its own martyrs!

The characteristic virtue of the martyrs is fortitude in bearing the trials of this life and the most violent persecution. Because of this their fortitude, or patience, in the estimation of the Church, they follow immediately after the Apostles. For patience is what makes saints: "You have need of patience that, doing the will of God, you may receive the promise" (Heb. 10:36). "Bear fruit in patience" (Luke 8:15). "Let patience have its perfect work" (James 1:4). Which souls make great progress in virtue? The patient. All the saints, not merely many, have passed through great suffering and temptations, and from these have drawn profit for eternal life.

The narrow but sure way to heaven is the one "that leads to life" (Matt. 7:14). It is the one our Divine Master invites us to take: "If anyone wishes to come after me, let him deny himself, and take up his cross, and follow me" (Matt. 16:24).

The true lovers of Christ prove their love with their blood, the same proof He gave us. They follow Him to Calvary. These are strong lovers, privileged souls. Others, instead, reduce piety to something mechanical and external. Those who truly love the Lord have a special love for mortification, penance, and the cross. Contrariwise, the program followed by the spiritually lazy and lukewarm is to avoid as much as possible all toil and mortification. The fervent and truly holy souls propose to embrace the greatest number of wearisome labors and mortifications. With the choice of a program of life there is the inevitable choice of being Christ's friend or enemy, being with Him in glory or far from Him in suffering. We either place ourselves in the company of the saints or in the band of the indolent and slothful.

The comfortable way is not the narrow way. But we must see where each road leads.... Let us, then, rejoice at the thought of the glory already being enjoyed by the martyrs as the reward of their sufferings.

A fit conclusion will be the recitation of the prayer to St. Paul for patience:

TO ST. PAUL TO OBTAIN PATIENCE

O glorious St. Paul, from a persecutor of Christianity, you became a most zealous apostle, and to make known the Savior Jesus Christ to the ends of the world you suffered with joy imprisonment, scourgings, stonings, shipwrecks and persecutions of every kind, and in the end shed your blood to the last drop. Obtain for us the grace to receive, as favors of the Divine mercy, infirmities, tribulations, and misfortunes of the present life, so that the vicissitudes of this our exile will not render us cold in the service of God, but will make us always more faithful and fervent. Amen.

The glory of the confessors

But the souls of the just are in the hand of God, and no torment shall touch them. They seemed, in the view of the foolish, to be dead; and their passing away was judged an affliction and their going forth from us, utter destruction. But they are in peace. For if before men, indeed, they be punished, yet is their hope full of immortality; chastised a little, they shall be greatly blessed, because God tried them and found them worthy of himself. As gold in the furnace, he proved them, and as sacrificial offerings he took them to himself. In the time of their visitation they shall shine, and shall dart about as sparks through stubble; they shall judge nations and rule over peoples, and the Lord shall be their King forever. Those who trust in him shall understand truth, and the faithful shall abide with him in love: because grace and mercy are with his chosen ones.

Better is childlessness with virtue; for immortal is its memory: because both by God is it acknowledged, and by men. When it is present men imitate it, and they long for it when it is gone; and forever it marches crowned in triumph, victorious in unsullied deeds of valor. But the numerous progeny of the wicked shall be of no avail; their spurious offshoots shall not strike deep root nor take firm hold. For even though their branches flourish for a time, they are unsteady and shall be rocked by the wind and, by the violence of the winds, uprooted; their twigs shall be broken off untimely and their fruit be useless, unripe for eating, and fit for nothing. For children born of lawless unions give evidence of the wickedness of their parents, when they are examined. But the just man, though he die early, shall be at rest. For the age that is honorable comes not with the passing of time, nor can it be measured in terms of years. Rather, understanding is the hoary crown for men, and an unsullied life, the attainment of old age. He who pleased God was loved; he who lived

among sinners was transported—snatched away,
lest wickedness pervert his mind or deceit beguile
his soul; for the witchery of paltry things obscures
what is right and the whirl of desire transforms
the innocent mind. Having become perfect in a
short while, he reached the fulness of a long career;
for his soul was pleasing to the Lord, therefore he
sped him out of the midst of wickedness. But the
people saw and did not understand; nor did they
take this into account: That God's grace and mercy
are with his holy ones and his care with his elect.
Yes, the just man dead condemns the sinful who
live, and youth swiftly completed condemns the
many years of the wicked man grown old. For they
see the death of the wise man and do not understand what the Lord intended for him, or why he
made him secure. They see, and hold him in contempt; but the Lord laughs them to scorn. And
they shall afterward become dishonored corpses
and an unceasing mockery among the dead. For he
shall strike them down speechless and prostrate
and rock them to their foundations; they shall be
utterly laid waste and shall be in grief and their
memory shall perish.

Fearful shall they come, at the counting up
of their misdeeds, and their transgressions shall
convict them to their face. (Wis. 3:1-9; 4:1-20.)

What is characteristic of the Confessor-Saints?
Their heroism in the most varied virtues. Some dis-
tinguished themselves for their faith, some for
charity, some for their spirit of obedience, some for
their practise of humility, and still others for
chastity.

Once a child said to his father, "We're not nobles, are we?" The wise answer he received was:
"You will be noble if you are virtuous." Many souls
would like to ask, "Will I become a saint? Do you
think I will?" The only answer is, "You will if you
practise virtue in the common everyday occasions
of virtue. Virtue that is in evidence only in moments
of fervor, when no difficulty presents itself, is not
great virtue. Real, robust virtue is the habit of
doing good. A good act becomes virtue when by
repetition it develops into a good habit. Hence, real
virtue consists of a habit of doing good continually.

Let us give glory to the saints, especially to
those whose names we bear, our holy patrons. Let
us read their lives, study their examples, and recommend ourselves to their prayers. They have marked
the path to heaven for us, so let us walk in their
footsteps.

May the Blessed Mother draw us to herself, to
heaven, where she is waiting for us. At the beginning of one August, St. Stanislaus Kostka had made
a good annual retreat. The preacher had spoken of
heaven so well that Stanislaus was on fire with the
desire to be there for the feast of the Assumption,
August 15th. He began to ask insistently for this
favor of the Blessed Virgin. He even entrusted his
plea to the Deacon, St. Lawrence, whose feast is the
tenth of August. Our Lady heard his prayers, and

on the day of the Assumption, this young man of angelic behavior appeared in heaven in the midst of the angels to chant forever the glories of Mary.

Ah, these saints–may they obtain for us the grace to imitate them and follow them on the path to heaven! Life is short; it was for them, too. Blessed is the faithful soul: "Blessed is the man who endures temptation; for when he has been tried, he will receive the crown of life" (James 1:12). Life is a trial, but happy the one who proves himself, for he will be crowned in the eternal life to come.

Uniting ourselves in spirit to all the Masses celebrated daily, let us offer the following prayer:

FOR THOSE WHO, LIKE CHRIST, THIRST FOR SOULS

Lord, in union with all Your priests who today offer Holy Mass, I offer You Jesus-Host and myself, a small victim—

1. In reparation for the many blasphemies, errors and impious acts which are diffused throughout the world by radio and television, motion pictures and the press.

2. To implore Your mercy on the many souls who, through deceit and allurement to sin, are snatched away from Your fatherly Heart by these modern means of evil.

3. For the conversion of the many servants of satan who, through radio and television, motion pictures and the press, have spread teachings in opposition to the Divine Master, corrupting the mind, heart and actions of men.

4. To follow only Him Whom You, O Heavenly Father, in Your boundless love, have given to the world, proclaiming: "This is My beloved Son; hear Him".

5. To know that only Jesus is the perfect Master, that is, the Truth that enlightens, the Way or Model of all sanctity, and the true Life of the soul, which is sanctifying grace.

6. That You may increase the number of priests and religious consecrated to the propagation of Christian doctrine and morals throughout the world by prayer and the most advanced and efficient means of good.

7. That apostolic writers, technical workers and propagandists may be holy and full of wisdom and zeal for the glory of God and the salvation of souls.

8. That all Catholic editions may prosper, increase in number and drown out the voices of error and evil.

9. That we may all recognize our ignorance and unworthiness, and our need to kneel humbly before Your holy Tabernacle, O Lord, imploring light, compassion and mercy.

XIX

THE BLESSED ETERNITY

In this meditation, we shall ask the virgins for holy purity, the Blessed Mother for her protection, and all the saints for faith, hope and charity.

The purity of the virgins

Now concerning virgins I have no commandment of the Lord, yet I give an opinion, as one having obtained mercy from the Lord to be trustworthy. I think, then, that this is good on account of the present distress—that it is good for a man to remain as he is. Art thou bound to a wife? Do not seek to be freed. Art thou freed from a wife? Do not seek a wife. But if thou takest a wife, thou hast not sinned. And if a virgin marries, she has not sinned. Yet such will have tribulation of the flesh. But I spare you that.

But this I say, brethren, the time is short; it remains that those who have wives be as if they had none; and those who weep, as though not weeping; and those who rejoice, as though not rejoicing; and those who buy, as though not possessing; and those who use this world, as though not using it, for this world as we see it is passing away. I would have you free from care. He who is unmarried is concerned about the things of the Lord, how he may please God. Whereas he who is married is concerned about the things of the world, how he may please his wife; and he is divided. And the unmarried woman, and the virgin, thinks about the things of the Lord, that she may be holy in body and in spirit. Whereas she who is married thinks about the things of the world, how she may please her husband.

(1 Cor. 7:25-34.)

Our life must produce love of God. Indeed, it is one long effort to combat evil, which separates us from God, and to adhere to Him, to unite ourselves to Him, the Highest Good, our eternal happiness. Eternal life is, in actual fact, love; even the theological virtues of faith and hope are themselves directed toward charity. The more we detach our hearts from creatures and adhere to God, the more progress we make on the path to perfection. The devils believe, but they tremble, whereas belief must lead to love; we believe and hope so as to love in eternity. The virgin saints, such as St. Aloysius, St. Joseph Cottolengo, St. Francis de Sales, St. Thomas Aquinas, St. Agnes, St. Teresa, and others avoided sin and even the appearance of evil, or what might possibly be a distant occasion of sin. They sought the Lord with their whole strength, with their whole mind, and with their whole heart. They sought Him to serve Him both directly and indirectly, without being diverted or held back.

Man is composed of body and soul. If the sensual part were to dominate, he would lean toward the animals; if the intellectual element dominated, he would live according to reason; and if the spirit reigned supreme, he would lead an angelic life. Thus, St. Aloysius is called "the angelic youth", and St. Thomas Aquinas, "the angelic doctor." Virgins possess love integrally; they almost rise above human nature. They have learned to live in heaven, not on this earth, in imitation of the life of Jesus Christ Himself.

The virgins and the pure of heart elevate themselves so as to become one with God, through the action of the Holy Spirit. This is the Spouse they have chosen, and who could be compared to Him in beauty or be more desirable? They will never leave Him, once they have found such a heavenly life while still on earth: "I took hold of him and would not let him go" (Cant. 3:4). "They will neither marry nor be given in marriage, but are as angels in heaven" (Mark 12:25). And is this life not heavenly, this life that only God could inspire the Blessed Mother and St. Joseph to embrace? that only the Son of God could bring us from heaven when He became incarnate? Not everyone understands this, but those who have the grace, let them take heed and follow it!

The flower of virginity needs a protecting hedge around it, and vigilance and mortification constitute that hedge. It needs the moisture and warmth of prayer and grace.

In heaven, the pure will have special glory. Let us, then, entrust ourselves to the Blessed Virgin, begging her to raise up many virginal souls:

Let us pray for religious vocations—Hear our prayer, Mary, our Mother and Queen. Beg your Son, the Lord of the harvest, to send good laborers into His vineyard!

Let us ask the protection of Our Lady

Now in the sixth month the angel Gabriel was sent from God to a town of Galilee called Nazareth, to a virgin betrothed to a man named Joseph, of the house of David, and the virgin's name was Mary. And the when the angel had come to her, he said, "Hail, full of grace, the Lord is with thee. Blessed art thou among women." When she had heard him she was troubled at his word, and kept pondering what manner of greeting this might be.

And the angel said to her, "Do not be afraid, Mary for thou has found grace with God. Behold, thou shalt conceive in thy womb and shalt bring forth a son; and thou shalt call his name Jesus. He shall be great, and shall be called the Son of the Most High; and the Lord God will give him the throne of David his father, and he shall be king over the house of Jacob forever; and of his kingdom there shall be no end."

But Mary said to the angel, "How shall this happen, since I do not know man?"

And the angel answered and said to her, "The Holy Spirit shall come upon thee and the power of the Most High shall overshadow thee; and therefore the Holy One to be born shall be called the Son of God. And behold, Elizabeth thy kinswoman also has conceived a son in her old age, and she who was called barren is now in her sixth month; for nothing shall be impossible with God."

But Mary said, "Behold the handmaid of the Lord; be it done to me according to thy word." And the angel departed from her.

(Luke 1:26-38.)

Mary was predestined to be the Mother of God, Mediatrix of all graces, and the Queen of all saints. In the Incarnation, she became the mother of Jesus; in heaven, she intercedes for all her children. Every saint has received from her, for Mary found not only grace, but the fullness of grace.

They who are devoted to Mary will be saved; they who are greatly devoted to her will become saints. In fact, Mary defends the innocent that they may overcome the devil, the call of the world, and the urgings of the flesh. The souls who consecrated their innocence to Mary and prayed to her perseveringly have obtained perpetual purity, e.g., St. Thomas Aquinas, St. Bonaventure, St. Aloysius, St. Stanislaus, St. Alphonsus de Liguori, St. Francis de Sales, St. Bernardine of Siena, and thousands of others.

Mary converts sinners, inspiring sentiments of sorrow, fortifying their will that they may persevere, and at times, even transforming them into great saints. She is the mother of sinners who wish to change their ways. St. Mary of Egypt, St. Margaret of Cortona, St. Andrew Corsini, and Alphonse Ratisbonne confirm this fact by their life stories.

Mary comes to the aid of beginners, supports the proficient, and is the delight of the perfect. She gives purity to virgins, fortitude to the weak and to the martyrs, zeal to the apostles, and virtue of every kind to the confessors, for she is the Queen of all saints.

Those who are nearest her on earth will be nearest her in heaven, and Mary's throne is next after her Son's.

Let us pray: "Be mindful, O Virgin Mother of God, when you stand in the sight of the Lord, to speak good things for us, and to turn away His anger from us." Then we shall consecrate ourselves to her:

CONSECRATION TO MARY MOST HOLY
QUEEN OF THE APOSTLES

Receive me, O Mary, Mother, Teacher and Queen, among those whom you love, nourish, sanctify and guide, in the school of Jesus Christ, our Divine Master.

You read in the mind of God the children whom He calls, and for them you have special prayers, grace, light and comfort. My Master, Jesus Christ, entrusted Himself to you, from the Incarnation to the Ascension. For me this is doctrine, example and an ineffable gift—I, too, place myself completely in your hands. Obtain for me the grace ever better to know, imitate and love the Divine Master, Jesus, the Way, the Truth, and the Life. Present me to Him. I am an unworthy sinner, and have no other recommendation but yours to be received into His school. Enlighten my mind, fortify my will, sanctify my heart, so that I may profit by so much mercy and reach the point of being able to say: "I live now, not I, but Christ lives in me."

Let us ask all the saints to obtain faith, hope and charity for us

And coming down with them, he took his stand on a level stretch, with a crowd of his disciples, and a great multitude of people from all Judea and Jerusalem, and the sea coast of Tyre and Sidon, who came to listen to him and to be healed of their diseases. And those who were troubled with unclean spirits were cured. And all the crowd were trying to touch him, for power went forth from him and healed all.

And he lifted up his eyes to his disciples, and said, "Blessed are you poor, for yours is the kingdom of God. Blessed are you who hunger now,

for you shall be satisfied. Blessed are you who
weep now, for you shall laugh. Blessed shall you
be when men hate you, and when they shut you
out, and reproach you, and reject your name as
evil, because of the Son of Man. Rejoice on that
day and exult for behold your reward is great in
heaven. For in the selfsame manner their fathers
used to treat the prophets.   (Luke 6:17-23.)

The basic virtues, also called the theologica
virtues, are faith, hope and charity. They are necessary in some degree to everyone to attain heaven
All the inhabitants of heaven, then, had faith, a
least in the existence of God, who rewards or punishes men for their actions; they all had hope o
receiving from God's bounty the eternal reward o
their good deeds; and they all loved the Lord ir
varying degrees as their highest Good and eterna
Happiness.

These virtues are necessary virtues. They lif
man to the supernatural state and are infused by
God at Baptism. All Christians in the state of grace
possess them.

To ask for these virtues is equivalent to asking
for eternal salvation. If we have them and put then
into practice in an outstanding way, we shall earr
a high place in heaven. We might call anyone in the
state of grace holy, on this earth, but the souls ir
heaven are far holier, and they are eternally confirmed in that state.

On the feast of All Saints, the Church honors all those who have gone to heaven, even if they are not listed on the calendar of the saints. She commemorates, therefore, the children who died after baptism and before reaching the use of reason; she remembers our ancestors and all the just souls of the Old and New Testament.

Let us ask them, therefore, for grace and the three theological virtues. The other virtues increase in proportion to a soul's depth of patience, humility and goodness of heart. Moreover, vocations to the religious state and to the priesthood rest on these virtues.

A lively faith produces humility and obedience. Strong, serene hope produces the spirit of poverty. Ardent charity inspires perfect chastity. Hence a religious is a person who possesses the theological virtues in a higher degree than the ordinary Christian.

In addition, if faith is a truly living faith, it produces priestly zeal. If hope is powerfully strong, it generates love for the toil and sacrifice of the apostle. If charity is on fire, it sets a soul seeking the greater glory of God and the salvation of men **with every ounce of its strength. Thus, the priestly** spirit is formed by the theological virtues possessed more profoundly.

Let us pray: "O Lord our God, multiply Your grace upon us, and grant that by leading a holy life, we may attain to the happiness of Your saints. Through our Lord."

Let us now say the Divine Praises, asking that we may one day praise God in heaven with his angels and saints.

THE DIVINE PRAISES

Blessed be God.
Blessed be His Holy Name.
Blessed be Jesus Christ, true God and true Man.
Blessed be the Name of Jesus.
Blessed be His Most Sacred Heart.
Blessed be His Most Precious Blood.
Blessed be Jesus in the Most Holy Sacrament of the Altar.
Blessed be the great Mother of God, Mary most Holy.
Blessed be her holy and Immaculate Conception.
Blessed be her glorious Assumption.
Blessed be the name of Mary, Virgin and Mother.
Blessed be St. Joseph, her most chaste Spouse.
Blessed be God in His Angels and in His Saints.

HELL

XX

HELL

The present meditation aims to obtain for us a horror of sin. Sin is an offense to God and the ruin of the soul. Many and bitter are its poisonous effects on the poor sinner, but the worst of these is eternal damnation. Just one mortal sin suffices to merit the condemnation to hell.

The nature of hell

There was a certain rich man who used to clothe himself in purple and fine linen, and who feasted every day in splendid fashion. And there was a certain poor man, named Lazarus, who lay at his gate, covered with sores, and longing to be filled with the crumbs that fell from the rich man's table; even the dogs would come and lick his sores. And it came to pass that the poor man died and was borne away by the angels into Abraham's bosom; but the rich man also died and was buried in hell. And lifting up his eyes, being in torments, he saw Abraham afar off and Lazarus in his bosom. And he cried out and said, "Father Abraham, have pity on me, and send Lazarus to dip the tip of his finger in water and cool my tongue, for I am tormented in this flame."

But Abraham said to him, "Son, remember that thou in thy lifetime hast received good things, and Lazarus in like manner evil things; but now here he is comforted whereas thou art tormented.

And besides all that, between us and you a great gulf is fixed, so that they who wish to pass over from this side to you cannot, and they cannot cross from your side to us."

And he said, "Then, father, I beseech thee to send him to my father's house, for I have five brothers, that he may testify to them, lest they too come into this place of torments." And Abraham said to him, "They have Moses and the Prophets: let them hearken to them." But he answered, "No, father Abraham, but if someone from the dead goes to them, they will repent." But he said to him, "If they do not hearken to Moses and the Prophets, they will not believe even if someone rises from the dead."

(Luke 16:19-31.)

The place called hell was created by God as punishment for those who refused to observe the commandments during life, to believe the Church, to pray.... These unfortunate souls abandon God on this earth. They draw away from Him with their mind by infidelity; they draw away from Him with their will by evil actions; they draw away from Him with their heart by giving up prayer. As long as they live, they can regain faith, change their will, and put themselves back into the grace of God. But once death strikes, the soul is confirmed in the state in which it is found at that moment. If it is separated from God, it can no longer hope for salvation, because the period of trial is over. The son will be forever separated from his Father, the creature from his Creator, the sinner from heaven. This state of a soul is called **hell.**

After describing the scene at the general judgment, Christ foretold the words He will use in sentencing souls, both good and bad, and He concluded: "And these will go into everlasting punishment, but the just into everlasting life" (Matt. 25:46).

At the present time, there is heaven, purgatory, and hell. The Church now is composed of three parts: the Church triumphant, comprising the blessed; the Church suffering, consisting of the souls who are preparing to ascend to heaven; and the Church militant, wherein we find ourselves, battling evil under the leadership of our great captain, Jesus Christ. At the universal judgment, the Church suffering and the Church militant will end. Only the Church triumphant will remain. All the souls who were found unworthy, because of the stains of sin, to enter into that eternity of bliss will be hurled far from God, into eternal fire. There Judas and many sowers of scandal and ruin have already been suffering for centuries. Moreover, it is greatly to be feared that other souls stubbornly clinging to sin will end by falling into that pit, for obstinacy is the way of perdition and many, unfortunately, follow this path.

Hell is the place of torments. God is both mercy and justice. On this earth, we experience the whole

of His utterly tender and fatherly love inviting us
to heaven, but after death, the sinner will taste His
justice. God will pile every kind of evil upon the
damned–pain for the spirit, pain for the body. Dante
pictured the following inscription over the gate of
hell:

"Through me you go into the city of grief,
"Through me you go into the pain that is eternal,
"Through me you go among people lost."

Just as there was a valley near Jerusalem in
which all the refuse was thrown to be burned, "the
fire of Gehenna," so also there is, in the moral sphere,
a place in which all evil will be gathered. There is
only one source of evil: sin. In hell all sin will be
accumulated, and with it its consequences–suffering.
"I will spend on them woe upon woe" (Deut. 32:23).

Let us reflect on eternity, gazing on paradise,
which is populated by saints, and on hell, swarming
with devils and every kind of sinner, a place wherein every type of torment is heaped up. Do we realize,
then, what sin is? Let us take a close look at hell, a
good long look at that spectacle. Then we shall turn
to Christ and hear Him say: "For what does it profit
a man, if he gain the whole world, but suffer the
loss of his own soul?" (Matt. 16:26).

After reciting the Sixth Psalm, we will close
with a prayer to St. Joseph.

PSALM 6

Prayer in Time of Distress

O Lord, reprove me not in your anger,
nor chastise me in your wrath.
Have pity on me, O Lord, for I am languishing;
heal me, O Lord, for my body is in terror;
My soul, too, is utterly terrified; but you, O Lord, how
    long . . . ?
Return, O Lord, save my life;
rescue me because of your kindness,
For among the dead no one remembers you;
in the nether world who gives you thanks?
I am wearied with sighing;
every night I flood my bed with weeping;
I drench my couch with my tears.
My eyes are dimmed with sorrow;
they have aged because of all my foes.
Depart from me, all evildoers,
for the Lord has heard the sound of my weeping;
The Lord has heard my plea;
the Lord has accepted my prayer.
All my enemies shall be put to shame in utter terror;
they shall fall back in sudden shame.

TO ST. JOSEPH

To you, O blessed Joseph, do we have recourse in our
tribulation, and having implored the help of your thrice-
holy Spouse, we confidently invoke your patronage also. By
that charity wherewith you were united to the immaculate
Virgin Mother of God, and by that fatherly affection with
which you embraced the Child Jesus, we beseech you and
we humbly pray you to look graciously upon the inheritance which Jesus Christ has purchased by His Blood and
assist us in our needs by your power and strength. Most

watchful guardian of the Holy Family, protect the chosen people of Jesus Christ; keep far from us, most loving father, all blight of error and corruption. Mercifully assist us from heaven, most mighty defender, in this our conflict with the powers of darkness; and, even as of old you rescued the Child Jesus from the supreme peril of His life, so now defend God's holy Church from the snares of the enemy and from all adversity. Keep us one and all under your continual protection, that we may be supported by your example and your assistance, and may be enabled to lead a holy life, die a happy death and come at last to the possession of everlasting blessedness in heaven. Amen.

The existence of hell

"And whoever causes one of these little ones who believe in me to sin, it were better for him if a great millstone were hung about his neck, and he were thown into the sea. If thy hand is an occasion of sin to thee, cut it off! it is better for thee to enter into life maimed, than, having two hands, to go into hell, into the unquenchable fire, 'Where their worm dies not, and the fire is not quenched.' And if thy foot is an occasion of sin to thee, cut it off! It is better for thee to enter into life everlasting lame, than, having two feet, to be cast into the hell of unquenchable fire, 'Where their worm dies not, and the fire is not quenched.' And if thy eye is an occasion of sin to thee, pluck it out! It is better for thee to enter into the kingdom of God with one eye, than, having two eyes, to be cast into hell-fire, 'Where their worm dies not, and the fire is not quenched.' For everyone shall be salted with fire, and every victim shall be salted. Salt is good; but if the salt becomes insipid, what shall you season it with? Have salt in yourselves, and be at peace with one another."

(Mark 9:41-49.)

The existence of hell is an article of our Faith. In the Athanasian Creed we say: The true Faith teaches that we must believe and confess that whoever does good will go into eternal life, whereas whoever does evil will go into eternal fire. This is the Catholic Faith, and he who does not faithfully and firmly believe it, will, beyond doubt, be damned.

The Gospel tells us: "At harvest time I will say to the reapers: Gather up the weeds first and bind them in bundles to burn; but gather the wheat into my barn" (Matt. 13:30). From the context it is clear that the wheat represents the just and the weeds the wicked. St. Irenaeus writes: All those to whom the Lord will have said, "Depart from Me, you cursed!" will be lost forever, and all those to whom Jesus Christ will have said, "Come, you blessed of My Father," will be forever saved.

Every nation and tribe of people has understood and believed in the existence of an eternal place of torment. Once Divine Justice is admitted, in fact, it becomes evident that evil must be punished, and it is obvious that this punishment does not always occur in this life. Do we not often find the good being persecuted and the wicked prospering?

Blessed be God, the Lawgiver! May His goodness be forever glorified, for He forgives the humble and contrite of heart. May His justice be glorified, for He punishes the obstinate sinner who passes into eternity with his sins.

The tree that falls to the right will remain for all eternity on the right; if, instead, it falls to the left, there it will remain forever.

The only cause of damnation is sin. Hence this realization must make us heartily sorry for sin. One drop of sinful pleasure brings on a sea of suffering. The damned cry out: What good was our wealth to us? what good the glory of this world? what good fun and pleasure? Everything passes like a shadow, and what remains forever is the bitter fruit of all this—hell! We enjoyed a bit of apple and were poisoned to death—eternally!

Let us fervently invoke the protection of St. Joseph, patron of a good death.

CHAPLET TO ST. JOSEPH

1. O St. Joseph, faithful cooperator in our redemption, have pity on poor mankind still enfolded in many errors, vices and superstitions. You were a docile instrument in the hands of the Heavenly Father, in all arrangements for the birth and infancy of Jesus, for the preparation of the Victim, the Priest, and the Divine Master of men. May you

be blessed, you who often, even without understanding, let yourself be guided entirely by heavenly inspirations and the words of the angel! Obtain for us the apostolic spirit, so that with prayers, words and works, we may humbly co-operate in the Christianization of the world. May iniquity be wiped out, and may everyone receive Jesus Christ, the Way, Truth and Life.

St. Joseph, pray for us.

2. O St. Joseph, model of every virtue, obtain for us the grace to possess your spirit. In loving, fruitful silence, in the practice of all religious and civil precepts, in docility to every manifestation of God's will, you arrived at a high degree of sanctity and of heavenly glory. Obtain for us an increase of faith, hope and charity, an ample infusion of prudence, justice, fortitude, and temperance, an abundance of the gifts of wisdom, understanding, knowledge, counsel, piety, fortitude and fear of God. From heaven assist us so that we may always better know the end for which we were created and the wisdom of those who do good. Direct every action of our life towards heaven.

St. Joseph, pray for us.

Sin and hell

Let us hold fast the confession of our hope without wavering, for he who has given the promise is faithful. And let us consider how to arouse one another to charity and good works; not forsaking our assembly as is the custom of some, but exhorting one another, and this all the more as you see the Day drawing near. For if we sin willfully after receiving the knowledge of the truth, there remains no longer a sacrifice for sins, but a certain dreadful expectation of judgment, and "the fury of a fire which will consume the adversaries." A man making void the Law of Moses dies without any mercy on the word of two or three witnesses; how much worse punishments do you think he deserves who has trodden under foot the Son of God, and has regarded as unclean the blood of the covenant through which he was sanctified, and has insulted the Spirit of grace? For we know him who has said, "Vengeance is mine, I will repay." And again, "The Lord will judge his people." It is a fearful thing to fall into the hands of the living God.

(Heb. 10:23-31.)

God is all-wise. And He has given His laws a just sanction: the threat of eternal suffering. The Lord gave men commandments which He wants observed. He cannot allow His creatures to take so much liberty that they seem almost independent of Him. The laws of God demand much sacrifice, for passions which are often violent must be denied, a world which drags man towards sin must be overcome, and many diabolic suggestions must be rejected. How would man obey at certain times were it not for the fear of God? The beginning of wisdom is the fear of the Lord. "Fear God and keep His commandments" (Eccles. 12:13). The two points are related, for the man who fears God obeys His commandments. And yet not even the thought of the tremendous sufferings of hell is sufficient to make some avoid sin.

Moreover, God grants man every kind of help and grace that he may observe the divine law. He created man for heaven and sent His only-begotten Son to save him. We have the Church, the Sacraments, prayer and innumerable means of saving ourselves . . . If, after all this, man disobeys God, what a punishment he deserves! Certainly he is asking for damnation! No one goes to hell without knowing it and wanting it. There is a hell but God warns us: "Keep away! your salvation is in your own hands." It is not God who is too severe, but the sinner who is senseless.

And furthermore, there is something infinitely malicious in sin. Through it, in fact, an infinite majesty is offended. Hence the punishment should be in some way infinite, and since it cannot be in intensity, it is in duration. Hell lasts forever.

Now let us say the third penitential Psalm, Psalm 37, followed by another part of the chaplet to St. Joseph.

PSALM 37 (1-11)

Prayer of an Afflicted Sinner

O Lord, in your anger punish me not,
in your wrath chastise me not;
For your arrows have sunk deep in me,
and your hand has come down upon me.
There is no health in my flesh because of your indignation;
there is no wholeness in my bones because of my sin,

For my iniquities have overwhelmed me;
they are like a heavy burden, beyond my strength.
Noisome and festering are my sores
because of my folly,
I am stooped and bowed down profoundly;
all the day I go in mourning,
for my loins are filled with burning pains;
there is no health in my flesh.
I am numbed and severely crushed;
I roar with anguish of heart.
O Lord, all my desire is before you;
from you my groaning is not hid.
My heart throbs; my strength forsakes me;
the very light of my eyes has failed me.

CHAPLET TO ST. JOSEPH

(Continued)

3. O St. Joseph, we venerate you as the model of workingmen, the friend of the poor, the consoler of the afflicted and exiled, the Saint of Providence. On earth you visibly represented the universal goodness and solicitude of the Heavenly Father. You were the carpenter of Nazareth and the teacher of work to the Son of God, Who became a humble laborer for us. At Nazareth, work was elevated to dignity as a means of sanctification and redemption. Aid with your prayers all who labor in intellectual, moral and material work. For the nations tormented by social problems obtain legislation in conformity with the Gospel; for everyone, the spirit of Christian charity, for the world a social order based on the teachings of the Supreme Pontiff. St. Joseph, provide for us.

4. O St. Joseph, foster-father of Jesus, I bless the Lord for your intimacy with Him during His infancy and youth

in Bethlehem, Egypt and Nazareth. You loved Him paternally and you were filially loved. Your faith made you adore in Him the Incarnate Son of God, while He obeyed you, served you, and listened to you. You had sweet conversations with Him, and with Him you shared work, great trials and tender consolations. Great is your joy and your power in heaven. Obtain for me the grace never to offend and lose Jesus through sin. Pray for me that I may always receive Holy Communion and confess myself well, attain to a great intimacy with Jesus and a tender and strong love for Him while on earth, and possess Him forever in Heaven. I ask you also for the grace which I desire most. . . . St. Joseph, take care of it.

St. Joseph, pray for us.

XXI

THE PAIN OF SENSE IN HELL

Mortification is a general law. We must check our passions, our desires, our will, and our heart always and everywhere. Otherwise, it is impossible to obey God's law and save ourselves. Hell is populated by people who gave free rein to their passions and to their senses. Now they suffer for the very things for which they sinned.

The pain of fire

Yes, working together with him we entreat you not to receive the grace of God in vain. For he says, "In an acceptable time I have heard thee, and in the day of salvation I have helped thee." Behold, now is the acceptable time; behold, now is the day of salvation! We give no offense to anyone, that our ministry may not be blamed. On the contrary, let us conduct ourselves in all circumstances as God's ministers, in much patience; in tribulations, in hardships, in distresses; in stripes, in imprisonments, in tumults; in labors, in sleepless nights, in fastings; in innocence, in knowledge, in long-sufferings; in kindness, in the Holy Spirit, in unaffected love; in the word of truth, in the power of God; with the armor of justice on the right hand and on the left; in honor and dishonor, in evil report and good report; as deceivers and yet truthful, as unknown and yet well known, as dying and behold, we live, as chastised but not killed, as

> sorrowful yet always rejoicing, as poor yet enriching many, as having nothing yet possessing all things.
>
> (2 Cor. 6:1-10.)

The suffering in hell which makes the greatest impression on us is fire. This is by no means the greatest suffering, but it does impress us tremendously. The fire of hell is indescribably fierce, for it was lit by the wrath of God to punish, not help man. It is almost a rational fire, since it directs itself especially to the senses and members which are most guilty, whether they be the heart, the eyes, or other members. It is an eternal fire, for while it burns constantly, it never burns itself out. What would it be like to grip a hot iron? What would it be like to be burned alive? The pain would be terrible, but it would be over in a few minutes. The fire of hell, instead, covers the damned entirely, penetrating right to the bone and to the very heart, so that the damned look like burning coals! "Who of us can live with the consuming fire? Who of us can dwell with everlasting burnings?" (Isa. 33:14). We who cannot stand a toothache, a burn, or the sweltering heat of summer—how would we bear the flames of hell? Whoever sins to satisfy one or another of his senses will be punished in that sense with inextinguishable fire. "Pool of fire, furnace of fire, fire of Gehenna"—how many times Sacred Scripture repeats approximately the same thought, even using the same words.

"Whoever wishes to come after me, let him deny himself, take up his cross, and follow me," Christ tells us. And to what suffering He subjected Himself! What a life of toil He willed to lead! The whole life of Christ was a cross and a martyrdom. The worldly, however, do not want to remember these fundamentals any longer; they declare every whim and inclination lawful. Thus, they are opposed to Christ.

In what should we mortify ourselves? In everything, both great and small, and always. St. Paul admonishes us to imitate him, "always bearing about in our body the dying of Jesus" (2 Cor. 4:10). We should direct our efforts in this regard against indolence and laziness, especially, for they strive to spare the body all weariness and keep it from doing its duty. Special mortification is also needed for what we call our temperament or nature—if not good, it must be corrected. And another special mortification must counteract the spirit of comfort, because of which life becomes enslaved to the senses, bound by a degrading selfishness, and deprived of all ideals. The pain of fire will strike at this type of sin, since "a man is punished by the very things through which he sins" (Wis. 11:16).

After Psalm 101, we shall continue with the chaplet to St. Joseph.

PSALM 101

Prayer in Time of Distress

O Lord, hear my prayer,
and let my cry come to you.
Hide not your face from me in the day of my distress.

Incline your ear to me;
in the day when I call, answer me speedily.

For my days vanish like smoke,
and my bones burn like fire.
Withered and dried up like grass is my heart;
I forget to eat my bread.

Because of my insistent sighing
I am reduced to skin and bone.

I am like a desert owl;
I have become like an owl among the ruins.

I am sleepless, and I moan;
I am like a sparrow alone on the housetop.
All the day my enemies revile me;
in their rage against me they make a curse of me.

For I eat ashes like bread
and mingle my drink with tears,
Because of your fury and your wrath;
for you lifted me up only to cast me down.

My days are like a lengthening shadow,
and I wither like grass.

But you, O Lord, abide forever, and your name through all
generations.

CHAPLET TO ST. JOSEPH

(Continued)

5. O St. Joseph, pure spouse of Mary, we humbly ask you to obtain for us a true devotion to our most tender Mother, Teacher and Queen. By divine will, your mission was associated with that of Mary. You were the head of the Holy Family, the model of fathers, the guardian of vocations. With Mary you shared trials and joys; with her you entered into a holy competition in virtue, work and merit; and union of mind and heart. O St. Joseph, pray for the fathers and mothers of families; pray for the innocence of youth; pray for religious and priestly vocations. Obtain for us the grace to know the Blessed Virgin Mary as you knew her, to imitate her, to love her, to pray to her always. Draw many souls to her maternal Heart.

St. Joseph, pray for us.

6. O St. Joseph, protector of the dying, we pray to you for all the dying, and beg your assistance in the hour of our death. You merited a happy departure from a holy life, and in your last hours you had the ineffable consolation of being assisted by Jesus and Mary. Deliver us from a sudden death. Obtain for us the grace to imitate you in life, to detach our heart from all worldly things and daily to store up treasures for the moment of our death. Obtain for us the grace to receive the last Sacraments well, and together with Mary, inspire us with sentiments of faith, hope, love and sorrow for sins, so that we many breathe forth our soul in peace.   St. Joseph, pray for us.

The suffering of sight and sound

We are frank with you, O Corinthians; our heart is wide open to you. In us there is no lack of room for you, but in your heart there is no room for us. Now as having a recompense in like kind— I speak as to my children—be you also open wide to us.

Do not bear the yoke with unbelievers. For what has justice in common with iniquity? Or what fellowship has light with darkness? What harmony is there between Christ and Belial? Or what part has the believer with the unbeliever? And what agreement has the temple of God with idols? For you are the temple of the living God, as God says, "I will dwell and move among them, I will be their God and they shall be my people." Wherefore, "Come out from among them, be separated, says the Lord, and touch not an unclean thing; and I will welcome you in, and will be a Father to you, and you shall be my sons and daughters, says the Lord almighty."

Having therefore these promises, beloved, let us cleanse ourselves from all defilement of the flesh and of the spirit, perfecting holiness in the fear of God.

Make room for us. We have wronged no one, we have corrupted no one, we have taken advantage of no one. I am not saying this to condemn you; for I have already said that you are in our hearts to die together and to live together. Great is my confidence in you, great my boasting about you. I am filled with comfort, I overflow with joy in all our troubles.

(2 Cor 6:11-18; 7:1-4.)

Let us listen to the Apostle and purify ourselves of every uncleanness and ugliness. Our sight and hearing are instruments of innumerable sins, when they are employed contrary to the will of God. If this be the case, what torments the sinner piles up for himself! Every sense will have its own torment. Sight will be punished with darkness. What pity wells up in us to hear that someone has gone blind! And if we had to go only one year without sunlight, without even the tiniest light, what would we feel? What if we had to stay locked in a pit of snakes awaiting at every moment either bites or swordblows of an enemy–what torment! Of the damned, it is said that they "shall never more see light" (Ps. 48:20).

Earthly fire gives light, but hellfire is darkness. St. Basil explains that the Lord separates the light from the fire, so that fire burns without illuminating. And St. Albert the Great says that God will divide the light from the heat. The very smoke coming from this fire will form the dark storm of which Sacred Scripture speaks, and it will blind the damned: "For whom the storm of darkness has been reserved forever" (Jude 1:13). According to St. Thomas, the only light they will glimpse will be what is necessary to increase their affliction.

The hearing of the wicked will also have its torment. Uninterrupted screams and desperate sobs will make that place horrible. In one way, each will suffer what all the rest are suffering, and will in his turn make the rest suffer. "The sound of terrors is in his ears" (Job 15:21). In a hospital where the patients all screamed and sobbed in an agony of pain the whole night through, the sound would chill the heart. It would be a really hard night to lie sleepless there hour after hour because of the pitiful cries and pleas of the wounded and helpless.

Imagine the plight of the damned who have to take that for all eternity, and far worse than that—as much, in fact, as human nature is capable of suffering.

When war correspondents tried to describe the terrors of certain nights during World War II, they used the strong expression: hellish nights. For the fire never ceased. From one minute to the next, another bomb, another hand grenade, another round of machine gun fire could have blasted them into eternity. But that terrible human carnage finally came to an end. Hell, on the other hand, will never cease. God will never end the sufferings that cause the shrieks and blasphemies in that prison of fire.

Ah, let us mortify our eyes and ears. We must check our sight with modesty always and everywhere, coming and going, reading, and even when alone with ourselves. As to our hearing, we must not listen to sinful songs or talk, which offend God. Is it not better to mortify ourselves now than damn ourselves eternally?

Often the first link in a chain of sins comes from some bad companion. But we have to remember that the damned are greatly tormented by their companions in hell. The expression, "If I go to hell, I won't be alone," is truly senseless. It does not matter how persuasive we find the words of someone trying to induce us to sin. The serpent spoke very appealingly to Eve, but what ruin that brought on!

Job said that he had made an agreement with his eyes that he would not so much as think upon a virgin (cf. Job 31:1). Sinful glances, in fact, lead to sinful thoughts.

Our Lord said, "My sheep hear My voice." To heed the voice of the Lord is a sign of salvation.

We shall now recite Psalm 126 and then the concluding point of the chaplet to St. Joseph.

PSALM 126

The Need of God's Blessing:
His Gift of Sons

Unless the Lord build the house,
they labor in vain who build it.
Unless the Lord guard the city,
In vain does the guard keep vigil.
It is vain for you to rise early,
or put off your rest,
You that eat hard-earned bread,
for he gives to his beloved in sleep.

Behold, sons are a gift from the Lord;
the fruit of the womb is a reward.
Like arrows in the hand of a warrior
are the sons of one's youth.
Happy the man whose quiver is filled with them;
they shall not be put to shame when they contend
with enemies at the gate.

CHAPLET TO ST JOSEPH

(Continued)

7. O St. Joseph, protector of the universal Church, look benignly upon the Pope, the Episcopate, the Clergy, the Religious and the laity. Pray for the sanctification of all. The Church is the fruit of the Blood of Jesus, your foster Son. We entrust to you our supplications for the extension, the liberty, and the exaltation of the Church. Defend her from errors, from evil and from the powers of hell, as you once saved the threatened life of Jesus from the hands of Herod. May Christ's desire come true: "That there be one fold under one shepherd." Obtain for us the grace to be living and active members of the Church militant, that we may eternally rejoice in the Church triumphant.

St. Joseph, pray for us.

Sufferings of the nostrils, the palate, and the tongue

For indeed when we came to Macedonia, our flesh had no rest; we had troubles on every side, conflicts without and anxieties within. But God, who comforts the humble, comforted us by the arrival of Titus. And not by his arrival only, but also by the comfort which he himself experienced in you. He told us of your longing, of your sorrow, of your zeal for me, so that I rejoiced yet more.

Wherefore, although I made you sorry by my letter, I do not regret it. And even if I did regret it, seeing that the same letter did for a while make you sorry, now I am glad; not because you were made sorry, but because your sorrow led you to repentance. For you were made sorry according to God, that you might suffer no loss at our hands. For the sorrow that is according to God produces repentance that surely tends to salvation, whereas the sorrow that is according to the world produces death. For behold this very fact that you were made sorry according to God, what earnestness it has wrought in you, nay, what explanations, what indignation, what fear, what yearning, what zeal, what readiness to avenge! In everything you have showed yourselves to be innocent in the matter.
(2 Cor. 7:5-11.)

The sense of smell will be tormented, for the damned will have to remain from judgment day through all eternity with thousands and thousands of others like himself, with deformed and evil-smelling bodies. The stench will be unspeakable. St. Bonaventure says that only one damned person from hell would be enough to contaminate the whole earth. It would be a terrible suffering to have to stay in a closed room with a corpse already in an advanced stage of putrefaction, but it will be a thousand times worse for the damned soul to remain in hell with heaps of corrupt corpses: "Like sheep they are herded into the nether world" (Ps. 48:15).

The sense of taste will be tormented, for the damned suffer a ravenous hunger without let-up. This seems indeed a humiliating pain, but the glutton, the drunkard, and the lover of good foods found their delight in satisfying the palate. They used their reasoning power to satisfy their senses first of all and hence lowered themselves to the level of the animals: "Man, for all his splendor, if he have not prudence, resembles the beasts that perish" (Ps. 48:21). Animals follow their instincts, but man cannot act that way without degrading his soul: "Their god is the belly" (Phil. 3:19). Therefore, they will suffer unheard-of hunger and thirst. In Christ's parable, the rich man, who had banqueted to his heart's content, called from hell: "Father Abraham, have pity on me, and send Lazarus to dip the tip of his finger in water and cool my tongue, for I am tormented in this flame" (Luke 16:24).

The tongue will be tormented. This tongue is the sum or manifestation of all sins: "the very world of iniquity" the Bible calls it (James 3:6). Hence in the tongue all the other torments of the damned will be manifested and gathered. The tongue of the heretic Arius was eaten by worms because he had blasphemed Jesus Christ and Our Lady. The damned's tongue will also be riddled by worms, and he will shriek, shout, and enumerate all the sufferings of his body and his soul, without being able fully to express them. That tongue will call for help, for compassion, but heaven will be closed. It will blaspheme and curse everything, everyone and itself. The only answer it will receive will be from the devils, always ready to torment him some more. Let us reflect, then. These descriptions are only earthly comparisons, and will always be insufficient to express the reality. Time cannot be compared to eternity. The sufferings of this life are light when compared to the pains of hell. All the pains of the present put together would not equal the smallest pain suffered by the damned.

O Lord, I detest all the satisfactions I have taken in eating and speaking. Self-indulgent and unmortified as I am, how would I be able to remain there amid such torments for all eternity?

Let me examine myself well, therefore, and make a firm resolution. For my past life, I beg you, Jesus, give me time and fervor in doing penance. With St. Augustine, I shall say, "Lord, here cut, here saw, and spare me not–as long as You spare me in eternity."

After saying the seventh penitential Psalm, we shall offer an Act of Contrition.

PSALM 142

Prayer of a Penitent in Distress

O Lord hear my prayer;
hearken to my pleading in your faithfulness;
in your justice answer me.
And enter not into judgment with your servant,
for before you no living man is just.
For the enemy pursues me;
he has crushed my life to the ground;
he has left me dwelling in the dark, like those long dead.
And my spirit is faint within me,
my heart within me is appalled.
I remember the days of old;
I meditate on all your doings,
the works of your hands I ponder.
I stretch out my hands to you;
my soul thirsts for you like parched land.
Hasten to answer me, O Lord, for my spirit fails me.
Hide not your face from me
lest I become like those who go down into the pit.
At dawn let me hear of your kindness,
for in you I trust.
Show me the way in which I should walk,
for to you I lift up my soul.
Rescue me from my enemies, O Lord,
for in you I hope.
Teach me to do your will,
for you are my God.
May your good spirit guide me on level ground.
For your name's sake, O Lord, preserve me;
in your justice free me from distress,
And in your kindness destroy my enemies;
bring to naught all my foes,
for I am your servant.

ACT OF CONTRITION

O my God, I am heartily sorry for having offended Thee, and I detest all my sins, because of Thy just punishments, but most of all because they offend Thee, my God, Who art all-good and deserving of all my love. I firmly resolve, with the help of Thy grace, to sin no more and to avoid the near occasions of sin.

XXII

THE PAIN OF LOSS IN HELL

We see the justice of God in punishing the damned particularly when we consider the pain of loss and the eternity of hell. There is something infinite about the malice of sin, for it boldly offends infinite majesty. Hence the obstinate sinner will be deprived in hell of the infinite Good, which is God.

The suffering of the intelligence

A man named Ananias with Sapphira his wife, sold a piece of land and by fraud kept back part of the price of the land, with the connivance of his wife, and bringing a part only, laid it at the feet of the apostles. But Peter said, "Ananias, why has Satan tempted thy heart, that thou shouldst lie to the Holy Spirit and by fraud keep back part of the price of the land? While it yet remained, did it not remain thine; and after it was sold, was not the money at thy disposal? Why hast thou conceived this thing in thy heart? Thou hast not lied to men, but to God." And Ananias, hearing these words, fell down and expired. And great fear came upon all who heard of it. And the young men got up and removed him and, carrying him out, buried him.

About three hours later his wife, not knowing what had happened, came in. And Peter said to her, "Tell me, did you sell the land for so much?" And she said, "Yes, for so much." And Peter said to her, "Why have you agreed to tempt the Spirit of the Lord? Behold the feet of those who have buried thy husband are at the door, and they will carry thee out." And she fell down immediately at his feet and expired. And the young men, coming in, found her dead, and carrying her out they buried her beside her husband.

(Acts 5:1-10.)

The suffering of the intelligence consists especially in understanding what a great good the damned has lost. St. Augustine says that this pain is so immense that if it should be taken away, hell would be changed into heaven. In fact, St. Thomas declares that the pain of loss is infinite, since the God the soul has lost is Himself infinite. Once the soul is separated from the body, its one, irresistible desire will be for God, but because it renounced God for sin, it will be rejected by God. Hell lies in those words: "Depart from Me!"

The soul will feel for its God a boundless love, the love of a son for his Father, but that very love will be its torment. It will glimpse heaven afar off, and the throne prepared there for it, realizing that never, never will it possess it. As from a distance it will see the angels and saints rejoicing, and understand that it will never know that incomparable, eternal happiness. It will recognize that it was made to love, and to love God, but with that knowledge will come the certitude that nothing remains but to hate–to hate everything and everyone, to hate the saints and angels, the other damned and the devils, the Blessed Mother, the Crucifix even more, the Blessed Trinity, and itself in eternal despair. Heaven is love, hell is hate.

The damned, says St. John Chrysostom, will be more tormented by heaven than by hell. For they were created for heaven (and they will all know it), but God left them free. "Before man are life and death, whichever he chooses shall be given him" (Sirach 15:17). Thus, they only have themselves to blame. Did not many of their friends and acquaintances reach heaven?

Sin is a great offense to God. It deprives Him of glory; it is despicable ingratitude toward Him; and in itself, it is a horrible rebellion, incomprehensible boldness. Who can ever fully explain what sin actually is?

At Christ's feet, we pray: Lord, how many times I have deserved hell because of my senseless passion! Poor me, had I died that night . . . or that day. Foolish trader I was—for one drop of pleasure that disappears in thin air I would have been handed eternal suffering. My Jesus, forgive me. Christ, have mercy on me! I ask it by Your cross, Your sacred wounds, and Your heart opened by the lance!

With Psalm 139 and a prayer to St. Paul, let us ask to be saved from hell.

PSALM 139

Prayer for Deliverance from the Snares of the Wicked

Deliver me, O Lord, from evil men;
preserve me from violent men,
From those who devise evil in their hearts,
and stir up wars every day.
They make their tongues sharp as those of serpents;
the venom of asps is under their lips.
Save me, O Lord, from the hands of the wicked;
preserve me from violent men,
Who plan to trip up my feet—
the proud who have hidden a trap for me;
They have spread cords for a net;
by the wayside they have laid snares for me.
I say to the Lord, you are my God;
hearken, O Lord, to my voice in supplication;
O God, my Lord, my strength and my salvation;
you are my helmet in the day of battle!
Grant not, O Lord, the desires of the wicked;
further not their plans.
Those who surround me lift up their heads;
may the mischief which they threaten overwhelm them.
May he rain burning coals upon them;
may he cast them into the depths, never to rise.
A man of wicked tongue shall not abide in the land;
evil shall abruptly entrap the violent man.
I know that the Lord renders
justice to the afflicted, judgment to the poor.
Surely the just shall give thanks to your name;
the upright shall dwell in your presence.

TO ST. PAUL THE APOSTLE

O holy Apostle who, with your doctrine and with your charity, has taught the entire world, look kindly upon us, your children and disciples.

We expect everything from your prayers to the Divine Master and to Mary, Queen of the Apostles.

Grant, O Doctor of the Gentiles, that we live in faith, that we save ourselves through hope, and that charity alone reign in us. Obtain for us, O Vessel of election, docile correspondence to divine grace, so that it may not remain unfruitful in us. Grant that we may better know you, love you and imitate you, that we may be living members of the Church, the mystical body of Jesus Christ.

Raise up many and holy apostles. Breathe over the world the warm breath of true charity. Grant that all men may know and glorify God and the Divine Master, the Way, Truth and Life.

And You, Lord Jesus, know that we do not have any faith in our own strength; in Your mercy, then, grant that we may be defended against all adversity through the powerful intercession of St. Paul, our teacher and father.

The suffering of the memory and the will

In the course of time Cain brought to the Lord an offering of the fruit of the ground. Abel also brought some of the firstlings of his flock with their fat portions. The Lord was pleased with Abel and his offerings; but for Cain and his offering he had no regard. Cain was very angry and downcast. The Lord said to Cain, "Why are you angry and why are you downcast? If you do well, will you not be accepted; but if you do not do well, will not sin crouch at the door! Its desire is for you, but you must master it."

Cain said to his brother Abel, "Let us go out into the field." Now when they were in the field, Cain turned against his brother Abel and slew him. Then the Lord said to Cain, "Where is your brother Abel?" He answered, "I do not know. Am I my brother's keeper?" And the Lord said, "What have you done? The voice of your brother's blood cries to me from the ground. And now cursed are you in the soil which has opened its mouth to receive your brother's blood from your hand. When you till the soil, it shall not give its fruit to you; a fugitive and a wanderer shall you be on the earth." Cain said to the Lord, "My punishment is too great to bear. You are driving me today from the soil; and from your face I shall be hidden. And I shall be a fugitive and a wanderer on the earth, and whoever finds me will kill me." But the Lord said to him, "Not so! Whoever kills Cain shall be punished sevenfold." Then the Lord gave Cain a token so that no one finding him should kill him.

(Gen. 4:3-15.)

Sacred Scripture tells us that the remorse of the damned will never end. "I lost my soul for nothing!" he will keep saying. Indeed, for what a miserable satisfaction he condemned himself to hell! A little money, some empty glory, or an earthy pleasure, that was all. With a small sacrifice he could have saved himself, instead.

After Esau had eaten the lentils for which he sold his birthright, he began to groan and shout in sorrow and remorse. With what cries of despair the damned will fill the air at the thought that for a passing, poisonous satisfaction, he lost an eternal reign of bliss and condemned himself to everlasting suffering!

Against the prohibition of his father, Jonathan had eaten some honey, and was therefore condemned to death. With infinite bitterness, he cried out: "I just tasted a bit of honey, and for that I must now die!" Imagine how the damned will suffer to think of the way he spent his life!

St. Thomas says that the souls in hell will suffer especially because they damned themselves for no good reason. "For nothing!" the wretched soul will say. "With a little prayer, with a little more care to avoid the occasions, to overcome human respect, to forgive my enemy, to make a good confession, I could have won heaven forever.

"I received much good advice, many inspirations and holy desires; all I had to do was to follow them. I could have learned from my friends, from the books I read, and from the sermons I heard; I could have put into practice what was told me in God's name. The Lord wanted me holy. Did not God the Father create me for heaven, God the Son die to save me, and God the Holy Spirit take possession of my soul? But I remained obstinate and was lost. Lost, despite my good parents, the holy Sacraments, and the care of my Mother Mary!"

The will, too, will be punished with torment. It will never again have the delights for which it sighed. Instead, its fare will be forever the very evils it fears. Hell is pure suffering. It is easy to understand, therefore, what it means to give scandal or bad example, to be the cause of harm to others, or even only to neglect to do good inasmuch as lies in our power! All sin, directly or indirectly, does harm to our neighbor. For this reason, the Psalmist prayed: "Thoroughly wash me from my guilt, and of my sin cleanse me" (Ps. 50:4).

Let us surrender to Divine Grace, saying: I love You, my God and Creator, my Jesus, and I want to love You always. O Mary, peacemaker between God and sinners, obtain mercy for me. I place myself under your mantle–enlighten me, defend me, save me.

We shall recite Psalm 140 and then two parts of the chaplet to the Sacred Heart.

PSALM 140

Prayer of a Just Man to Be saved from Wickedness

O Lord, to you I call; hasten to me;
hearken to my voice when I call upon you.
Let my prayer come like incense before you;
the lifting up of my hands, like the evening sacrifice.

O Lord, set a watch before my mouth,
a guard at the door of my lips.
Let not my heart incline to the evil
of engaging in deeds of wickedness
With men who are evildoers;
and let me not partake of their dainties.
Let the just man strike me; that is kindness;
let him reprove me; it is oil for the head,
Which my head shall not refuse,
but I will pray under these afflictions.
Their judges were cast down over the crag,
and they heard how pleasant were my words.
As when a plowman breaks furrows in the field,
so their bones are strewn by the edge of the nether world.
For toward you, O God, my Lord, my eyes are turned;
in you I take refuge; strip me not of life.
Keep me from the trap they have set for me,
and from the snares of evildoers.
Let all the wicked fall, each into his own net,
while I escape.

CHAPLET TO THE SACRED HEART

O Jesus, our Master, I, an unworthy sinner, prostrate before You, adore Your Heart, which has so greatly loved mankind and has not spared anything for it. I believe in Your infinite love for us. I thank You for the great gifts which You gave to mankind, especially the Gospel, the Holy Eucharist, the Church, the Priesthood, the religious state, Mary as our Mother, and Your very life.

1. O Jesus, Divine Master, I thank and bless Your most generous Heart for the great gift of the Gospel. You have said: "I was sent to evangelize the poor." Your words bear eternal life. In the Gospel, You have revealed divine mysteries, taught the way of God with truthfulness, and offered the means of salvation. Grant me the grace to preserve

Your Gospel with veneration, to listen to it and to read it according to the spirit of the Church and to spread it with the love with which You preached it. May it be known, honored, and received by all! May the world conform to its life, laws, customs, and doctrines. May the fire You brought upon the earth inflame, enlighten, and give warmth to all.

Sweet Heart of my Jesus, make me love You more and more.

2. O Jesus, Divine Master, I thank and bless Your most amiable Heart for the great gift of the Holy Eucharist. Your love makes You dwell in our tabernacles, renew Your passion and death in the Mass, and make Yourself food of our souls in Holy Communion. May I know You, O hidden God! May I draw salutary waters from the font of Your Heart. Grant me the grace to visit You every day in this Sacrament, to understand and assist devoutly at Holy Mass, to receive Holy Communion often and with the right dispositions. May all mankind heed Your invitation: "Come to Me all of you."

Sweet Heart of my Jesus, make me love You more and more.

The eternity of hell

The next day we reached Sidon and Julius treated Paul kindly, allowing him to go to his friends and receive attention. And putting to sea from there, we passed under the lee of Cyprus, as the winds were against us and sailing over the sea that lies off Cilicia and Pamphylia, we reached Myra in Lycia. There the centurion found a ship of Alexandria bound for Italy and put us on board her.

For many days we made slow progress and had difficulty in arriving off Cnidus. Then as the wind kept us from going on, we sailed under the lee of Crete off Salmone and coasting along it with difficulty we came to a place called Fair Havens, near the town of Thalassa.

But as much time had been spent and navigation was now unsafe, for the Fast was already over, Paul began to admonish them, saying to them, "Men, I see that this voyage is threatening to bring disaster and heavy loss, not only to the cargo and the ship, but to our lives also."

(Acts 27:3-10.)

Evil that lasts but little is a small evil. But if it endured forever, even were it but just one small pain, it would be indescribable agony. Now, of the damned it is said: "They will be tormented day and night forever and ever" (Apoc. 20:10). That is their lot: eternal fire, eternal loss of God, eternal torment of every kind, without the slightest hope of relief.

Eternity is not like time, which passes, and brings with each hour only the pain of that hour. Eternity weighs all at once and always, with all its sufferings, upon the damned, just as the whole weight of a ball of ivory presses upon one point, when it rests on a perfect plane. In hell, guilt is punished, but not expiated. The fire burns, but does not consume. Desperation prevails, not repentance; in fact, the desire to sin is never satiated in the damned. Innocent III wrote: "The reprobate will never humble themselves; rather the malice of their hatred will increase."

Their eternity has a beginning, but no succession and no end. Even though the sinner feared death while on this earth, in hell he would desire it. Yet it will never come. "Men will seek death and will not find it; and they will long to die and death will flee from them" (Apoc. 9:6). Hence St. Jerome wrote: "O death, how welcome you would be to these souls who found you so bitter before!"

"Always! Never!" These are the only two words heard unceasingly in hell. There is no change of suffering, for everything continues unchanging, mercilessly.

It would be useless to fear the pains of hell if we do not fear sin, which merits those pains. For it is sin which closes heaven, opens hell and condemns the soul to an unspeakable series of punishments and remorse. And if death overtakes him before he has been reconciled to God, he will be thrown into that eternal dungeon of fire and agony–and who will suffer the consequences?

Therefore, St. Alphonsus prayed: "Lord, if I had fallen into hell, I would be doing nothing but suffering and moaning. Yet, through Your mercy, I am still living and can still save myself. You love me, and I, too, love You. I deserve every punishment, but in Your goodness, give it to me now, while I am on this earth. Only save me from eternal punishment. Forgive me!"

After reciting Psalm 141, let us continue the chaplet to the Sacred Heart.

PSALM 141

Prayer of a Prisoner in Dire Straits

With a loud voice I cry out to the Lord;
with a loud voice I beseech the Lord.
My complaint I pour out before him;
before him I lay bare my distress.
When my spirit is faint within me,
you know my path.
In the way along which I walk
they have hid a trap for me.
I look to the right to see,
but there is no one who pays me heed.
I have lost all means of escape;
there is no one who cares for my life.
I cry out to you, O Lord,
I say, "You are my refuge,
my portion in the land of the living."
Attend to my cry,
for I am brought low indeed.
Rescue me from my persecutors,
for they are too strong for me.
Lead me forth from prison,
that I may give thanks to your name.
The just shall gather around me
when you have been good to me.

CHAPLET TO THE SACRED HEART

(Continued)

3. O Jesus, Divine Master, I bless and thank Your most sweet Heart for the great gift of the Church. She is the

Mother who instructs us in the truth, guides us on the way to heaven, and communicates supernatural life to us. She continues Your mission of salvation here on earth as Your Mystical Body. She is the ark of salvation. She is infallible, indefectible, catholic. Grant us the grace to love her as You loved and sanctified her in Your Blood. May the world know her; may all enter Your fold; may everyone humbly cooperate in Your reign.

Sweet Heart of My Jesus, etc.

4. O Jesus, Divine Master, I bless and thank Your most loving Heart for the institution of the priesthood. Priests are sent by You, as You were sent by the Father. To them You have committed the treasures of Your doctrine, Your law, and your grace, and souls themselves. Grant me the grace to love them, to listen to them, and to let them guide me in your ways. Send good laborers into Your vineyard, O Jesus. May Priests be the purifying and preserving salt of the earth; may they be the light of the world; may they be the city placed on the mountaintop; may they all be according to Your own Heart; and may they have one day in heaven, as their crown and joy, a multitude of souls conquered for Christ.

Sweet Heart of My Jesus, etc.

THE GENERAL
JUDGMENT

XXIII

THE GENERAL JUDGMENT

At the particular judgment, each soul is assigned its merited reward or punishment.

The purpose of the general judgment is 1) *to give glory to God by showing His Providence in governing the world;* 2) *give glory to Jesus Christ by making known, even to His enemies, His power, sanctity, and wisdom;* 3) *glorify the saints for their good works; and* 4) *humiliate the wicked, the devils, the people rebellious to God and to His Christ.*

God is almighty

And Jesus left the temple and was going away, when his disciples came forward to show him the buildings of the temple. But he answered and said to them, "Do you see all these things? Amen I say to you, there will not be left here one stone upon another that will not be thrown down."

And as he was sitting on the Mount of Olives, the disciples came to him privately, saying, "Tell us, when are these things to happen, and what will be the sign of thy coming and of the end of the world?"

And in answer Jesus said to them, "Take care that no one leads you astray. For many will come

in my name, saying, 'I am the Christ,' and they
will lead many astray. For you shall hear of wars
and rumors of wars. Take care that you do not be
alarmed, for these things must come to pass, but
the end is not yet. For nation will rise against nation, and kingdom against kingdom; and there will
be pestilences and famines and earthquakes in
various places. But all these things are the begin-
nings of sorrows.

"Then they will deliver you up to tribulation,
and will put you to death; and you will be hated
by all nations for my name's sake. And then many
will fall away, and will betray one another, and
will hate one another. And many false prophets
will arise, and will lead many astray. And because
iniquity will abound, the charity of the many will
grow cold. But whoever perseveres to the end, he
shall be saved.   (Matt. 24:1-13.)

In the beginning, God created the heavens and
the earth and all that they contain (Genesis 1). He
created the sun, the moon, and the stars and arranged all the planets according to his wisdom.
He created the animals and plants, separated the
waters from the dry land, established the succession
of night and day, the seasons, the years, the ages.
God rules over the history of man, setting up and
overthrowing empires, and governing every creature with loving providence.

God the Father adorned Adam with grace and
marvelous prerogatives. God the Son redeemed the
world with His death on the cross. God the Holy

Spirit is the soul of the Church, Who strengthens it against tyrants and guides it for the salvation of men. This our God is the true, almighty, and all-good Lord.

In heaven and earth, God does as He wishes. By His power, the sun will be darkened, as though wrapped in thick blackness. The moon will be eclipsed and look as though it were covered with dark blood. The earth will be shaken and the stars will fall from heaven. The sea will tremble and overflow its bounds. The earth will open to display gaping abysses. Horrifying earthquakes will rock the mountains and everything else, while wars, discord, and pestilences desolate the earth.

And all this will take place almost suddenly, when the measure of good and evil has reached its fullness before God. In other words, these things will occur when the world least expects them, when it is most given over to sin, when there is no more time for reparation.

God is Lord of the elements; fire, hail, floods and lightning obey Him. Hence from heaven a torrent of consuming fire will set everything ablaze—men and animals, plains and forests, great buildings and forts.

If the whole world will be shaken and terrified, what will be the case of the sinner, who will realize that the day of reckoning has come?

Let us pay homage to the omnipotence of God, adored by the angels and, with sincere hearts, ask forgiveness for our sins. Our confidence does not fail us, for we know that Almighty God awaits the sinner to forgive him.

We conclude with the first Psalm and the chaplet.

PSALM 1

True Happiness

Happy the man who follows not
the counsel of the wicked
Nor walks in the way of sinners,
nor sits in the company of the insolent,
But delights in the law of the Lord and meditates on his law
day and night.
He is like a tree
planted near running water,
That yields its fruit in due season,
and whose leaves never fade.
(Whatever he does, prospers.)
Not so the wicked, not so;
they are like chaff which the wind drives away.
Therefore in judgment the wicked shall not stand,
nor shall sinners, in the assembly of the just.
For the Lord watches over the way of the just,
but the way of the wicked vanishes.

CHAPLET TO THE SACRED HEART

(Continued)

5. O Jesus, Divine Master, I thank and bless Your most holy Heart for the institution of the religious state. Through it, You have called many to evangelical perfection. You have

made Yourself their model, their help, and their reward. O Divine Heart, multiply religious vocations. Sustain them in the faithful observance of the evangelical counsels. May they be the Church's most fragrant gardens. May they be prayerful souls who console You and work for Your honor in every form of apostolate.

Sweet Heart of My Jesus, etc.

6. O Jesus, Divine Master, I thank and bless Your most merciful Heart for having given us Mary as our mother, teacher, and queen. On the Cross You placed us all in her hands. You gave her a big heart, and great wisdom and power. May all men know her, love her, and pray to her! May all permit themselves to be led by her to You, the Savior of mankind. I place myself in her hands, as You did. May I be with Mary Most Holy now, in the hour of my death, and for all eternity.

Sweet Heart of My Jesus, etc.

God is good

And this gospel of the kingdom shall be preached in the whole world, for a witness to all nations; and then will come the end.

"Therefore when you see the abomination of desolation, which was spoken of by Daniel the prophet, standing in the holy place—let him who reads understand—then let those who are in Judea flee to the mountains; and let him who is on the housetop not go down to take anything from his house; and let him who is in the field not turn back to take his cloak. But woe to those who are with child, or have infants at the breast in those days! But pray that your flight may not be in the winter, or on the Sabbath. For then there will be great tribulation, such as has not been from the beginning of the world until now, nor will be. And unless those days had been shortened, no living creature would be saved. But for the sake of the elect those days will be shortened.

"Then if anyone say to you, 'Behold, here is the Christ,' or, 'There he is,' do not believe it. For false christs and false prophets will arise, and will show great signs and wonders, so as to lead astray, if possible, even the elect. Behold, I have told it to you beforehand. If therefore they say to you, 'Behold, he is in the desert,' do not go forth; 'Behold, he is in the inner chambers,' do not believe it. For as the lightning comes forth from the east and shines even to the west, so also will the coming of the Son of Man be. Wherever the body is, there will the eagles be gathered together.

"But immediately after the tribulation of those days, the sun will be darkened, and the moon will not give her light, and the stars will fall from heaven, and the powers of heaven will be shaken. And then will appear the sign of the Son of Man in heaven; and then will all tribes of the earth mourn, and they will see the Son of Man coming upon the clouds of heaven with great power and majesty. And he will send forth his angels with a trumpet and a great sound, and they will gather his elect from the four winds, from one end of the heavens to the other.

"Now from the fig tree learn this parable. When its branch is now tender, and the leaves break forth, you know that summer is near. Even so, when you see all these things, know that it is near, even at the door. Amen I say to you, this generation will not pass away till all these things have been accomplished. Heaven and earth will pass away but my words will not pass away.

(Matt. 24:14-35.)

God's goodness is infinite. Heaven and earth chant the mercy of God, and the just will praise it for all eternity.

Our body was taken from the earth, and because of sin, it will be humiliated in the earth, where death will wreak complete havoc on it. But this flesh of ours was glorified in Jesus Christ. The Son of God, in fact, clothed Himself with it: "And the Word was made flesh". It was in human flesh that He was viewed in the manger, at Nazareth, and at Capharnaum. It was as a man that He instituted the Holy Eucharist, suffered pain and humiliation, and by shedding His Blood, saved all mankind.

In the flesh, He rose from the grave, was touched by the Apostles, and ascended into heaven, where He sits at the right hand of the Father. From there, still in human flesh, He will return a second time to judge humanity.

In Jesus Christ, our flesh is ennobled; it becomes an instrument of merit; it is glorified and led into heaven. Through Holy Communion, Christ incorporates us into Himself, making us His members. Christ's resurrection and glory gives us a picture of the glory that awaits our body. "We are . . . joint heirs with Christ, provided, however, we suffer with him that we may also be glorified with him" (Rom. 8:17).

St. John Chrysostom exhorts us: "Picture the splendor of Saints Peter and Paul when those glorious bodies rise from their graves, victorious over the world, over tyrants, and over death!"

May Christ be blessed for desiring to have His brothers, whom He redeemed, as companions in His glory, in His triumph on the great day.

Each of us must think: I shall rise from the site wherein my body is buried. My soul will be called from eternity to join my body, and from that time on, my body will be immortal along with my soul. Already I hear the call of the last trumpet: "Arise, O you dead, and come to the judgment."

Blessed then will be the penance of a St. Aloysius, of a St. Peter of Alcantara, of a holy Curé of Ars! Blessed will be the labors of a St. Francis Xavier, of a St. Alphonsus de Liguori, of a St. Peter Canisius! Blessed the rocks suffered by St. Stephen, the flames endured by St. Lawrence, the wild animals, the swords, the various instruments of torture, the prisons of thousands of martyrs! Heaven will reward and crown them all.

Let us recite the second Psalm and the chaplet.

PSALM 2

The Universal Reign of the Messias

Why do the nations rage
and the peoples utter folly?
The Kings of the earth rise up,
and the princes conspire together
against the Lord and against his anointed:
"Let us break their fetters
and cast their bonds from us!"
He who is throned in heaven laughs;
the Lord derides them.
Then in anger he speaks to them;
he terrifies them in his wrath:
"I myself set up my king
on Sion, my holy mountain."
I will proclaim the decree of the Lord:
The Lord said to me, "You are my son;
this day I have begotten you.
Ask of me and I will give you
the nations for an inheritance
and the ends of the earth for your possession.
You shall rule them with an iron rod;
you shall shatter them like an earthen dish."
And now, O kings, give heed;
take warning, you rulers of the earth.
Serve the Lord with fear, and rejoice before him;
with trembling pay homage to him,
Lest he be angry and you perish from the way,
when his anger blazes suddenly.
Happy are all who take refuge in him!

CHAPLET TO THE SACRED HEART

(Continued)

7. O Jesus, Divine Master, I thank and bless Your most meek Heart, which led You to give Your life for me. Your blood, Your wounds, the scourges, the thorns, the cross, and Your bowed head speak to my heart: no one loves more than he who gives his life for the loved one. The Shepherd died to give life to the sheep. I, too, want to spend my life for You. Grant that You may always, in all things and everywhere dispose of me for Your greater glory. May I always say: "Thy will be done." Inflame my heart with a holy love for souls, so that I may love them even to the greatest sacrifice.

Sweet Heart of My Jesus, etc.

The King of the ages

"But of that day and hour no one knows, not even the angels of heaven, but the Father only. And as it was in the days of Noe even so will be the coming of the Son of Man. For as in the days before the flood they were eating and drinking, marrying and giving in marriage until the day when Noe entered the ark, and they did not understand until the flood came and swept them all away; even so will be the coming of the Son of Man.

"Then two men will be in the field; one will be taken, and one will be left. Two women will be grinding at the millstone; one will be taken and one will be left.

"Watch therefore, for you do not know at what hour your Lord is to come. But of this be assured, that if the householder had known at what hour the thief was coming, he would certainly have watched, and not have let his house be broken into. Therefore you also must be ready, because at an hour that you do not expect, the Son of Man will come. Who, dost thou think, is the faithful and prudent servant whom his master has set over his household to give them their food in due time? Blessed is that servant whom his master, when he comes, shall find so doing. Amen I say to you, he will set him over all his goods. But if that wicked servant says to himself, 'My master delays his coming,' and begins to beat his fellow-servants, and to eat and drink with drunkards, the master of that servant will come on a day he does not expect, and in an hour he does not know, and will cut him asunder and make him share the lot of the hypocrites. There will be the weeping, and the gnashing of teeth.   (Matt. 24:36-51.)

The Judge will appear in tremendous majesty. "All judgment he (the Father) has given to the Son" (John 5:22). The cross, once an instrument of shame, will precede, shining above the clouds as a trophy of victory. Next will come an immense court of angels, apostles, martyrs, confessors, and virgins. Lastly Jesus Christ Himself will appear in all His justice and goodness. He was given to the world as Master, Redeemer, and Model. To Him everything was subjected, but some received Him and obeyed Him, whereas others rejected Him and persecuted Him. And now He comes–

as the glory and comfort of the good;

as the vindicator of His Father's honor;

as the triumphant conqueror of His enemies.

He is the King of the ages, the judge of the living and the dead, the absolute and eternal arbiter of the fortunes of nations and individuals.

As the Creator, He will ask an account of all the gifts and means He made available to men for their eternal salvation. In front of all, He will manifest His divine bounty and universal providence.

As the Redeemer, He will ask an account of all the gifts of grace which He brought down from heaven and merited with His Passion and Death. What an accusing sight the cross will be for obstinate unbelievers! But what a comfort to fervent souls, to faithful Christians!

As the Sanctifier, He will ask an account of the observance of His law, of faith in His words, of the use made of the Sacraments.

How beautiful is the scene described by the Psalm: "The Lord said to my Lord: 'Sit at my right hand till I make your enemies your footstool.' The scepter of your power the Lord will stretch forth from Sion: 'Rule in the midst of your enemies.' Yours is princely power in the day of your birth, in holy splendor" (Ps. 109:1-3).

To Jesus Christ belongs supreme authority and greatness;

In Jesus Christ is to be found all goodness and justice;

Jesus Christ is the joy of the elect;

Jesus Christ is the terror of the reprobate.

The entire human race will appear before Him, the good exultant in their reception of Him, and the wicked utterly crushed by His powerful majesty.

After the third Psalm, we shall pray to St. Paul to ask him to obtain for us the grace to give glory to the Divine Master by submitting our minds to Him.

PSALM 3

Trust in God in Time of Danger

O Lord, how many are my adversaries!
Many rise up against me!
Many are saying of me,
"There is no salvation for him in God."
But You, O Lord, are my shield;
my glory, you lift up my head!
When I call out to the Lord,
he answers me from his holy mountain.
When I lie down in sleep,
I wake again, for the Lord sustains me.
I fear not the myriads of people
arrayed against me on every side.
Rise up, O Lord!
Save me, my God!
For you strike all my enemies on the cheek;
the teeth of the wicked you break.
Salvation is the Lord's!
Upon your people be your blessing!

PRAYER TO ST. PAUL

O glorious Apostle of the Gentiles, St. Paul, who with so much zeal spent yourself to destroy in Ephesus those writings which you knew would have perverted the minds of the faithful, now, too, look upon us benignly. You see how an unbelieving press, unhindered, seeks to snatch from our hearts the precious treasures of faith and of purity. O holy Apostle, enlighten the minds of so many perverse writers, we beg you, so that they may cease to bring ruin to souls through their false doctrines and wicked suggestions. Move their hearts to detest the evil that they do to the elect flock of Jesus Christ. Obtain for us the grace always to be docile to the voice of the Supreme Pontiff, and never to read perverse writings. May we seek, instead, to read, and as much as we are able, to distribute those writings whose salutary contents will help everyone to promote the greater glory of God, the exaltation of His Church, and the salvation of souls. Amen.

XXIV

THE PURPOSE OF THE JUDGMENT

At the general judgment, we shall come face to face with Jesus. Now, on our altars, He is in a position of lowliness, and almost, we might say, of weakness. Then, instead, He will appear in all His majesty.

Let us put these questions to ourselves:

Will I arise with a beautiful and glorious body, or rather with a deformed one?

Will I be placed at the right, with the elect, or on the left, with the damned?

What will my meeting with Jesus be like—joyous or terrifying?

When consciences are revealed, will I be more honored than ashamed, or vice-versa?

What will my sentence be? Into which of the two eternities will I go?

The glory of the elect

Then Jesus spoke to the crowds and to his disciples, saying, "The Scribes and the Pharisees have sat on the chair of Moses. All things, therefore, that they command you, observe and do. But do not act according to their works; for they talk but do nothing. And they bind together heavy and oppressive burdens, and lay them on men's shoulders; but not with one finger of their own do they choose to move them. In fact, all their works they

341

do in order to be seen by men; for they widen their phylacteries, and enlarge their tassels, and love the first places at suppers and the front seats in the synagogues, and greetings in the market place, and to be called by men 'Rabbi.' But do not you be called 'Rabbi'; for one is your Master, and all you are brothers. And call no one on earth your father; for one is your Father, who is in heaven. Neither be called masters; for one only is your Master, the Christ. He who is greatest among you shall be your servant. And whoever exalts himself shall be humbled, and whoever humbles himself shall be exalted.

(Matt. 23:1-12.)

On this earth, the good and the wicked live together, like weeds and good grain. Even in the cemetery, the coffins of the good and bad are laid side by side. But at the judgment, the angels will come to separate them. The just will be put on the right, and the reprobate hurled to the left. Sons will be separated from fathers, husbands from wives, one friend from another: "One will be taken, and one will be left" (Matt. 24:40).

At present, the rich, the powerful, the ruling classes are considered fortunate, whereas often the poor and the lowly are looked down upon with a compassionate glance, even if they are holy.

O you who are faithful to God, do not be dismayed at seeing yourselves despised or troubled on this earth. Remember that the poor in spirit, the clean of heart, the meek, and the patient are blessed. On judgment day, you will be honored and placed in the glorious court of Jesus Christ. What splendid dignity will enfold a St. Felix of Cantalice, a St. Lydwina, and others who seemed so lowly in this world! Think of the glory that will come to St. Agnes, St. Agatha, St. Cecilia, and St. Clare! Contrariwise, how far abased will be men like Herod, Nero, Pilate, who were great here below but perhaps are not even saved! At present, men often do not receive what is coming to them in fairness (considering just this life), but wait for the day of truth and justice. It will be an overwhelming reality for the wretched, and everlasting exaltation for the good. Then, only virtue will be of any import.

Thus, the elect will be placed on the right. In fact, to their greater glory, according to St. Paul, they will be caught up on the clouds to meet Christ and the angels: "We . . . shall be caught up together with them in clouds to meet the Lord in the air" (1 Thess. 4:16). The damned, instead, will be banished to the left, to wait for the Judge to condemn their lives publicly.

The sight of Jesus Christ will be for them a greater pain than hell itself, according to St. Jerome. And St. Teresa used to say: "My Jesus, give me every suffering, only do not let me see Your face frowning at me on that day!"

God is faithful! He promised to comfort the good, and not one word of His promise will fall short: "He who overcomes, I will permit him to sit with me upon my throne" (Apoc. 3:21).

Glory to the elect! Persevere, just ones, in expectation of that great day. The rejoicing of the wicked lasts but a moment, while your rejoicing will endure forever. "We shall ever be with the Lord" (1 Thess. 4:17). "If God is for us, who is against us? Who shall make accusation against the elect of God? It is God who justifies! Who shall condemn? It is Christ Jesus who died; yes, and rose again, he who is at the right hand of God, who also intercedes for us!" (Rom. 8:31, 33-34). Glory to the elect!

We shall say the fourth Psalm, and then invoke the Queen of the elect so that after this exile, she may show unto us the Fruit of her virginal womb.

PSALM 4

Joyful Confidence in God

When I call, answer me, O my just God,
You who relieve me when I am in distress;
Have pity on me, and hear my prayer!
Men of rank, how long will you be dull of heart?
Why do you love what is vain and seek after falsehood?
Know that the Lord does wonders for his faithful one;
the Lord will hear me when I call upon him.
Tremble, and sin not;
reflect, upon your beds, in silence.

Offer just sacrifices,
and trust in the Lord.
Many say, "Oh, that we might see better times!"
O Lord, let the light of your countenance shine upon us!
You put gladness into my heart,
more than when grain and wine abound.
As soon as I lie down, I fall peacefully asleep,
for you alone, O Lord,
bring security to my dwelling.

HAIL, HOLY QUEEN

Hail, holy Queen, Mother of mercy, our life, our sweetness, and our hope. To thee do we cry, poor banished children of Eve; to thee do we send up our sighs, mourning and weeping in this valley of tears. Turn then, most gracious advocate, thine eyes of mercy toward us; and after this our exile, show unto us the blessed fruit of thy womb, Jesus. O clement, O loving, O sweet Virgin Mary.

Glory to God!

"But woe to you, Scribes and Pharisees, hypocrites! because you shut the kingdom of heaven against men. For you yourselves do not go in, nor do you allow those going in to enter.

("Woe to you, Scribes and Pharisees, hypocrites! because you devour the houses of widows, praying long prayers. For this you shall receive a greater judgment.)

"Woe to you, Scribes and Pharisees, hypocrites! because you traverse sea and land to make one convert; and when he has become one, you make him twofold more a son of hell than yourselves.

"Woe to you, blind guides, who say, 'Whoever swears by the temple, it is nothing; but whoever swears by the gold of the temple, he is bound.' You blind fools! for which is greater, the gold, or the temple which sanctifies the gold? 'And whoever swears by the altar, it is nothing; but whoever swears by the gift that is upon it, he is bound.' Blind ones! for which is greater, the gift, or the altar which sanctifies the gift? Therefore he who swears by the altar swears by it, and by all things that are on it; and he who swears by the temple swears by it, and by him who dwells in it. And he who swears by heaven swears by the throne of God, and by him who sits upon it.

"Woe to you, Scribes and Pharisees, hypocrites! because you pay tithes on mint and anise and cummin, and have left undone the weightier matters of the Law, right judgment and mercy and faith. These things you ought to have done, while not leaving the others undone. Blind guides who strain out the gnat but swallow the camel!

"Woe to you, Scribes and Pharisees, hypocrites! because you clean the outside of the cup and the dish, but within they are full of robbery and uncleanness. Thou blind Pharisee! clean first the inside of the cup and of the dish, that the outside too may be clean.

"Woe to you, Scribes and Pharisees, hypocrites! because you are like whited sepulchres, which outwardly appear to men beautiful, but within are full of dead men's bones and of all uncleanness. So you also outwardly appear just to men, but within you are full of hypocrisy and iniquity.

"Woe to you, Scribes and Pharisees, hypocrites! you who build the sepulchres of the prophets, adorn the tombs of the just, and say, 'If we had
lived in the days of our fathers, we would not
have been their accomplices in the blood of the
prophets.' Thus you are witnesses against yourselves that you are the sons of those who killed
the prophets.

"You also fill up the measure of your fathers.
Serpents, brood of vipers, how are you to escape
the judgment of hell?   (Matt. 23:13-33.)

Consciences will be revealed. "The court was
convened, and the books were opened" (Dan. 7:10).
On the body and soul of every man the good and
evil of his whole life will be read–in all the circumstances, from both the objective and subjective point
of view. The good will be manifest, which is only
right, for on earth, good is often unknown, misun-
derstood, and made an object of contradiction. How
many times virtue is forced under cover, while vice
is celebrated! Can we believe that the Lord will let
Himself be deceived by men or let falsehood triumph? Can we think that He will not defend His
good children, or that evil will always have the last
word? No! After the trial, comes glory; after the
shame of the cross, the Father has taken it upon
Himself to glorify His Son, by showing Him to be
the true God, the Holy One in Whom He is well
pleased. On the great day, good deeds done in secret
will shine, and the just will have eternal praise:

"Then everyone will have his praise from God"
(1 Cor. 4:5).

God is truth, and every sin is the opposite: a
deception of the devil, who was a liar from the beginning of the world. Indeed, did he not say to Eve,
to entice her to eat the forbidden fruit: "You shall
not die; for God knows that when you eat of it, your
eyes will be opened and you will be like God, knowing good and evil" (Gen. 3:4-5). And Eve fell into
his snare, dragging Adam with her.

Already Satan had deceived a great many of
the angels in heaven, urging them to rebel against
God, since he wanted divine honors for himself, and
obedience from his fellows. He tried what was a
black deception: "I will ascend above the tops of
the clouds; I will be like the Most High!" (Isa. 14:14).
But St. Michael revenged the truth: "Who is like
God?"

In the same way, the devil tricks man, when
man sins. He promises him all kinds of good things,
while he steals from him the grace of God and his
highest good. Even to Christ, he boldly lied: "All
these things will I give thee, if thou wilt fall down
and worship me" (Matt. 4:9).

Sin is, in fact, a deception of passion. Man
seeks his happiness in something which becomes his
torment. From a momentary delight comes a biting
remorse and an eternity of suffering.

As a rule, a man tries to cover up his sins, keeping them hidden from the knowledge of others. But sin is a worm that dies not, unless repentance steps into the picture. Even if others are deceived and think the sinner a holy man, God is truth. Everything will be pulled out into the open on the tremendous day of judgment. Let the good rejoice and the wicked shake! Everything will be uncovered, in front of everyone, forever.

Let the light, which is God the Truth, shine, and all the upright of heart who seek the Lord with sincerity rejoice. Let the workers of deceit and iniquity flee to hide themselves and their hypocrisy if they can. But they cannot. Glory to God, the God of Truth! He will make known that which was hidden. Let the secret works of grace and the Holy Spirit be made manifest. Let the fruits of the Redemption by the Son be evident in every soul. Let the goodness of God the Father to His children be made known.

Glory to God in the highest! Peace to men of good will!

Let us conclude with the fifth Psalm and with the chaplet to St. Paul, to ask him his help, that we may become his companions in the glory of heaven.

PSALM 5

Prayer for Divine Help

Hearken to my words, O Lord,
attend to my sighing.
Heed my call for help,
my king and my God!
To you I pray, O Lord;
at dawn you hear my voice;
at dawn I bring my plea expectantly before you.
For you, O God, delight not in wickedness;
no evil man remains with you;
the arrogant may not stand in your sight.
You hate all evildoers;
you destroy all who speak falsehood;
The bloodthirsty and the deceitful the Lord abhors.
But I, because of your abundant kindness,
will enter your house;
I will worship at your holy temple
in fear of you, O Lord;
Because of my enemies, guide me in your justice;
make straight your way before me.
For in their mouth there is no sincerity;
their heart teems with treacheries.
Their throat is an open grave;
they flatter with their tongue.
Punish them, O God;
let them fall by their own devices;
For their many sins, cast them out
because they have rebelled against you.
But let all who take refuge in you
be glad and exult forever.
Protect them, that you may be the joy
of those who love your name.
For you, O Lord, bless the just man;
you surround him with the shield of your good will.

CHAPLET TO ST. PAUL

1. I bless You, O Jesus, for the great mercy granted to St. Paul in changing him from a bold persecutor to an ardent apostle of the Church. And you, O great Saint, obtain for me from Jesus and Mary Most Holy a heart docile to grace and a complete conversion from my predominant fault.

Jesus Master, Way, Truth, and Life, have mercy on us.
Queen of Apostles, pray for us.
St. Paul, the Apostle, pray for us.

2. I bless You, O Jesus, for having elected the Apostle Paul as a model and preacher of holy virginity. And you, O Saint Paul, my dear Father, guard my mind, my heart, and my senses, in order that I may know, love, and serve only Jesus, and employ all my energies for His glory.

Jesus Master, Way, Truth, and Life, have mercy on us.
Queen of Apostles, pray for us.
St. Paul, the Apostle, pray for us.

3. I bless You, O Jesus, for having given, through St. Paul, examples and teachings of perfect obedience. And you, O great Saint, obtain for me from Jesus and Mary Most Holy, a humble docility to all my Superiors, certain that in obedience I shall be victorious over my enemies.

Jesus Master, Way, Truth, and Life, have mercy on us.
Queen of Apostles, pray for us.
St. Paul, the Apostle, pray for us.

4. I bless You, O Jesus, for having taught me by the deeds and words of St. Paul the true spirit of poverty. And you, O great Saint, obtain for me from Jesus and Mary Most Holy the evangelical spirit of poverty so that after having imitated you in life, I may share in your heavenly glory.

Jesus Master, Way, Truth, and Life, have mercy on us.

Queen of Apostles, pray for us.
St. Paul, the Apostle, pray for us.

5. I bless You, O Jesus, for having given to Saint Paul a heart so full of love for God and for the Church, and for having saved so many souls through his zeal. And you, beloved Patron, obtain for me from Jesus and Mary Most Holy, an ardent desire to labor for the Kingdom of Christ through prayer, example, word and deed, so that I may merit the reward promised to good apostles.

Jesus Master, Way, Truth, and Life, have mercy on us.
Queen of Apostles, pray for us.
St. Paul, the Apostle, pray for us.

Glory to Jesus Christ

Therefore, behold, I send you prophets, and wise men, and scribes; and some of them you will put to death, and crucify, and some you will scourge in your synagogues, and persecute from town to town; that upon you may come all the just blood that has been shed on the earth, from the blood of Abel the just unto the blood of Zacharias the son of Barachias, whom you killed between the temple and the altar. Amen I say to you, all these things will come upon this generation.

"Jerusalem, Jerusalem! thou who killest the prophets, and stonest those who are sent to thee! How often would I have gathered thy children together, as a hen gathers her young under her wings, but thou wouldst not! Behold, your house is left to you desolate. For I say to you, you shall

not see me henceforth until you shall say, 'Blessed
is he who comes in the name of the Lord!'"
(Matt. 24:34-39.)

Jesus prayed: "Do thou, Father, glorify me
with thyself, with the glory that I had with thee
before the world existed" (John 17:5). Christ is the
beloved Son, who is always heard by reason of His
infinite merit. He is so perfect that whoever wants
to be loved by God must be found similar to Jesus
Christ. "For those whom he has foreknown, he has
also predestined to become conformed to the image
of his Son, that he should be the firstborn among
many brethren. And those whom he has predestined, them he has also called; and those whom he
has called, them he has also justified, and those
whom he has justified, them he has also glorified"
(Rom. 8:29-30).

Hence, whoever is glorified is glorified in
Christ. And Christ is glorified in every one of His
elect. The members live and act through the head;
and the head receives glory from the activities of
the members.

Furthermore, a reward will go to those who
serve and come to the aid of Jesus Christ in His
members. Similarly, punishment will strike those
who scorn their neighbor, and in their neighbor,
Jesus Christ Himself: "Then the king will say to
those on his right hand, 'Come, blessed of my Fa-

ther, take possession of the kingdom prepared for you from the foundation of the world; for I was hungry and you gave me to eat; I was thirsty and you gave me to drink; I was a stranger and you took me in; naked and you covered me; sick and you visited me; I was in prison and you came to me.' Then the just will answer him, saying, 'Lord, where did we see thee hungry, and feed thee; or thirsty, and give thee drink? And when did we see thee a stranger, and take thee in; or naked, and clothe thee? Or when did we see thee sick, or in prison, and come to thee?' And answering the king will say to them, 'Amen I say to you, as long as you did it for one of these, the least of my brethren, you did it for me.'

"Then he will say to those on his left hand, 'Depart from me, accursed ones, into the everlasting fire which was prepared for the devil and his angels. For I was hungry, and you did not give me to eat; I was thirsty and you gave me no drink; I was a stranger and you did not take me in; naked, and you did not clothe me; sick, and in prison, and you did not visit me.' Then they also will answer and say, 'Lord, when did we see thee hungry, or thirsty, or a stranger, or naked, or sick, or in prison, and did not minister to thee?' Then he will answer them, saying, 'Amen I say to you, as long as you did not do it for one of these least ones, you did not do it for me.'

And these will go into everlasting punishment, but the just into everlasting life." (Matt. 25:34-46.)

Once again, Jesus Christ is constituted heir of the universe. He humbled Himself, taking the nature of a slave, being made like unto man in all things except sin. He was obedient to death on a cross. For which reason, God has exalted Him and has bestowed upon Him the name that is above every name, power and a kingdom (Cf. Phil. 2:7-9). Before Him, the blessed, the damned, and all men must prostrate themselves, for everyone must recognize the glory He has with the Father. Thus He exercises his legislative authority, his executive and judiciary power. He will say, therefore, to those who have despised His law or His grace: Depart from me, you cursed, into eternal fire, prepared for the devil and his followers. And they will be plunged into everlasting damnation.

Then he will say to His faithful servants: Come, you blessed, into the kingdom of my Father! And they will join the angels and the Lord Jesus in an eternity of bliss.

This will be Christ's hour of triumph. The damned will form the footstool of His justice, and the blessed His crown of victory! "Lift up, O gates, your lintels; reach up, you ancient portals, that the king of glory may come in! Who is the king of glory?

The Lord of hosts; he is the king of glory" (Ps. 23:9-10).

May Our Lady, Mother of the Divine Master, intercede for us. In renewing our baptismal promises, let us declare our fidelity to Our Lord.

RENEWAL OF BAPTISMAL VOWS

I believe in God, the Father almighty, Creator of Heaven and earth.

R. *I believe.*

I believe in Jesus Christ, His only Son, God and man, Who died on the cross for our salvation.

R. *I believe.*

I believe in the Holy Spirit, the Holy Catholic Church, the Communion of Saints, the forgiveness of sins, the resurrection of the body, life everlasting.

R. *I believe.*

I promise with the help which I ask and hope from God, to observe His Holy Law, and to love Him with my whole heart above all things, and my neighbor as myself for the love of God.

R. *I promise.*

I renounce the devil, his pomps and his works, that is, sin.   R. *I renounce.*

I promise to unite myself to Jesus Christ and follow Him, and I will to live and die for Him.

R. *I promise.*

In the Name of the Father, and of the Son, and of the Holy Ghost.   R. *Amen.*

ACT OF CONSECRATION TO MARY MOST HOLY

I am all Yours, and all that I possess I offer to You, My amiable Jesus, through Mary, Your most holy Mother.

CONCLUSION

There are three great means of saving ourselves: 1) *believe,* 2) *observe the Commandments,* 3) *pray and in particular, frequent the Sacraments.*

At Baptism, we take upon ourselves the duty of believing, keeping the Commandments, and making use of the Sacraments.

When they receive the Sacrament of Matrimony, Christian couples take each other for life as man and wife for the procreation and rearing of children and the cherishing of one another in a common life.

At their profession, religious take the vows of chastity, poverty, and obedience for their whole lives.

At their Ordination, priests assume the obligation of giving themselves totally to the worship of God and the quest for souls.

When life comes to an end, we shall be judged according to the promises we have made.

Also Available from St. Paul Editions:

Call to Total Consecration

Rev. James Alberione, SSP, STD
Beginners and experienced religious alike will certainly treasure this inspiring and encouraging book which gives a deep understanding of the great privilege that is theirs. 94 pages
cloth \$3.00; paper \$2.00 — SP0020

Growing in Perfect Union

Rev. James Alberione, SSP, STD
"Father Alberione, as founder of several religious congregations, is exceptionally equipped for the task he sets before him: to provide religious not only with solid doctrine, upon which their vocations must be founded, but also to delineate for them practical guidelines for fruitful practice." "Spiritual Book News"
132 pages
cloth \$3.00; paper \$2.00 — SP0210

Insights Into Religious Life

Rev. James Alberione, SSP, STD
These previously unedited lectures of the renowned author and expert on the spiritual life offer

rich and highly practical reflections on fundamental aspects of religious life and topics pertaining to consecrated life in the service of God. 152 pages
cloth $3.00; paper $2.00 — SP0310

Lest We Forget

Rev. James Alberione, SSP, STD
Reflecting on the deceased brings: relief for those beloved souls, since we arouse ourselves to offer prayers and sacrifices for them; benefit for ourselves, because the thought of eternity helps us to shun sin and grow in perfection. 252 pages
cloth $3.95; paper $2.95 — SP0360

Living Our Commitment

Rev. James Alberione, SSP, STD
In accord with the conciliar spirit of the decree "Adaptation and Renewal of Religious Life," Father Alberione has given a series of practical meditations on the cardinal and moral virtues so that the religious may attain to a more total living of his special commitment and a truly Christlike personality. 168 pages
cloth $4.00; paper $3.00 — SP0400

Meditation Notes on Paul the Apostle, Model of the Spiritual Life

Rev. James Alberione, SSP, STD
These writings of Father James Alberione, Founder of the

Pauline Family, were discovered after his death in November, 1971. They are meditation notes and resolutions made during a course of spiritual exercises. The theme is St. Paul and the priest. Every priest and spiritual guide can find in these pages a great wealth of material. 100 pages cloth $2.00 — SP0420

The Paschal Mystery and Christian Living

Rev. James Alberione, SSP, STD

Meditations on the passion, resurrection and ascension of our Lord Jesus designed to deepen the Christian's understanding of that pivotal event in time—the Paschal Mystery—and the event's transcendence of time and space to permeate the lives of each of us at every moment. An excellent volume of meditations for everyone—religious and laity alike—for to the living of this Mystery all of us are called. 200 pages cloth $3.95; paper $2.95 — SP0570

Personality and Configuration with Christ

Rev. James Alberione, SSP, STD

Father Alberione's masterful and challenging blend of psychological insight and ageless wisdom. Writing in the spirit of

the Second Vatican Council and emphasizing, as did Vatican II, the importance of the person, he presents step by step the process of personality development and fulfillment that culminates in the final goal of configuration with Christ, Way, Truth and Life. 192 pages
cloth $3.50; paper $2.50 — SP0520

Pray Always
Rev. James Alberione, SSP, STD
A solid and fundamental explanation of the need and value of prayer, various methods of speaking with God and the reward of closer living with God in daily life. 264 pages
cloth $4.00; paper $3.00 — SP0550

The Spirit in My Life
Rev. James Alberione, SSP, STD
The Holy Spirit is the animator of the Church and of believers. This volume contains the theology of the Holy Spirit, His transforming action in our souls, the talk of Paul VI to Catholic charismatics, a novena and prayers. 78 pages
paper 95¢ — SP0700

Thoughts
Rev. James Alberione, SSP, STD
The reader is introduced to the guidelines behind Father Alberione's amazing activity, evan-

gelical spirit of prayer, and his far-seeing vision. This work of Father Alberione covers a wide range of topics: a vision of man and of history, Jesus Christ: center of thought and action, the presence of the Mother of God, St. Paul today, the Word of God, the Church, the Pope, vocations, prayer, the apostolate as a radiation of Christ, the media as a means of evangelization—all in his very original style, striking for its brevity and power. 211 pages cloth, $4.00; paper $3.00 — SP0750

Please order from addresses on the following page, specifying title and item number.

Daughters of St. Paul

IN MASSACHUSETTS
    50 St. Paul's Ave., Jamaica Plain, Boston, MA 02130;
      617-522-8911; 617-522-0875
    172 Tremont Street, Boston, MA 02111; **617-426-5464;**
      617-426-4230
IN NEW YORK
    78 Fort Place, Staten Island, NY 10301; **212-447-5071**
    59 East 43rd Street, New York, NY 10017; **212-986-7580**
    625 East 187th Street, Bronx, NY 10458; **212-584-0440**
    525 Main Street, Buffalo, NY 14203; **716-847-6044**
IN NEW JERSEY
    Hudson Mall — Route 440 and Communipaw Ave.,
      Jersey City, NJ 07304; **201-433-7740**
IN CONNECTICUT
    202 Fairfield Ave., Bridgeport, CT 06604; **203-335-9913**
IN OHIO
    2105 Ontario St. (at Prospect Ave.), Cleveland, OH 44115; **216-621-9427**
    25 E. Eighth Street, Cincinnati, OH 45202; **513-721-4838**
IN PENNSYLVANIA
    1719 Chestnut Street, Philadelphia, PA 19103; **215-568-2638**
IN VIRGINIA
    1025 King St., Alexandria, VA 22314
IN FLORIDA
    2700 Biscayne Blvd., Miami, FL 33137; **305-573-1618**
IN LOUISIANA
    4403 Veterans Memorial Blvd., Metairie, LA 70002; **504-887-7631;**
      504-887-0113
    1800 South Acadian Thruway, P.O. Box 2028, Baton Rouge, LA 70821
      504-343-4057; 504-343-3814
IN MISSOURI
    1001 Pine Street (at North 10th), St. Louis, MO 63101; **314-621-0346;**
      314-231-1034
IN ILLINOIS
    172 North Michigan Ave., Chicago, IL 60601; **312-346-4228**
      312-346-3240
IN TEXAS
    114 Main Plaza, San Antonio, TX 78205; **512-224-8101**
IN CALIFORNIA
    1570 Fifth Avenue, San Diego, CA 92101; **714-232-1442**
    46 Geary Street, San Francisco, CA 94108; **415-781-5180**
IN HAWAII
    1143 Bishop Street, Honolulu, HI 96813; **808-521-2731**
IN ALASKA
    750 West 5th Avenue, Anchorage AK 99501; **907-272-8183**
IN CANADA
    3022 Dufferin Street, Toronto 395, Ontario, Canada
IN ENGLAND
    128, Notting Hill Gate, London W11 3QG, England
    133 Corporation Street, Birmingham B4 6PH, England
    5A-7 Royal Exchange Square, Glasgow G1 3AH, England
    82 Bold Street, Liverpool L1 4HR, England
IN AUSTRALIA
    58 Abbotsford Rd., Homebush, N.S.W., Sydney 2140, Australia